JESUS
of Nazareth
our
Liberator

BEATRICE FRANCIS CAREY

CITI OF
BOOKS

CITIOFBOOKS, INC.
3736 Eubank NE Suite A1
Albuquerque, NM 87111-3579
www.citiofbooks.com
Hotline: 1 (877) 389-2759
Fax: 1 (505) 930-7244

Ordering Information:
Quantity sales. Special discounts are available on quantity purchases by corporations, associations, and others. For details, contact the publisher at the address above.

Printed in the United States of America.

ISBN-13:	Softcover	979-8-89391-225-8
	Hardcover	979-8-89391-226-5
	eBook	979-8-89391-227-2

Library of Congress Control Number: 2024915394

This work is dedicated to Her Majesty, the Queen of England (DEFENDER OF THE FAITH).

Contents

Foreword..11

1. Fame...13

2. His Name...40

3. His Word..75

4. Early..98

5. A Voice...127

6. Making God Great Again 153

7. Hell..176

8. The Exalted Word 204

9. Knowest Thou Not.......................................232

10. The Loss of All 263

11. Repent..285

12. Jerusalem..311

Bibliography...337

Notes 339

*Then said Jesus to those Jews
which believed on Him,
If ye continue in MY WORD,
then are ye My Disciples indeed;
And ye SHALL KNOW
THE TRUTH,
AND THE TRUTH SHALL
MAKE YOU FREE.*

—*John 8:31-32*

America

Samuel-Francis Smith - Henry Carey

My country, 'tis of thee, sweet land of lib-er-ty, Of thee I sing. Land where my fa-thers died! Land of the Pilgrim's pride! From ev-'ry mountain side, Let freedom ring!

My na-tive coun-try, thee, Land of the no-ble free, Thy name I love. I love thy rocks and rills, Thy woods and templed hills, My heart with rapture thrills Like that a-bove.

Let mu-sic swell the breeze, And ring from all the trees Sweet freedom's song. Let mortal toung-ues awake, Let all that breathe partake, Let rocks their silence break, The sound prolong.

Our fathers' God, to Thee, Author of lib-er-ty, To Thee we sing. Long may our land be bright With freedom's ho-ly light; Protect us by Thy might, Great God, our King.

Foreword

These words are best read out loud. *Out loud* gives the devil less room to snatch away the importance of the message. Jesus is the message, and the devil wants to distract and stop your ears from hearing about Jesus. To know Jesus is salvation. Therefore, read out loud and put the devil to flight. He hates the spoken Word. The devil is the prince of the power of the air. Let us put him to flight with a counterattack. Read the Scriptures out loud, and you yourself will see how well this works to fortify Jesus's message.

Moses read out loud to the Hebrew children from the door of the Tabernacle. Joshua read all the *words* of Moses out loud to the congregation. Ezra the high priest and Scribe (and so much more) read to all the congregation all the *words* of the book out loud from morning to evening and the list is endless.

The author has no intention of ill play here—only this, the Word says, warn them. And it is in my heart to say that if there is any doubt of things in your life—even the slightest, minutest, miniscule to infinity of doubt about anything, friend, it behooves us to examine ourselves closely and to our utmost to please the Master. Let things in doubt go; get rid of them, do not hang onto them, for missing heaven is not worth anything this side of Earth, not gold, not sex, not power, not beauty—nothing, nothing here can compare to losing happiness for eternity. So in a most compassionate state of mind, I have set these things forth in my work; only and only in kindness do I speak.

Jesus's own words are, we cannot serve two masters, and He is our Master, for we will love the one and despise the other. Now if you are putting any of the aforesaid things between or before the Master, then you will love the object of your desire and hate the other. Jesus and Jesus alone must be our object of desire.

A note of thanks is extended to those who helped type and retype drafts of this manuscript. Especially Jim Brown and a certain young lady who patiently deciphered my own handwriting of the entire work. As the Apostle said, in my own handwriting.

Thank you again.

Fame

---

*Since the world began was it not heard that any man opened the eyes of
one that was born blind. If this man were
not of GOD he could do nothing.*

—John 9:32–33

And Jesus said, *"I proceeded forth and came from GOD;
neither came I of Myself, but the Father sent ME."*

—John 8:42

*And Jesus returned in the power of the Spirit
into Galilee and there went
out a FAME of Him through all the region
round about. And He taught in their
synagogues, being glorified of all.*

—Luke 4:14–15

*And they were all amazed and spake among themselves, saying, "What
a WORD is this! For with authority and
power He commandeth the unclean
spirits, and they come out. And the FAME
of Him went out into every place
of the country round about."*

—Luke 4:36–37

There has never been anything like Jesus in the history of the world. He shot across the landscape of Israel like a cannonball of heavenly power sent on the wings of mercy to comfort the poor, heal the sick, and set the captives free. He stormed the strongholds of Satan's powers with *words* of love, compassion, and mercy. Jesus was the greatest thing since sliced bread. The country was taken with amazement; they were utterly astonished. His fame went abroad throughout all the countryside and roundabout. Jesus asked many of those healed not to tell anyone. He did not want them to come and take Him to be their king; that was not His mission. He came into the world to suffer and die for our sins. He was no earthly king—not yet, not now. He declared His mission in the Nazareth synagogue as He stood to read Isaiah where it said, *"The Spirit of the LORD is upon ME, because He hath anointed ME to preach the Gospel to the poor, deliverance to the captives, recovering of sight to the blind…and them that sit in darkness to bring them out of the prison house"* (Isa. 42:7).

They brought their sick and possessed to Him, and He healed all; every one of them He healed. Jesus is the Great Physician, and He had compassion on all. He looked at them as lost sheep, having no shepherd. Some even touched His garments and were healed. He turned no one away. He laid His Hands on all and with a *word*, they were healed. No doubt the Kingdom of God has come nigh unto you and your sons, O, Israel, had you only known the hour of your Peace.

> *"There was brought unto Him one possessed with a devil, blind and dumb: and Jesus healed him, so he both spake and saw. And all were amazed and said, Is not this the son of David and the son of Joseph?"* (Matt. 12:22–23).

Upon seeing this notable miracle, the Pharisees accused Jesus of sorcery. But Jesus said, "Not even you, hypocrites and fools," for He knew their heart. Jesus said, *"I cast out devils by the Spirit of God therefore the kingdom of God is come unto you"* (verse 28). But they heard Him not and sought other occasions to catch Him at his *word*. The children of the kingdom heard Jesus's *words* and marveled and praised Him and worshipped Him. *"He that is of God heareth God's WORDS"* and *"Never man spake like this MAN."* No because Jesus said these are not my *words* but the Father's *words* filled with miracles and power. Jesus only asked, *"Do you believe?"* And said, *"To him that believeth all thing are possible."*

> Now as the sun was setting all they that had any sick…brought them unto Jesus; and He laid His Hands on every one of them and healed them. And devils also came out of many, crying out, and saying Thou art Christ the Son of God. And He rebuked them suffering them not to speak: for they knew that he was Christ. (Luke 4:40–41)

And Jesus went from city to city, healing and preaching, though they constrained Him to stay. Everything Jesus did was phenomenal; next He picked out twelve men to be His disciples. He ordained them to help Him do His work. These twelve were gifted by Jesus to heal, deliver, and forgive sins as He did. They went before Jesus to the cities to prepare the way for Him. And they came back rejoicing, saying, *"Even the spirits are subject to us, but Jesus said rather rejoice because your names are written down in Heaven."* They were turning the world upside-down and even Herod heard the rumors and wanted to see some miracles. But Jesus taught that we ought not cast our pearls before swine, lest they turn and rend you again. God knew all men's hearts and Jesus said, *"A good man out of the good treasure of the heart bringeth forth good things: and an evil man out of the evil treasure bringeth forth evil things. O generation of vipers, how can ye being evil, speak good things? For out of the abundance of the heart the mouth speaketh"* (Matt. 12:35, 34). And Herod, wicked, evil Herod boasted, *"John have I beheaded: but who is this of whom I hear such things? And Herod also desired to see Jesus"* (Luke 9:9). Evil, evil Herod killed the one person on Earth that Jesus loved and thought the most of. Jesus said, *"For I say unto you, among those that are born of women there is not a greater prophet than John the Baptist"* (Luke 7:28). *"Wisdom is vindicated by her fruits."* The kingdom of God was growing, and Jesus had a great following; He even had an entourage to go before Him into the cities.

Jesus's divinity was being witnessed every day by signs and wonders, but He was not seeking glory for Himself but for His Father. Jesus said, *"The father and I are one"* and *"I seek not Mine own glory,"* *"Verily, verily I say unto you, if a man keep My WORD He shall never see death"* (John 8:49–51). Now the Jews said for sure Jesus has a devil, for no mere man should dare make such godlike proclamations. The Jews insisted all men die. "Even our Father Abraham is dead. Now are you greater than our Father Abraham?" they said. Jesus replied, *"Verily, verily I say to you, before Abraham was I AM"* (verse 58). Now the crowd went berserk and picked up stones to cast at Him, but Jesus vanished. Jesus is like a baby glorified Lamb in the midst of these tyrants, manslayers, evening wolves, and lions that have a taste for human blood. But the Father and the Holy Spirit know and are supplying Jesus lamp with oil, and the heavenly angels have their shields as tight as piranha scales. Jesus is safe; He knows until His appointed hour. So Jesus goes about from city to city, synagogue to synagogue, and to countryside and houses. He kills the vipers with His *words*, and He slays the dragon with His faith and belief in God the Father. These are not mere words; they are substance. They are whatever He says they are! It was a double-edged *sword* that proceeded out of the mouth of the Heavenly Father. And the Word accomplishes that which it is sent forth to do.

"For which good work do you stone Me?" Jesus says. Were they not like a flock of vultures constantly circling in the sky over their prey? Constantly, every day, the enemy to our souls would lie in wait, thinking to kill Jesus and snuff out our redemption plan in a second. And they said, "Tell us plainly, are you the Christ?"

Jesus said, *"I have told you but you are not of My flock therefore you do not hear what I say"* (John 10:24, 27), And Jesus said plainly, *"'I and My FATHER are ONE' then the Jews took up stones to stone Him"* (verses 30–31). For according to them, Jesus was blaspheming by saying He was *one* with the Father. Jesus persisted saying, "Maybe you don't believe *me*, but please believe the works I do. These are great miracles of God." And back when John was imprisoned by Herod, his disciples sent word to Jesus and asked,

> *"Art Thou He that should come? Or look we for another."*
> *Then Jesus answering said unto them. Go your way, and tell John what things ye have seen and heard; how that the blind see, the lame walk, the lepers are cleansed, the deaf hear the dead are raised, to the poor the gospel is preached.* (Luke 7:20, 22)

Jesus did not hesitate to tell all the truth. He answered to John and the crowds that He was the Christ. They just did not yet know He was the *Lamb of God*. He was both the *Lamb* and the *Good Shepherd* and the Christ of God.

Jesus's list of notable miracles is endless; as the author says, if everything had been recorded, the world could not contain the volumes. And that is quite a big library. David says, *"Show me thy marvelous loving kindness… For Thou art Great and doest wondrous things Thou art God Alone"* (Ps. 86:10, 17, 7). The miracles are revealing the majesty of God. His great and tender mercy and His power as God Almighty. God is making Himself known to man. He is exalting His Great Name and is telling us peons, "Look up, your redemption draweth nigh."

"Let them praise the NAME of the LORD: for He commanded, and they were created" (Ps. 148:5).

Malachi 1:11 says, *"For from the rising of the Sun even unto the going down of the same, MY NAME shall be GREAT among the Gentiles"* (and in the Earth).

He is making a *name* for Himself; He is building His kingdom in the Earth.

I want us to go to the country of the Gadarenes now and witness one of Jesus's many fabulous miracles.

> *As Jesus* [and His motley crew] *arrived…a certain man met him, which had devils a long time, and wore no clothes, neither abode in any house, but in the tombs. When he saw Jesus, he cried out and fell down before Him, and with a loud VOICE said, What have I to do with Thee, Jesus Thou Son of God Most High? I beseech Thee torment me not"* [for Jesus had commanded the unclean spirit to come out of the man, and he was kept bound with chains]. *Jesus asked him, what is thy name? and he said Legion: because Many Devils were entered into him… There was a herd of swine close by and the devils besought Jesus not to send them back to the pit* [hell], *so… Jesus suffered them. Then went the devils out of the man, and entered into the swine and the herd ran violently down a steep place into the lake, and were choked."* [You see, even the pigs could not tolerate these miserable demons, it is a wonder the poor man was still alive, that those demons had not killed him, and the compassion, love and mercy of God shines here, it glitters as the stars, is radiant as the heavenly; yes the love of GOD that passes all understanding.] *"When they that fed the swine saw what was done, they fled, and went and told it in the city and in the country. Then they went out to see what was done; and they came to Jesus, and found the man, out of whom the devils were departed, sitting at the feet*

of Jesus, clothed, and in his right mind: *and they were afraid."* [He will keep him in perfect peace whose *mind* the Bible says, "is staid on THEE"; the devils had driven this man CRAZY.]

"Then the whole multitude of the country of the Gadarenes besought Him to depart from them; for they were taken with great FEAR, so Jesus went to the ship and returned back again" (Luke 8:26–35). I think the problem was not only the possessed but the folks that were fearful also had, it seems, no belief. No belief leaves a vacuum for the devil, these folks had no joy in seeing this man delivered, or so it seems to me—correct me if I'm wrong. There was no God in their midst, it seems.

Now the delivered Gadarenan besought Jesus that he might stay with Him but Jesus sent him away saying, Return to thine own house, and show how great things GOD hath done unto thee. And he went his way and published throughout the whole city how great things Jesus had done unto him. (Luke 8:38–39)

Now we know for sure the healed man turned his city upside-down. For this miracle is a stellar testimony to the powers Jesus possessed. Jesus removed dark spiritual powers from this man. The demons knew Jesus and were begging Him for mercy. Can you believe that? Wow! The Father has seen fit to place Jesus over all the powers that be. Jesus is in control of heaven, hell, and the Earth. He is the *head over all*; the Father has placed Him over all. This one miracle alone would be enough to bring salvation to all, but no the town was blinded. The Jews are blinded still; the veil is still over their eyes. And Jesus worked hundreds and thousands of miracles; just think about it. If that happened now in our country, that would seem like heaven. Heaven has come to Earth, almost like the thousand-year reign of Jesus on Earth—almost, a little. So they were fearful, but Jesus's star performance made Him a household *name*; everybody knew Him.

Let us go to the notable, glorious miracle of Jesus's transfiguration. This one seems to be in a higher category because it, like His birth, death, and resurrection, was about His glory, and about Himself, and the Father and the Holy Ghost, because they all function and glorify each other. But prior to this great event, Jesus is talking to His disciples and asked them, "'Whom say ye that I am?' And Peter said, 'The Christ of God.' And Jesus commanded them to tell no man this thing" (Luke 9:20–21). Likewise, Jesus will tell them the same thing after this next event. His transfiguration taken from Matthew 17:1–9:

> *And after 6 days Jesus taketh Peter, James and John up into a high mountain apart, and Jesus was transfigured before them: and His face did shine as the Sun, and His raiment was as the light. And behold there appeared Moses and Elijah talking with Jesus"* [of His decease which He should accomplish at Jerusalem (Luke 9:31)]. *"And Peter said LORD it is good for us to be here let us make 3 tents… While he yet spake a bright cloud overshadowed them: and a Voice out of the cloud said, This is My Beloved Son, in Whom I am well pleased; HEAR YE HIM. And when the disciples heard it, they fell on their faces, and were afraid and in terror. But Jesus came and touched them and said, Arise and be not afraid. And when they lifted up their eyes they saw none but JESUS only. As they came down from the mountain, Jesus commanded them, Tell no man this vision until the Son of man be risen again form the dead."* *"(And they kept this vision secret) questioning one with another what the rising from the dead should mean."* (Mark 9:10)

This was big: Jesus in His glorified body and having a talk with two of the great ones from heaven. Everything Jesus did was out-of-this-world spectacular. He put on no little show. The transcript of these three was exhilarating for Jesus. For they were discussing His victory and His glorified state, which reminded Him of His Father and how He was going to return back to the Father and be in His glorified state for the rest of eternity. And they must have assured Jesus that the Father and the Holy Spirit and the angels believed in His victory for Him and that all would go well. And Jesus would come through shining just as He was then. I bet that conversation was X amount of cool, then the Father stamps it with His signet ring by shining through the cloud and saying, yes, *"This is My Beloved Son, in Whom I am well pleased, hear ye Him."* I never tire of quoting that line; three important facts are here, but the last one I will remark on: "Hear ye Him." You see, here we have the direct command from heaven, God Almighty telling us, "Yes, this is really *My Son*, and this is our plan of redemption." So hear Him and do what He says.

And the Father not just once, or twice, but several times came out of heaven with the same *voice*, declaring His great love for His Beloved Son. His great love! This event was an encouragement for Jesus and His three disciples. He knew things would get tough in the future, and they would need some tangible memories to see them through the dark days ahead. Yes, they would say Jesus is the Christ of God; we saw Him ourselves in His glorified body. They were rock solid, and Jesus knew how to boost their morale, and the Father had just told these men "Hear My Son." As the Father is also telling us, *"Hear Him,"* how do we hear Jesus? By reading His WORDS, His Gospels?

Jesus did need encouragement because He was in a man's body and suffered as any human would. On the other side of the equation, Jesus knew the book of *Isaiah* well. I believe it was His favorite book; Jesus could read about Himself in Isaiah, and His mission is foretold there. Isaiah received Messianic Revelation and is considered the fifth gospel because of His insights. All of chapter 53 tells of His suffering: *"For the transgression of My people was He stricken"* (verse 8).

Then back in chapters 8 and 9, we have Jesus as *the stone of stumbling and the rock of offence"* in verse 14. And 9:6 says, "For unto us a child is born, unto us a son is given: and the government shall be upon His shoulder and His Name shall be called *Wonderful, Counselor,* the *Mighty God,* the *Everlasting Father,* and the *Prince of Peace."*

Isaiah talks much about Jesus. Jesus's first appearance after His temptation by the devil in the wilderness was at the synagogue in Nazareth where He had been brought up. And as the custom was, He stood to read and He read Isaiah 42:7, which spoke of His ministry: *"The spirit of the LORD is upon ME, because He hath anointed ME to preach the Gospel"* (Luke 4:16–18). All of chapter 42 describes Jesus's mission. Verse 4 says, *"He shall not fail nor be discouraged, till He have set judgement in the Earth."* And in verse 6, *"I the LORD have called Thee in Righteousness, and will hold Thine hand, and will keep Thee, and give Thee for a covenant of the people, for a LIGHT to the Gentiles."* And verse 8 says, *"I am the LORD: that is MY NAME"...* *"I am the LORD thy GOD, the Holy One of Israel, Thy Savior"* (43:3). Yes, Jesus had this book hid in His heart, and He quoted often from the Old Testament books and the prophets. The transfiguration sealed in Jesus's heart His mission; it was a private time of encouragement for Him and the boys.

Let's go back to His public that is anxiously awaiting Him; I am a little out of sequence, but I wanted to visit the crowds that ran after Jesus to hear this Rockstar preach and heal. Now Herod had just celebrated his birthday and decided that the Baptist's head on a platter would amuse his guests. Jesus, upon hearing this, wanted some time alone so He departed by ship into a desert place.

As St. Matthew tells us in 14:13–21,

> But great multitudes followed Him, and Jesus had compassion on them and *healed their sick At evening His disciples said, "This is a desert place, it is late send them away that they may buy food." "But Jesus said they need not depart give them to eat" "And they said we have only five loaves*

and two fishes. Jesus said bring them to ME. He commanded the crowd to sit down, and Jesus took the five loaves and two fishes, and looking up to Heaven, He blessed and brake, and gave the loaves to His disciples, and the disciples to the multitude. They all ate and were full; and they took up the fragments that remained which was twelve baskets full. And they that had eaten were about five thousand men and the women and children were not even counted.

Jesus repeated this same miracle with another crowd of four thousand-plus women and children. So as you see, with this size of crowd, Jesus had a great following; cities of people were coming out to hear Him and get healed. Jesus was God's Rockstar, and they were getting interested in taking Him by force, if need be to be their king. These people were poor, hungry, overtaxed, and tired of Roman occupation and oppression. They needed a miracle, a strongman to deliver them from out of Roman hands, and Jesus fit the ticket. St. John explains in 6:14–15:

Then those men when they had seen the miracle that Jesus did, said, This is of a truth, that prophet that should come into the world. When Jesus therefore perceived that they would come and take Him by force, to make Him a KING, He departed again into a mountain." Then some said to Jesus, "*If Thou do these things show thyself to the world…* Then Jesus said, *"My time is not yet come: but your time is always ready."* (Jn. 7:4–6)

Jesus is so popular, they want to make Him king. Every miracle Jesus did got Him a standing ovation. What if your president or prime minister or emperor could, from five pounds of food, wink an eye and turn it into millions of pounds of food to feed cities of the world? How great would that be? Very great; that miracle alone would turn the world upside-down, and we would no doubt reelect Him or her. Hail, King Jesus, on a scale of 1 to 10, how popular is Jesus. Jesus is at five thousand times five thousand times billions and trillions and on and on…

I try to imagine myself being there and witnessing these mighty *acts* of God. The crowds were electrified and this was an ongoing process of three and a half years. Jesus literally had to sneak away to make time for rest. He was walking, talking, gesticulating, and He would feel it in His earthly body when the power went out of Him; this all sounds very exhausting. The crowds held on, watching the blind, lame, and lepers cured. Jesus's compassion was never-ending. "And all were seized with astonishment; they glorified GOD and were filled with awe, saying, 'We have seen incredible things today' (Luke 5:26). Miracles are God in action, which is LOVE revealed (Moffatt). *"For God is LOVE."* and as the hymn says, *"You know nothing until you know God and His LOVE."* Amen!

Now here come the hypocrites, the Pharisees, asking for a *sign*. This seems like intolerable stupidity because every miracle Jesus did was a *sign*. Each one was a witness that Jesus was God; who else could do these miracles? Only one: God, and Jesus was God. They watched with their own eyes and saw the miracles themselves. What is wrong with these people, talking crazy like always; they wanted a *sign*. Jesus flatly refused and said, *"This generation is evil and seeks a SIGN but no sign shall be given to it except the sign of Jonah. For as Jonah became a SIGN to the men of Nineveh, so will the Son of man be a SIGN to this generation"* (Matt. 12:38–40). Jonah warned the people of Nineveh, so also Jesus was preaching repentance to all Israel. Jesus warned, *"The Queen of the South will arise at the judgement with the men of this generation and condemn them; for she came from the ENDS of the EARTH TO HEAR THE WISDOM OF SOLOMON, and behold, A GREATER THAN SOLOMON IS HERE"* (Matt. 12:42).

Folks, Solomon was so popular the world was taken under with him. God bestowed such great majesty on Solomon as had never been seen before. Kings paid handsomely for an audience with him. He was literally the king of the Earth in his day. God had given him a divine heavenly wisdom, which had never been seen upon a man before or after him; plus, He bestowed him with riches and honor such as no king ever had before or after him. God is good. Can we have an *amen* in the balcony? With all that said, Jesus is shouting at them, *"Behold a greater than Solomon is here; Right here."* And Jesus said kings and prophets have desired to see and hear those things which you are witnessing, because ever since the fall, mankind has looked for a Savior. Did Solomon work miracles? No, no, no way; he just had wisdom to govern and rightly divide.

Solomon wrote Proverbs and many of them. But Jesus is saying, "My wisdom is mightier." The comparison is like comparing God to man. Solomon, yes, was great, but even all believers today put on the mind of Christ through the Holy Scriptures. God is able to make the simple wise through His Word, and the average Joe, He can elevate to genius level through His Word, because to take on the mind of Christ is to put on the *love* of God, which surpasses all knowledge. The *love* of God makes man a genius, it is a genius who *loves God*. So yes, Solomon had Proverbs, but Jesus preached with power because He sealed His *words* with miracles. And Jesus's teachings made Solomon's pale in comparison. Jesus taught parables that had astonishing *wisdom*; listen as Luke tells us about the unrighteous judge.

> *Jesus spoke this parable about our need to pray and not lose heart; There was in a city a Judge which feared not GOD, neither regarded man: And there was a widow in that city; and she came unto him saying, avenge me of mine adversary. And he would not for a while: But later said, though I fear not GOD nor regard man; yet because this widow troubleth me, I will avenge her, lest by her continual coming she weary me. And Jesus said; Hear what the unjust Judge saith. And shall not God avenge His own elect (that's us) which cry day and night unto Him, though He bear long with them. I tell you That HE WILL AVENGE THEM SPEEDILY.* (18:1–8)

The Moffatt version reads, *"Though I have no reverence for GOD and no RESPECT even for man, still, as this widow is bothering me, I will see justice done for her, so as not to have her forever coming and pestering me"* (18:4–5).

Quite a picture, quite a parable—the parable shows us how to persist with our prayers, for surely, God will hear us and answer speedily. Jesus's parable says it, and Jesus is not a liar. He says *"speedily."* And the judge was right; even though he was wicked, I need to get rid of her. She's driving me crazy, so I'll give her what she wants, and I'll be rid of my headache. And what does James 5:16 say? *"The effectual fervent prayer of a righteous man availeth much."*

Jesus's parables were seemingly simple yet profound. The key is that Jesus's *words* and *actions* are heavenly; they were not the normal of this world. Heaven is spiritual and invisible, and Earth is worldly and corrupt. The two have the beat of different drummers. His sayings and miracles were not ordinarily seen or heard of man; they were extraordinary. Jesus knew how big this was; Jesus knew how great things He was doing. Jesus knew His Words were not His *words*, but the Father's *words* and these miracles were not His but the Father's. Thus His righteous indignation was stirred within Him.

> *And Jesus began to upbraid the cities where in most of His mighty works were done, because they repented not: Woe unto thee Chorazin and Bethsaida! For if the mighty works which were done in you, had been done in Tyre and Sidon, they would have Repented long ago in sack cloth and ashes... (Woe unto you on Judgement Day) And thou Capernaum which art exalted to heaven shalt be brought down to Hell: for if the mighty works, which have been done in thee had been done in SODOM, it WOULD HAVE REMAINED UNTIL THIS DAY. But I say unto you, that it shall be more TOLERABLE FOR SODOM in the Day of Judgement than for thee.* (Matt. 11:20–24)

Strong *words*, strong message, and big condemnation. Jesus warned His followers of the Pharisees, *"Woe to you Pharisees, Scribes, Lawyers and hypocrites!... You tithe, but justice and the LOVE of God you disregard... You load men with burdens that you will not dare touch. Woe to you, you build the tombs for the prophets which your fathers killed"* (Luke 11:42–48). Jesus had their number and called them on it. There was no hope for their stiff-necked and rebellious ways. On the contrary, when His apostles saw Him walking on the water, they honored Him. When Jesus and Peter got into the ship, the sea became calm and they worshipped Jesus right there in the boat. And said, *"Of a truth thou art the Son of God."* Capernaum had wealth and riches, and Jesus said this will corrupt a man, for it is hard for a rich man to enter heaven. Wealth is a fortress of power and security that tends to ignore God. Wealth blinds humans of their need of God. Riches will be for naught on Judgement Day; those fists full of dollars will seem like monopoly money. Judgement Day will be pretty ugly for all the rebels. Getting into Jesus's ship is the sure thing; all other ships are sinking fast and won't last. Jesus said there will be wailing and gnashing of teeth as they are cast into the furnace of fire. All of Jesus's words are truth—the absolute *truth*.

Jesus's righteous indignation is shown through on several occasions as in the cleansing of the temple. Jesus is trying to point humanity into a righteous path by showing us what does and does not please the Father. His mission was to deliver unto us all the information possible that would be of assistance unto His flock to make it into the Kingdom of Heaven. Jesus had a treasure trove of sayings and parables. How did this man come up with all this stuff? Did He have a staff of writers, a team, a network, or was it the Father and the Holy Spirit? All in all, these writings are totally amazing. I bow in adoration at the feet of He who did so much for us. Jesus is indeed the *Author* of our salvation.

Now Jesus's disciples came to Him and asked, "Why are you speaking in parables to the people?" And Jesus said, *"Because it is given unto you to know the mysteries of the Kingdom of Heaven, but to them it is not given."* Then Jesus spoke this parable, "Again the Kingdom of Heaven is like unto a merchant man, seeking goodly pearls: who when he had found the *one pearl of great price*, he went and sold all that he had, and bought it" (Matt. 13:45–46).

Friends, Jesus is that *Pearl of great price*. He is it. He is the *prize*. So let us get our priorities straight and fly right. The man sold all that he had to apprehend this one costly pearl; it was his life's dream to have a treasure so costly. Elizabeth Taylor had the costly black pearl, but Jesus is the Priceless Pearl, the Great Prize. Paul says, "I have suffered the loss of all things to lay hold on the Pearl of Great Price." Moses forsook all the treasures of Egypt to win the Pearl of Great Price. John the Baptist gave up all the comforts of a couch, a TV, and TV dinners and dwelt with snakes, heat, cold, no food, and condemned Herod for taking his brother's wife to gain the Pearl of Great Price. Elijah walked forty days across the desert without food or water to lay hold of the Pearl of Great Price; the list is endless. Jesus has an endless list of suitors, all in search for the lover of their souls. And without a parable, Jesus did not speak to them, but many, many parables and saying Jesus did preach and teach. The parables were Jesus's genius.

However, Jesus's Words were not without power.

> *"Now Jesus loved Martha, Mary and Lazarus."*
> [And Word came to Jesus that Lazarus was sick.]
> *"When Jesus heard this He said This sickness is not unto death, but for the glory of GOD, that the SON of GOD might be glorified thereby" "and Jesus said Where have ye laid him"… Take the stone away… And Jesus lifted up His eye heavenward and said Father I thank Thee that Thou hast heard ME… And then Jesus cried with a LOUD VOICE Lazarus come forth, and he came forth."* (John 11:1–44)

This miracle of miracles shows that Jesus is Lord of both the living and the dead and has power over both life and death. When has this ever happened in the history of the world that a man could raise a decomposing corpse back to life? Yes, Lazarus was already decomposing. But the Lord told Martha, "Said I not unto thee that if thou wouldest believe, thou shouldest see the Glory of GOD" (verse 40). And that is precisely what this miracle is: the glory of *God Almighty*. This is God revealed unto man, the miraculous being unveiled. And yes, this is a high point in Jesus's ministry; now, many, many more believed that Jesus was God. These people all knew Lazarus and knew for sure he had died and knew for sure Jesus had raised him from the dead. Now the Pharisees had said it was a hoax and were trying to dissuade the people, but the Holy Spirit triumphed on this one.

I believe Jesus had deep thoughts and emotions about this whole ordeal. On the one hand, He is very troubled; here, Lazarus was at peace and in a better place, but his relatives want to call him back into this old painful world. Maybe Lazarus was happy where he was and "Jesus wept"—the shortest verse in the Bible. Maybe that is why Jesus wept; "Come back, Lazarus, and suffer some more." The other thought is that Jesus is very happy because He is foretelling His own resurrection from the dead. No man has ever raised himself from the dead, but Jesus did. He raised himself out of the grave after three days without seeing any corruption to His body, as King David foretold. And Jesus foretold, "I am the resurrection"; it is because of Jesus that we will all be raised from the dead. Without Jesus's resurrection, none of us would be able to see God; that is how big a message this miracle had. Jesus is glorified here because now the Jews are believing that God sent Jesus and that He is their long-awaited Messiah, *"the desire of ages."* "Believe," Jesus says, "and you will see God at work," and they did see. God raised the dead Lazarus for the crowd so that they would believe in Him. And many believed.

Belief is tantamount to Jesus's entire ministry. Again in this miracle, Jesus is saying only believe. I hold to the fact that Jesus was the greatest teacher ever to live. In the course of my studies, I became acquainted with lots of teachers and theorized that a really good teacher could make the simplest of students grasp their studies. A good teacher can make the lessons understandable to everyone. What I see through His parables and miracles is that He kept it simple and had three major points, which were repeated often.

First, He said *believe*, an absolute command to us; just accept and believe. Just do it. Jesus's chief question, do you believe, or only believe because all things are possible with God? He only asks that we would believe in Him.

Second, have faith, Jesus said. He became man to understand our weaknesses and Jesus, the Father, and the Holy Spirit are in an invisible realm. Therefore, we must trust and believe and have Faith. *"Jesus saith, have Faith in God"* (Mark 11:22).

"Jesus said, Because of your unbelief: [you could not cast the devil out] *for verily I say unto you, If you have Faith as a grain of mustard seed* (very small)*ye shall say unto this mountain Remove…and it shall Remove"; and nothing shall be impossible unto you"* (Matt. 17:20). For unto God and in God's Kingdom, *faith* is everything. Galatians 5:6 talks about faith: *"For in Jesus Christ* (nothing) *availeth anything… but Faith which worketh by Love."* And 1 John 5:4 nails it by saying, *"For whatsoever is born of GOD overcometh the world: and this is the VICTORY that overcometh the WORLD even OUR FAITH."* And Paul gives us the definition in Hebrews 11:1, *"NOW FAITH IS the substance of things hoped for, and the evidence of things not seen."* This is why our good, great teacher Jesus said over and over, "Have faith in God."

And the *third point* that Jesus repeated often is, "Your *sins* are forgiven you." Now this was not said at Lazarus's tomb, but may have been implied. For the Word says, *"Whatsoever is not of Faith is sin."* Jesus wants us to know that when we believe and have faith in Him, our sins are forgiven; they are washed away never to be remembered. This is a fact. Jesus wants us to know His precepts, His doctrines, the facts, and the *truth.* We can rest on the fact that when we *believe* and have *faith,* our *sins* are forgiven us. Easy, Jesus is an easy teacher, but repetition implies that these three points are very important; and Jesus wants us to do, to know, and remember His sayings, His miracles.

Jesus showcased this miracle as none other. He is the star performer here and will not give His glory to another. He set the stage for this grand event by stalling out a little and coming in for a home-run later in the game. Jesus wants to be noticed for who He is—God Almighty. He points to His Father and to Himself. Why? "Because the Father and I are one. And if you do not believe in ME, at least believe in the works, for the works cry; He is God alone, there is no other and no one like Him. And now that you have met the BEST you can forget the REST… [of all your vanities].” Jesus's performance is crying, “LOVE ME, BELIEVE ME, for I am God and I and the Father are one” (Deut. 6:4–5).

> *Hear O Israel: The LORD our GOD is ONE LORD!*
> *And thou shalt love the LORD thy GOD*
> *with all thine heart,*
> *and with all thy soul,*
> *and with all thy might.*

And Isaiah echoes the same sentiment in 45:5–8:

> *I am the LORD, and there is none else. There*
> *is no GOD besides ME. That they*
> *may know from the rising of the Sun, and*
> *from the West, that there is None*
> *besides ME. I am the LORD, and there is*
> *none else. I form the light, and create*
> *darkness: I make peace and create evil: I the*
> *LORD do all these things. Drop down,*
> *ye heavens, from above,… Let the Earth open*
> [and receive her KING].

“Open your eyes and see and believe that it is I the LORD Jesus that do these miracles. Come unto ME and love ME for I am He, the LORD thy God in the midst of thee. I work a work in your day that will be hard to believe.” Jesus knew He had a home run. He had truly gotten their attention. Now their faith in Him was being built, for they had said, “LORD build our faith.” *“But without FAITH it is impossible to please Him: for he that cometh to GOD must believe that HE IS, and that He is a rewarder of them that diligently seek Him”* (Heb. 11:6).

This was their faith-building miracle; it was definitely a “look at ME” moment. *“Look unto ME, and be ye saved, all the ends of the*

Earth: for I am GOD, and there is none else" (Isa. 45:22). And Isaiah 52:6 says, *"Therefore My people shall know My NAME: they shall know in that day that I am He that doth speak: behold it is I."*

And many believed on Him this day; Lazarus walked out of the tomb and many believed. Jesus had won their hearts on this day. Now they would believe because seeing is believing. They witnessed an act of God, a performance by their creator. Earth had been kissed by her Maker and the power of His Holy arm revealed for every eye to see.

But not everyone in Zion was thrilled on this day. After knowing that Jesus had raised Lazarus, the Pharisees went berserk again. They assembled one of their kangaroo courts and decided enough was enough. They said,

> *"What are we to do, for this Jesus doeth many miracles. If we let Jesus alone all men will BELIEVE ON HIM, and the Romans will come and take away both our Holy Place and Our NATION."* *"Then from that day forth they took counsel together to put Jesus to death."* (John 11:47, 53)

And as a matter of record, the chief priests and Pharisees wanted to put Lazarus to death also because he was the proof of this mighty miracle, which Jesus did, and many more Jews had come to believe in Jesus because of it.

At this point, Jesus's popularity was so rock-solid and grounded. His following so large that He, if He had wished, could have established His Kingdom here on Earth. The disciples were already bringing out the red carpet and arguing over what percentage of gold leaf to use in the precipices of the palace. The throne would be solid gold and the twelve of them would rule His Kingdom as princes.

This, however, was not the Father's plan. No, this idea was insignificant against the magnificent plan the Father had for His Real Kingdom here on Earth. Jesus's desire was always to please the Father and all Scripture of the Holy Prophets must be fulfilled; the Scriptures cannot be broken. Now they were on their way to Jerusalem and

Jesus reminded His disciples again that the Son of Man had yet to be mocked, shamed, and crucified for our sins.

It was *sin* that stood yet in the path of victory. Jesus could do forty more years of miracles and cures, and raising the dead, but *sin*, *sin* had to be removed. Sin had yet to be taken out of the picture, with the atoning ransom at the *cross*. The *just one* for the unjust and unlovely had to die in our place and redeem us (the world) unto the Father. Colossians 2:15 tells us, *"And having SPOILED principalities and powers, He made a SHOW of them openly, TRIUMPHING OVER THEM IN IT."* Jesus's *victory* was the *cross*, and He had yet to tread the winepress *alone* up Golgotha's hill. The disciples and the crowds would suffer disappointment until the Father sent the *Holy Spirit* to interject understanding on the behalf of our human weakness. An Earthly Kingdom just was not in the plan (quite yet)! Later, a short time later, it will be happening soon; soon to come! Jesus was born to die and was anxiously awaiting to be baptized in His mission and be *glorified*.

The Holy Word says, "For envy they sought to kill Jesus." And envy kills. The chief priests who thought, "Wow, we are so religious, we are so zealous, we are like so of GOD. [Hah!] We fast, pray, read, study, in fact I have the Torah memorized, and mine is the biggest library around. I tithe myself poor."

And Jesus said, "Depart from ME, ye wicked and unbelieving. Ye do build the Sepulchers of the Most Holy Prophets, and by the way do not say Abraham is your Father. Abraham is the father of the righteous, the Holy of God, and the believing. If you do not believe Me, you would not believe *My Father*, for we are One and the same. God is one. Hear, O, Israel, God is One, you hypocrites. One, you blind guides, one, you deaf of hearing.

Filthy vermin are ye all, a froward generation with the Spirit of your father the devil in you. A riotous mob of debauchery. You belong in the stone age and in the stone age you will stay, never ever coming to the *light* because you don't want your deeds manifest that you are of the devil.

Jesus, being God, read their minds and hearts. He was the Messiah, and at any given moment or hour, could call upon legions of angels for reinforcement. He would lay down His life. He had the power to lay it down and take it up again. He was not forced or commanded to. Jesus offered to the Father to lay down His life as a pure sacrifice for our sins. He was never required. He offered okay willingly. "For this purpose, I was born and came into the world," Jesus said.

Jesus continued His preaching throughout all the cities, towns, and villages, spreading the good news of the Kingdom of God. And all people came out to see and hear what the Master was saying. And with a Word, He healed them all. *Therefore the Pharisees said among themselves, Perceive how ye can do nothing? BEHOLD THE WORLD IS GONE AFTER HIM"* (John 12:19).

Even the officers they sent to apprehend Jesus were amazed saying, *"Never man spake like this Man"* (John 7:46).

And the centurion of Capernaum sent word to Jesus saying, *"Wherefore neither thought I myself worthy to come unto thee: but say the WORD and my servant shall be healed"* (Luke 7:7).

The power of a Word is real with Jesus. With a Word, everything in the universe obeys Him. His Words are so real and important that Jesus claims,

> *He that rejecteth ME, and receiveth not MY WORDs, hath one that judgeth him: the WORD that I have spoken, the same shall judge him in the LAST DAY. For I have not spoken of Myself; but the Father which sent ME* [He it was who ordered ME what to say and what to speak, Moffatt]. *And I know that His commandment* [His WORD] *is life everlasting: whatsoever I speak therefore even as the Father said unto ME so I speak.* (John 12:48–50)

Jesus Words are power, and they are *life*. That's why the Gospels and the Holy Scriptures are called the "Living Word," and that is why the Father said, "Hear ye Him; this is MY BELOVED SON. Hear Him, hear His WORDS." And the whole world went after Jesus because of His Words and miracles. And rightly so because He is God, and the whole world should run after Jesus and apprehend *life*.

Jesus continued His bold statements and claims saying,

> *For I am come down from Heaven not to do Mine own will, but the will of Him* [the Father] *that sent ME…*
> *And this is the will of Him that sent ME, that everyone which seeth the SON and believeth on HIM, may have everlasting life: and I will raise him up at the Last Day* [to be with ME]. (John 6:38, 40)

"Just like I raised Lazarus up and just like I raised Myself up out of the grave, this same way I will raise you up out of the grave and you will then be forever with ME in heaven." This is Jesus's total message: *everlasting life.* The miracles were proof that He was God sent from heaven above. His miracles were an overflow of His love because His compassion is automatic. God is the antithesis of *love*; His love embraced mercy. He used His divine nature to heal all the broken-hearted. Miracles are just God's nature; they are automatic with Him.

Jesus tells us how He worked the miracles. He says, *"But if I with the finger of GOD cast out devils* [and we can add here, heal the sick and raise the dead] *then no doubt the Kingdom of GOD is come upon you"* (Luke 11:20).

Jesus brought heaven to Earth and declared in every way, with every breath and action, that He was God: "I am God alone and there is none other." And he that is of God hears *Me*, hears *My Words*, believes *My miracles* and knows that I am the *Son* of *God* sent to Earth to save man, and this was all sanctioned by His miracles: God in action. These people were seeing the mystery of God, which had been hid from mankind for centuries. Jesus takes His disciples aside and tells them so,

> *Blessed are the eyes which see the things that ye see. For I tell you, that many prophets and kings have desired to see those things which ye see, and*

have not seen them; and to hear those things which ye hear, and have not heard them. (Luke 10:23–24)

And there is a further blessing, for the Lord said, "Blessed are they that have not seen, yet believe." That's us! We were not present, only in Spirit were we there. God hath spoken…

> *O Earth, Earth, Earth, hear the WORD of the LORD.*
> Drop down O Heavens, *"God who at sundry times and in divers manners spake in times past unto the fathers by the prophets, Hath in these last days spoken unto us by His Son, whom He hath appointed heir of all things, by whom also He made the worlds."* (Heb. 1:12)

God spoke to Abraham, Moses, and all the prophets, but now He speaks to us directly through Jesus.

"And Jesus taught daily in the temple. But the chief priests and the scribes and the chief of the people sought to destroy Him." Why? Because this is an ongoing controversy with Satan, our archenemy. Satan does not want us to have what he lost, *heaven: "And they could not find what they might do: for ALL the people were very attentive to hear Jesus"* (Luke 19:47–48).

Jesus had the people in the palm of His hand; they were mesmerized by the perfection of heaven's Master. They were on cloud 9. Imagine Jesus waking up each day to go work miracles, and the people waking up each day to see and hear Him. *"Since the World began was it not heard."* Jesus had taken the whole world by a perfect storm, and they were loving it.

The reality of all, Jesus did bedazzles me, as it did them. How could anyone in their right mind believe anything less than the *truth* that Jesus Christ is the Almighty God of heaven and Earth. His rap sheet speaks volumes:

- He fed the five thousand plus, then the seven thousand plus.
- He raised the dead.
- He delivered demoniacs.
- He made crooked limbs straight.
- He healed lepers.
- The Father spoke out of heaven at various times, blessing His Son, and all the people heard.
- He gave hope to the poor and oppressed, confirming that evil would not escape punishment.
- And he gave us hope of eternal life by His death and resurrection.

How quickly we forget, just as the Hebrew children quickly forgot all the signs and wonders performed before Pharaoh and all Egypt. Those were outstanding miracles, revealing the arm of God's power. And we have only seen the tip of the iceberg. Because Paul says, "Eye has not seen nor ear heard of the wonderful things GOD has prepared for those that love Him." And God proclaims, "Is there anything too hard for ME?"

Belief is the key to Jesus's heart.

So if you are like me, you maybe can't wait to see God and be with this miracle God of wonders who has done so incredibly much for us. Like Paul Harvey says, "And now you know the rest of the story." No, we will only know if we make heaven our home and see Jesus for ourselves. That alone is incentive enough for me. I want to find out the rest of the story. Take the limits off your imagination and that will be a good starting point because we "ain't seen nothin' yet."

Oh, heaven is looking brighter all the time. All aboard, this train is bound for *glory*. "Let me see your ticket, sir." That's it. The one that has your name written on it, like in the Lamb's Book of Life. That's the ticket, that's it: your *name* on the ledger in the Lamb's Book of Life is the only available entry into *His Eternal Glory…*

Your name in the Book of Life.
Is your name there?

PS: Put your name there by kneeling before Jesus today and saying, "Jesus, Thou Son of God, I want you to be my Lord and Savior today. Right now, from this minute, and forever for all eternity."

His Name

—⟨∾⟩—

Wherefore God also hath highly exalted HIM,
and given HIM a NAME which is above every NAME:
That at the NAME OF JESUS every knee should bow,
of things in Heaven, and things in earth, and things under
the Earth; And that every tongue should confess that JESUS
CHRIST is LORD, to the glory of God the Father.

—Philippians 2:9–11

Give unto the Lord the glory due unto HIS NAME:
bring an offering, and come into his courts.
O worship the Lord in the beauty of holiness:
fear before HIM, all the Earth. Say among the heathen
that the LORD REIGNETH.

—Psalm 96:8–10

But these are written, that ye might believe that Jesus
is the Christ, the Son of God; and that believing ye
might have LIFE THROUGH HIS NAME.

—John 20:31

Everyone is known by his *name* and the Almighty is no exception. For ages, man has inquired, asked, pleaded, and begged for a name that they might affix to the Most High God that dwelleth in the heavens, the object of their worship and adoration. Listen to what Moses writes as Jacob puts forth his request for a name.

> *And Jacob was left alone; and there wrestled a man with him until the breaking of the day. And when he saw that he prevailed not against him, he touched the hollow of his thigh; and the hollow of Jacob's thigh was out of joint, as he wrestled with him. And he said, Let me go, for the day breaketh. And he said, I will not let thee go, except thou bless me. And he said unto him, What is thy name? And he said, Jacob. And he said, Thy name shall be called no more Jacob, but Israel: for as a prince hast thou power with God and with men, and hast prevailed. And Jacob asked him, and said, TELL ME, I pray thee, THY NAME. And he said, Wherefore is it that thou dost ask after my NAME? And he blessed him there. And Jacob called the name of the place Peniel: for I have seen God face to face, and my life is preserved.* (Gen. 32:24–30)

Until now, the Lord was referred to as the most high God, or the Lord God, Maker of heaven and Earth, and all that there is. Now, God taps Moses for service as a deliverer of His People who were in bondage to Pharaoh of Egypt because God heard the cries of His children, and He said, "I will send them a deliverer to free them from the iron furnace of Egypt."

> *And Moses said unto God, Behold, when I come unto the children of Israel, and shall say unto them, The God of your fathers hath sent me unto you; and they shall say to me, WHAT IS HIS NAME? what shall I say unto them? And God said unto Moses, I Am That I Am: and HE said, Thus shalt thou say unto the children of Israel, I Am hath sent ME unto you. And God said moreover unto Moses, Thus shalt*

thou say unto the children of Israel, the Lord God of your fathers, the God of Abraham, the God of Isaac, and the God of Jacob, hath sent ME unto you: this is MY NAME for ever, and this is My Memorial unto all generations. (Ex. 3:13–15)

This is MY NAME for all time, This is MY TITLE for all ages. (Moffatt)

Furthermore, if they need proof, "I am that I am," I will show them My *mighty power* through all the signs and wonders that you will perform before the children and before Pharaoh and the Egyptians. God is now going to manifest His identity to the world through Moses and confirm that yes, He is the Mighty God, Lord, and King of heaven and Earth, and He has a Name that is above all names and all gods. Now God is making His presence and Name known in the entire Earth and teaching His chosen nation, Israel, to trust alone in the Living GOD, who would lead them through the wilderness providing for them and protecting them from all their enemies.

For the Lord said, surely these are MY PEOPLE…so He was their Savior He led them by the right hand of Moses with a glorious arm, dividing the water before them, to make Himself an EVERLASTING NAME… So Thou didst lead Thy people, to make Thyself a glorious NAME. (Isa. 63:8, 12, 14)

Through His strong arm, God was revealing to His Chosen ones that His Name was glorious and Holy, He was to be reverenced and honored all the days of their lives.

Hear O Israel the LORD our GOD is ONE LORD: And thou shalt love the LORD thy God with all thy heart, with all thy soul, and with all thy might. Thou shalt fear the LORD thy God and serve HIM, and shalt swear by His NAME… That it may be well with thee. (Deut. 6:4, 13, 18)

Thou shalt not take the NAME of the LORD thy GOD in vain; for the LORD will not hold him guiltless that taketh HIS NAME in vain. (Exod. 20:7)

His name is One, one God; whereas the heathen had many gods, our God is one and his Name One. And since we serve a holy God, His very Name is to be revered. This is of course one of His ten most holy commandments, which are forever carved in *stone* by the finger of God. God said My Name shall be great and glorious for I am a Great King and a Great God. My Name shall be reverenced and Holy for I am a Holy God. In fact He absolutely commands this saying,

If thou wilt not observe to do all the WORDS of this LAW that are written in this BOOK, that thou mayest fear this GLORIOUS and FEARFUL NAME, THE LORD THY GOD; Then the Lord will make thy plagues (horrific), *and the plagues of thy seed, even great plagues, and of long continuance, and sore sicknesses, and of long continuance. Moreover he will bring upon thee all the diseases of Egypt, which thou wast afraid of; and they shall cleave unto thee.* (Deut. 28:58–60)

But if thou wilt hearken and obey the LORD thy GOD I will set thee on HIGH, above ALL NATIONS OF THE EARTH. And all these blessings shall come upon Thee (thou shalt be blessed, blessed and blessed) and the LORD shall establish thee as holy people unto Himself, as He hath sworn unto thee, if thou shalt keep the commandments of the LORD thy GOD, and walk in all His Ways. And all the people of the Earth shall see that thou art CALLED BY THE NAME OF THE LORD

THY GOD; and they shall be afraid of thee. (Deut. 28:1–2, 9–10)

The standard has been set; He is God. He writes the rules, this is it MY MOST HOLY NAME is to be feared above everything in life. I am the Great I Am that works miracles without end. I am your Maker, your Creator, and I teach my children the things that make for their good always. Remember My wonders that I performed before Pharaoh's courts. All of Egypt, all of Israel, and all of the known world saw firsthand a display of My majesty and power. Praise is due unto My Name forever. Lift up holy hands enter His courts with praise and the King of Glory shall come in. Who is this King of Glory? The Lord mighty in power. Again lesson #2: what does the Baltimore Catechism[1] say? Yes, the whole duty of man is to glorify the Name of Our God, that is our whole and entire duty. Thou, oh, God, art the great Alpha and Omega and *"Thy NAME is from everlasting."* In Moses's song, He says,

> *Give ear, O ye heavens, and I will speak and hear O Earth, the words of my mouth. Because I will publish the NAME of the LORD: ascribe ye greatness unto our God. He is the ROCK, His work is perfect.* (Deut. 32:1–4)

David, also a man after God's own heart, understood the significance of the Lord's Name. He fought His battles in the Name of the LORD. He built the great temple at Jerusalem to the glory of the Lord's Name. The Lord delivered his enemies into His hands because he never failed to call on the Name of the Lord. His enemies knew that David fought to bring honor to the Name of his God. And David knew that He was chosen king and anointed of God for the Lord's Great Namesake. That through Him, Israel would as a nation bring great honor to the Mighty and Powerful Name of the Lord. He would cause the enemies of the Lord to fear before His Holy NAME, the Name that is above every Name. God caused David to always triumph in the Name of His God, because he did cleave unto his God.

David says,

> *Because Thy loving kindness is better than life, my lips shall praise Thee. Thus will I bless Thee while I live: I will lift up my hands in THY NAME.* (Ps. 63:3–4)
>
> *Praise ye the LORD. Praise, O ye servants of the LORD, praise the NAME of the LORD. Blessed be the NAME of the LORD from this time forth and for evermore. From the rising of the sun unto the going down of the same, the LORD'S NAME is to be praised. The LORD is High above all the Nations and His glory above the Heavens. Who is like unto the LORD our GOD, who dwelleth on High. Who humbleth HIMSELF to behold the things that are…in the Earth!* (Ps. 113:1–6)
>
> *Through Thee will we push down our enemies: through Thy NAME will we tread them under that rise up against us. In GOD we boast all the day long, and praise Thy NAME forever. Selah.* (Ps. 44:5, 8)

(Oh yes, the Lord God of Abraham, Isaac, and Jacob went before David into battle, the Lord is on my side David says. Yes, His Captain and the Lord of Hosts is His Name.)

> *In Judah is God known HIS NAME is GREAT in ISRAEL. There brake He the arrows of the bow, the shield, and the sword, and the battle. Selah. Thou art more glorious and excellent than the mountains of prey. Thou even Thou, art to be feared: and who may stand in Thy sight when once Thou art angry.* (Ps. 72:1, 3–4, 7)
>
> *According to Thy NAME, O GOD so is Thy praise unto the ends of the Earth. For this GOD is*

our GOD forever and ever: HE will be our GUIDE even unto death. (Ps. 48:10, 14)

> *HIS NAME shall endure forever: HIS NAME shall be continued as long as the Sun… Blessed be the LORD of Israel, who only doeth wondrous things. And blessed be His Glorious NAME forever: And let the whole Earth be filled with His Glory. Amen and Amen. The prayers of David the son of Jesse are ended.* (Ps. 76:17–20)

From the meekest man ever in the earth, the only man to speak face to face with God, our man of God Moses we go to David, the anointed king of Israel, the sweet psalmist to a man most revered the prophetic prophet Isaiah. A prophet of vision and insight, the rocket scientist genius of prophets is this cum laude writer. Why genius, you say? Because the man that exalts God and sets Him in His rightful place on His Throne is a man of genius. It takes a genius to realize he needs God and it takes a genius to worship and adore his Maker unto whom belongs all our adoration. And so is the great one, Isaiah, a genius.

> *"The ox knoweth His owner, and The ass His Master's crib: But Israel doth not know, My People doth not consider"* (Isa. 1:3).

The man who penned these words deserves a PhD from the University of Heaven, for Isaiah is indeed provocative. And his Names for God leave nothing for our imagination for he refers to the Almighty as the Holy One of Israel. Is there anything left to say? A perfect description and Name tag for the object of our worship, the desire of ages. Hear, O, Israel, our God is One. Isaiah had everything to say and tell about our Savior, our King, our Holy One. He foretold all that Israel would suffer for turning her back on God. He also foretold all Jesus's birth, ministry, death, and resurrection, even to the end of days he foretold. There is so much information in his book; we call it the fifth gospel. Yes, read it; it will be the best read of your life. Nearly every Word and phrase is anointed by the Blessed Holy

Spirit. His Words are profound. I see where Jesus got so much of His learning from this book; no doubt he had chapters memorized and every day was realizing more and more that the Words of prophecy were speaking of Him. Because from a newborn babe, Jesus was filled with the Holy Spirit and it is the Blessed Holy Spirit that gives us understanding and insight into the Holy Writ, the Scriptures, the Words of Jesus and God. No, you do not need a priest to tell you its meaning—you, my friend, are the priest.

Jesus has made us kings and priests unto God.

Yes, my blessed Catholic friends, read on and you will understand all these concepts out of His Holy Book. Yes, we will reign with Him and judge the Earth with Him. To him that overcomes this world and the devil and the flesh and its lusts, this *reward* is guaranteed us by the death and resurrection of Jesus Christ.

> *Beloved, now are we the sons of God, and it doth not, YET APPEAR what we shall be: but we know that, when he shall appear, we shall be like HIM; for we shall see HIM as HE is. And every man that hath this HOPE in him purifieth himself, even as HE is PURE.* (1 John 3:2–3)

Isaiah's revelations are peppered with multiple Names for God. He renewed the people's *hope* that the Messiah that was to come was near. Once God had purged their iniquities through captivity they were again ready to listen to God and His Holy *men*, the prophets. This was indeed the prodigal son, crying, "Yes, Father, here I am. I'm back. I want you, O, God, my Lord, my Savior, my Redeemer. Hear, O, Israel, our God is One. Listen as the Master of verse and revelation puts sweet music in your ears! The Lord our God is One Lord."

> *Seek ye out of the book of the Lord and Read: not one of these (prophecies) shall fail.* (Isa. 34:16)
> *Now go, write it before them in a table, and note it in a book, that it may be for the time to come for ever and ever.* (Isa. 30:8)

Woe to them that go down to Egypt for help and stay on horses and trust in chariots…because they are strong but they look not unto the HOLY ONE of ISRAEL. Neither seek the LORD! But it shall come to pass that the remnant that ESCAPE… shall now stay upon the LORD the HOLY ONE of ISRAEL in TRUTH. (Isa. 31:1, 10:20)

I am the Lord: that is MY NAME: and my glory will I not give to another, neither my praise to graven images. (Isa. 42:8)

Even every one that is called by MY NAME: for I have created him for my glory, I have formed him; yea, I have made him. (Isa. 43:7)

Ye are my witnesses, saith the Lord, and my servant whom I have chosen: that ye may KNOW AND BELIEVE ME, and understand that I AM HE: before ME there was no God formed, neither shall there be after ME. I, even I, AM THE LORD; and beside me there is no saviour (Isa. 43:10–11). Thus saith the LORD, I AM GOD.

I have declared, and have saved, and I have shewed, when there was no strange god among you: therefore ye are my witnesses, saith the Lord, that I AM GOD. Yea, before the day was I AM HE; and there is NONE that can deliver out of my hand: I will work, and who shall let it? Thus saith the Lord, your redeemer, the Holy One of Israel; For your sake I have sent to Babylon, and have brought down all their nobles, and the Chaldeans, whose cry is in the ships. (Isa. 43:12–14)

I am the Lord, your Holy One, the creator of Israel, your King. Behold, I will do a new thing; now it shall spring forth; shall ye not know it? I will even make a way in the WILDERNESS, and RIVERS IN THE DESERT.(Isa. 43:15, 19)

Thus saith the Lord the King of Israel, and HIS REDEEMER the Lord of HOSTS; I am the FIRST, and I am the LAST; and beside ME there is no God. (Isa. 44:6)

Look unto me, and be ye saved, all the ends of the earth: for I AM GOD, and there is NONE else. (Isa. 45:22)

I bring near My righteousness; it shall not be far off, and My salvation shall NOT TARRY: and I will place Salvation in Zion for Israel My glory. (Isa. 46:13)

As for our REDEEMER, the Lord of HOSTS is HIS name, the Holy One of Israel. (Isa. 47:4)

The people that walked in darkness have seen a great LIGHT: they that dwell in the land of the Shadow of Death, upon them hath the LIGHT shined. For unto us a Child is born, unto us a SON is given.' And the government shall be upon His shoulder: and HIS NAME shall be called, WONDERFUL COUNSELLOR THE MIGHTY GOD THE EVERLASTING FATHER THE PRINCE OF PEACE The zeal of the LORD OF HOSTS will perform this. (Isa. 9:2, 6, 7)

From the rising of the SUN unto the going down of the same the LORDS NAME is to be praised. (Ps. 113:3)

For thus saith the high and Lofty One that inhabiteth eternity, whose NAME is HOLY; I dwell in the High and Holy place, with him also that is of a contrite and humble spirit, to revive the spirit of the humble, and to revive the heart of the contrite ones. (Is. 57:15)

For, behold, I create New Heavens and a New Earth: and the former shall not be remembered, nor come into mind. (Is. 65:17)

And the Lord shall be King over all the Earth: in that day shall there be ONE LORD, and HIS NAME ONE. (Zech. 14:9).

For from the rising of the sun even unto the going down of the same MY NAME shall be great among the Gentiles; and in every place incense shall be offered unto MY NAME, and a pure offering: for MY NAME shall be great among the heathen, saith the Lord of HOSTS. (Mal. 1:11)

So how was the Script of masterpiece theater with the renowned prophet and priest Isaiah? Anointed and called of God with a vision of the Lord of Hosts in the temple, *"High and lifted up and His train filled the temple."* And the angelic ones singing *"Holy, holy, holy is the LORD of HOSTS,"* then the angel brought a live coal and placed it on Isaiah's lips and said, *"Thy sin is purged."* The Lord cleansed Isaiah for his work and as He said to Jeremiah,

And if thou take forth the precious from the vile, thou shalt be as MY MOUTH. And Jeremiah says, Thy WORDS were found and I did eat them, and Thy WORD was unto me the joy…of my heart: for I am called by Thy NAME, O LORD GOD of HOSTS, and I do stand before Thee O LORD. (Jer. 15:19, 16)

And Isaiah says,

> *Also I heard the voice of the Lord, saying, Whom shall I send, and who will go for us? Then said I, Here am I; send me. And he said, Go, and tell this people, Hear ye indeed, but understand not; and see ye indeed, but perceive not... Moreover the Lord spake again unto Ahaz, saying, Ask thee a SIGN of the Lord thy God; ask it either in the depth, or in the height above... Therefore the Lord HIMSELF shall give you a sign; Behold, a virgin shall conceive, and bear a SON, and shall call HIS NAME IMMANUEL. (6:8–9, 7:10–11, 14)*

How many names did Isaiah assign to our GOD, many but the most precious is the *Holy One of Israel*; it just has a nice ring to it. *Prince of Peace* is a good runner up, though all His Names are wonderful just as *He is*. HEAR, O, ISRAEL, THE LORD OUR GOD IS ONE HIS NAME IS ONE.

Isaiah ushers us right to the apex and crucible of our *victory*. Not only did he give us the alpha and omega of the whole Bible storyline. He has brought us to the one Name that is above *all names*; that at the Name of Jesus, every knee shall give obeisance. The Name that terrorizes our enemy, melts, disintegrates, and causes the devil to flee at this great Name. Demons curse this *Name of Jesus* or Immanuel, which is God with us. Friend, if God be for us, or with us, "Who then can stand against us," and the Israelite king said to his enemy on the battlefield, "The LORD GOD of HOSTS is with us, He is even our CAPTAIN." What did the boy David say to Goliath?

> *Then said David to the Philistine, Thou comest to me with a sword, and with a spear, and with a shield: but I come to thee in the NAME of the LORD of HOSTS, the God of the Armies of Israel, whom thou hast defied. This day will the Lord deliver thee into mine hand; and I will smite thee, and take thine head from thee; and I will give*

the carcasses of the host of the Philistines this day unto the fowls of the air, and to the wild beasts of the earth; that ALL THE EARTH may know that there is a GOD IN ISRAEL. (1 Sam. 17:45–46)

And what did our Mighty Elijah do on the Mt. Carmel to glorify the NAME of the LORD of HOSTS.

And with the stones he built an altar in the NAME of the LORD: and he made a trench about the altar, as great as would contain two measures of seed... And Elijah came unto all the people, and said, HOW LONG HALT YE BETWEEN TWO OPINIONS? If the Lord be God, follow him: but if Baal, then follow him. And the people answered him not a word. Then said Elijah unto the people, I, even I only, remain a prophet of the Lord; but Baal's prophets are four hundred and fifty men. Let them therefore give us two bullocks; and let them choose one bullock for themselves, and cut it in pieces, and lay it on wood, and put no fire under: and I will dress the other bullock, and lay it on wood, and put no fire under: And call ye on the NAME of your gods, and I will call on the NAME OF THE LORD: and the God that answereth by FIRE, let him be GOD. And all the people answered and said, It is well spoken. Hear me, O Lord, hear me, that this people may know that thou art the Lord God, and that thou hast turned their heart back again. Then the FIRE of the Lord fell, and consumed the burnt sacrifice, and the wood, and the stones, and the dust, and licked up the water that was in the trench. And when all the people saw it, they fell on their faces: and they said, The LORD, he is the GOD; the LORD, he is the GOD. (1 Kings 18:32, 21–24, 37–39)

And to David's dying breath, he was working on the financial backing for the building of the Lord's house that the majesty of His *Name* might be exalted forever and ever and ever.

> *And it was in the heart of David My Father to build a house for the NAME of the Lord God of Israel. (For they shall hear of Thy great NAME and of Thy strong hand, and stretched out arm) when the stranger shall come and pray toward this house; Then hear thou O GOD in Heaven Thy dwelling place, and do according to all that the stranger calleth to THEE for; that all people of the earth may know Thy NAME, to fear Thee, as thy people Israel do fear thy NAME, and that they may know that this House which I have built is called by THY NAME.* (1 Kings 8:17, 42–43)

You hear the great majesty and honor that these men of God seek for their King of kings. Why? Because they obeyed the Lord their God and feared His Holy Name for their good, for their good always. The Lord's Name is exalted from Genesis, as Creator, all through each chapter of the Holy Writ to the final book of Revelation where John exalts Him as the Word, the Lamb that was slain and our victorious LORD, who has taken again to Himself His great power and *glory*. So the Father was instructing us since the beginning about this Great Name and the power exuding from the mere mention and worship and obedience and reverence to His Name. Now the plot thickens. Enter one Jesus of Nazareth. Predestined before the foundations of the Earth to be the lamb of God that taketh away the sins of the world.

Yes, the Father God has dazzled us with all His power. The creator God He is; He made everything out of nothing. How do you not want to worship that? God continues through all His Holy prophets, judges, kings, and priests to do wonders and miracles. And as if that is not enough the Father then sends *His Only Begotten Son* to the Earth to be a man.

> *And she shall bring forth a SON, and thou shalt call his NAME JESUS: for He shall save His people from their sins… Behold, a virgin shall be with child, and shall bring forth a SON, and they shall call HIS NAME EMMANUEL, which being interpreted is, God with us.* (Matt. 1:21, 23)
> *For unto you is born this day in the City of David a Saviour, which is Christ the Lord…his NAME was called JESUS, which was so NAMED of the angel before He was conceived in the womb.* (Luke 2:11, 21)

As Matthew says it is through this one NAME Jesus that the Earth was finally visited with a full pardon for its sins. Now God goes from being Creator and Deliverer to Savior and Immanuel, for now God, Himself, the very God of heaven and Earth is now living among His creation. The God of heaven is now on Earth robed in flesh, His Temple is flesh and blood just like you and me. Think about it. God was here stomping our grounds, and we knew it not and still some know it not. Because if you know His NAME and receive Him, He gives you power to become His actual SON; we are Sons of GOD, if you believe on His NAME you become SONS of GOD. The Only Begotten of the Father, this LAMB of GOD takes our sins away and we become reinstated as the SONS of GOD. (Think about it.)

> *And Nathaniel says unto Jesus, Rabbi, Thou art the Son of God; Thou art the King of Israel.* (John 1:49)
> *And John the Baptist says, I saw and bare record that this is the SON OF GOD.* (John 1:34)
> *And there came a voice from Heaven, saying, "THOU ART MY BELOVED SON, IN WHOM I AM WELL PLEASED."* (Mark 1:11)

Why then is this NAME JESUS so fabulous, so superlative, because He is the Son of GOD and also at once the King of the universe and the Creator GOD. Hear O ISRAEL the LORD Our God is ONE. Jesus said "I am in the Father and the Father in ME" the great mystery the three in ONE GOD. John explains it.

> In the beginning was the Word (Jesus is the WORD), and the Word was with God, and the Word was God. (you see He says I am the WORD). The same was in the beginning with God. All things were made by Him; and without Him was not any thing made that was made. In Him was LIFE; and the life was the LIGHT OF MEN. (John 1:1–4)

Jesus's Name starts realizing Power. He, Jesus created all things and verse 10 says the world knew Him not. Some said He was a teacher or prophet, some thought maybe, but didn't know how He could be Messiah. They denied Him, He was God incarnate and they denied Him. Jesus delegated disciples then to go forth in His NAME and cast out demons, heal the sick and deliver the poor and forgive sins; In His NAME. All in the NAME of JESUS, whatever you do, pray, eat, sleep, work, walk, talk, whatever you do; do all in the NAME of JESUS. Remember what David says. Blessed is the man who trusts in the NAME of His LORD.

> He leadeth me in the paths of righteousness for his NAME'S SAKE. (Ps. 23:3)
> Let all those that put their trust in Thee rejoice: let them that love THY NAME be joyful in Thee. (Ps. 5:11)
> I am the vine; ye are the branches:…without ME ye can do NOTHING. (John 15:5)
> And Jesus said to them ALL POWER is given unto ME in Heaven and in Earth. (Matt. 28:18)

All the power rests with Jesus. The Father has seen fit to put all power into Jesus's hands. Jesus paid the price, Jesus did the work and the Father has rewarded HIM with supreme authority. He is the Head over all PRINCIPALITY AND POWER, CHRIST JESUS REIGNS. We see Jesus in Luke, delegating His power just as Moses was told to lay hands on Joshua and give him some of his power.

> *After these things the Lord appointed other seventy also, and sent them two and two before His Face into every city and place, whither He Himself would come... And the seventy returned again with joy, saying, Lord, even the devils are subject unto us through THY NAME. And Jesus said unto them, I beheld Satan as lightning fall from Heaven. Behold, I give unto you power to tread on serpents and scorpions, and over all the power of the enemy: and nothing shall by any means hurt you. Notwithstanding in this rejoice not, that the spirits are subject unto you; but rather rejoice, because your names ARE WRITTEN IN HEAVEN.* (Luke 10:1, 17–20)

The power in Jesus's Name is at this point bringing Him crazy amounts of FAME. He is healing, delivering, saving men's souls, even raising the dead. He is wielding infinite power in Israel and the wicked Pharisees are denying it all. Jesus works His works in the Name of His Father and His disciples do their miracles in Jesus's Name.

Jesus's Name is now noised abroad, all people hear of Him and His power, so can this Name take on more significance? Yes, Jesus has not yet come to the heart of His Mission, which is His crucifixion, resurrection, and ascension. Jesus came into the world so that He could die as a sacrifice to the Father for our sins, and He brought heaven down to us. This Name will get bigger yet.

> *"Jesus says, But if I with the finger of God cast out devils, no doubt the Kingdom of God is come upon you"* (Luke 11:20).

His name is about to conquer the world, and this is the victory that overcometh the world even your faith. Jesus says to them, "It is now the time for the Father to glorify ME, and then I will return back to My Father just as He sent ME to Earth for this reason; that you might know ME. To know ME is LIFE ETERNAL." Here is the backdrop as Jesus describes to His own twelve disciples: how His Name will be glorified and lifted up above this world. Had the devil only known, he would have stopped the crucifixion, but no, he thought, "I will get this Jesus out of my world and back to heaven where He belongs."

> *But now I go My way to Him that sent Me; and none of you asketh Me, Whither goest thou? Nevertheless I tell you the truth; It is expedient for you that I go away: for if I go not away, the Comforter will not come unto you; but if I depart, I will send him unto you. And when He is come, He will reprove the world of sin, and of righteousness, and of judgment: Of sin, because they believe not on ME; Of righteousness, because I go to MY Father, and ye see ME no more; Of judgment, because the prince of this world is judged. I have yet many things to say unto you, but ye cannot bear them now. Howbeit when He, the Spirit of truth, is come, He will guide you into ALL TRUTH: for he shall not speak of himself; but whatsoever he shall hear, that shall he speak: and he will shew you things to come. And in that day ye shall ask (what ye will). Verily, verily, I say unto you, Whatsoever ye shall*

ask the Father in MY NAME, he will give it you. Hitherto have ye asked nothing in MY NAME: ask, and ye shall receive, that your joy may be full. I came forth from the Father, and am come into the world: again, I leave the world, and go to the Father. These things I have spoken unto you, that IN ME ye might have PEACE. In the WORLD ye shall have TRIBULATION: but be of good cheer; I HAVE OVERCOME THE WORLD. (John 16:5, 7–13, 23–24, 28, 33)

Jesus's High Priestly Prayer

These words spake Jesus, and lifted up his eyes to heaven, and said, Father, the hour is come; glorify Thy Son, that Thy Son also may glorify thee: As thou hast given Him power over all flesh, that he should give ETERNAL LIFE to as many as thou hast given him. And this is LIFE ETERNAL, that they MIGHT KNOW THEE the ONLY TRUE GOD, and JESUS CHRIST, whom thou hast sent. I have glorified Thee on the Earth: I have finished the work which thou gavest me to do. And now, O Father, glorify Thou Me with Thine Own Self with the glory which I had with THEE BEFORE THE WORLD WAS. (John 17:1–5)

This is our victory, and this is why this one Name is above every name. Satan was judged, condemned, and overcome at the cross. Oh yes, he still sputters around a bit, but he is finished. And with Jesus's resurrection from the dead in three days' time, our salvation through the Name of Jesus Christ was signed, sealed, and delivered, Jesus went to hell and took the keys to His Kingdom out of Satan's hands.

Jesus says to Pilate I AM A KING. To this end was I born, and for this CAUSE came I into the world, to bear witness to the TRUTH... The cup that my Father gave ME, I shall drink. (John 18:37, 11)

And they cried, crucify him, crucify him. (John 19:6)

And after Jesus's ascension the Apostles arrived at Jerusalem and on Pentecost Jesus sent them His Holy Spirit, this is the same Spirit Jesus had when He appeared in the Upper Room.

"Then came Jesus the doors being shut, and stood in their midst" (John 20:21).

This same Holy Spirit that Jesus has here, He gives to us for the asking. *"Ask and ye shall receive."* It is this Holy Spirit that Jesus gave the apostles and said wait and ye shall receive the Holy Spirit power from on High. The Baptist said, *"I baptize with water, but He* (Jesus) *shall baptize with fire"*—the fire, the strength, and power of the Holy Ghost. Jesus is *"the SAME—the SAME, yesterday, today, and FOREVER,"* and this same Holy Spirit is ours. If you do not think you have yet received the Holy Spirit, just ask. Jesus always says, "Ask, Lord in Jesus's Name give unto Thy servant, Thy child, Thy Holy Spirit. And bubba that is what all the hubbub is about." The Holy Spirit, the gift of the Holy Spirit, which in essence puts God Jesus within US. He is in us and with us. He is our power, our strength, our testimony because He gives witness to the *truth*. That there is One Name under heaven whereby men can be saved, by the Name Christ Jesus Our Lord and Savior. And the power is in His Name *alone*. You can call on *none* other to be *saved*. Only Jesus!

"And whosoever shall call upon the NAME of the LORD shall be saved" (Acts 2:21).

(WHOSOEVER, WHOSOEVER! Fabulous, remarkable.)

> *Then Peter said to them, REPENT and be baptized everyone of you in the NAME of JESUS CHRIST for the remission of SINS, and ye shall receive the GIFT of the Holy Ghost. For the promise is unto you and to your children, and to ALL, to ALL of us... Save yourselves from this untoward generation. (Acts 2:21, 38–40)*

From Peter's Pentecostal Sermon:

> *Now Peter and John went up together into the temple at the hour of prayer, being the ninth hour. And a certain man lame from his mother's womb was carried, whom they laid daily at the gate of the temple which is called Beautiful, to ask alms of them that entered into the temple; Who seeing Peter and John about to go into the temple asked an alms. And Peter, fastening his eyes upon him with John, said, Look on us. And he gave heed unto them, expecting to receive something of them. Then Peter said, Silver and gold have I none; but such as I have give I thee: In the* name *of Jesus Christ of Nazareth rise up and walk. And he took him by the right hand, and lifted him up: and immediately his feet and ankle bones received strength. And he leaping up stood, and walked, and entered with them into the temple, walking, and leaping, and praising God. And all the people saw him walking and praising God: And they knew that it was he which sat for alms at the Beautiful gate of the temple: and they were filled with wonder and amazement at that which had happened unto him. And as the lame man which was healed beheld Peter and John, all the people ran together unto them in the porch that is called*

Solomon's, greatly wondering. And when Peter saw it, he answered unto the people, Ye men of Israel, why marvel ye at this? Or why look ye so earnestly on us, as though by our own power or holiness we had made this man to walk? The God of Abraham, and of Isaac, and of Jacob, the God of our fathers, hath glorified his Son Jesus; whom ye delivered up, and denied him in the presence of Pilate, when he was determined to let him go. But ye denied the Holy One and the Just, and desired a murderer to be granted unto you; And killed the Prince of LIFE, whom God hath raised from the dead; whereof we are witnesses. And HIS NAME through FAITH in HIS NAME hath made this man strong, whom ye see and know: yea, the faith which is by him hath given him this perfect soundness in the presence of you all. And now, brethren, I wot that through ignorance ye did it, as did also your rulers. But those things, which God before had shewed by the mouth of all his prophets, that Christ should suffer, he hath so fulfilled. REPENT ye therefore, and be converted, that your SINS may be blotted out, when the times of refreshing shall come from the presence of the Lord. (Acts 3:1–19)

The power, all power is in Jesus's Name. He was there in the beginning, and by Him, all things were created that are. Think about it: The King, the one and ONLY KING allowed Himself to be mocked, spit on, flogged, crucified, and did not bat an eye. Greater love, greater love, hath no man than this. Don't ask where the power is, friend. Jesus is the power. His Name represents all the *power* that has ever existed or ever will. He is the Great "I Am," I Am that I Am, think on that awhile. There is no greater love than a man lay down

His life for His, friend. Jesus laid down His power and then took it up again to save you and me. Jesus, Jesus, Name *above all names.*

> *And when they had set them in the midst, they asked, By what POWER, or by what NAME, have ye done this? Then Peter, filled with the Holy Ghost, said unto them, Ye rulers of the people, and elders of Israel, If we this day be examined of the good deed done to the impotent man, by what means he is made whole; Be it known unto you all, and to all the people of Israel, that BY THE NAME OF JESUS CHRIST OF NAZARETH, whom ye crucified, whom God raised from the dead, even by HIM doth this man stand here before you whole. This is the STONE which was set at nought of you builders, which is become the HEAD OF THE CORNER. Neither is there SALVATION in any other: for there is NONE OTHER NAME under heaven given among men, whereby we must be saved... For of a truth against the NAME of the HOLY CHILD JESUS* [did the heathen rage]. (Acts 4:7–12, 27)

From time immemorial, the Father has set His Name on *high.* The Lamb predestined before the foundations of the Earth. The Father even made a holy decree and command, saying, *"Thou shalt not take the NAME of the LORD Thy GOD in vain."* His Name was only to be spoken in reverence. And what did the Father bellow from heaven? *"This, this is MY BELOVED SON in whom I am well pleased."* What does instruction tell us?

> *The LAW of the Lord is perfect converting the soul: the testimony of the LORD is sure, making wise the simple. More to be desired are they than GOLD, yea, than much FINE GOLD.* (Ps. 19:7, 10)

> *Yet have I set MY KING upon MY Holy Hill of ZION.* (Ps. 2:6)
>
> *I was set up from everlasting from the beginning, or ever the Earth was... Then I was by Him, as one brought up with Him and I was daily His delight, rejoicing always before Him.* (Prov. 8:23, 30)

Friend, your soul is so valuable that no amount of bulls burnt on all the altars of Israel for thousands of years could buy your soul. All the *gold* in China cannot buy your soul. It took, it took, the blood spilt at the cross to buy your soul. Jesus has bought your soul back from the grip of Satan and damnation. His *blood alone* could only do this, that is why the Father said, "This is MY BELOVED SON in Whom I am well pleased." And that is why His Name *alone* is set on *high*. That Name Jesus wields all the power of heaven and Earth. This is the *mystery* Paul speaks about that had been hid from the foundations of the Earth. Salvation is of Jesus Christ, the hope of glory, the desire of ages, your dream come true. Eternal life through that One Name Jesus the carpenter of Nazareth. Great revelations were given to the Apostle Paul of the Mystery of Christ. Read his Epistles and see.

> *(Whereby, when ye read, ye may understand my knowledge in the MYSTERY OF CHRIST) Which in other ages was not made known unto the sons of men, as it is NOW revealed unto his Holy Apostles and Prophets by the Spirit of the LORD. That the Gentiles should be fellowheirs, and of the same body, and partakers of his promise in Christ* by the gospel: *Whereof I was made a minister, according to the gift of the grace of God given unto me by the effectual working of his power. Unto me, who am less than the least of all saints, is this grace given, that I should preach among the Gentiles the unsearchable riches of Christ; And to make ALL*

MEN SEE what is the fellowship of the MYSTERY, which from the beginning of the WORLD HATH BEEN HID in God, who created all things by Jesus Christ: To the intent that now unto the principalities and powers in heavenly places might be known by the church the manifold wisdom of God, According to the ETERNAL PURPOSE which he purposed in CHRIST JESUS OUR LORD: In whom we have boldness and access with confidence by the faith of him. Wherefore I desire that ye faint not at my tribulations for you, which is your glory. For this cause I bow my knees unto the Father of OUR LORD JESUS CHRIST, Of whom the whole family in heaven and earth IS NAMED. (Eph. 3:4–15)

Jesus was God's eternal *purpose*, it was His *purpose* always even from before creation to manifest Jesus Christ and bring Him to Earth for our benefit. Man was promised a Messiah and they waited and looked for Him from the time of Abraham, Isaac and Jacob they looked for a revelation of the Almighty. Psalm 106:8 says, *"Nevertheless He saved them for His Name's sake, that he might make his MIGHTY POWER to be KNOWN."* The key here is *Name's sake*. The Lord God Almighty wanted to make Himself known to the planet Earth, to us, His creation. He wanted to be with us and in us, and this was and is now possible by His ascension at which He promised to then send His very own spirit to Earth, so He could keep dwelling in us and with us. He is here, folks; Jesus is here among us. Paul goes on explaining about the Mystery of Christ in his Epistle to the Colossians.

"Whereby I am made a minister (to reveal the word of God to you). To reveal the mystery which hath been hid from ages and from generations, but now is made manifest to His saints" (1:25–26).

Jesus tells His disciples how privileged they are to be the first ones that the mystery is revealed to.

> *"For I tell you Jesus says that many prophets and Kings have desired to see and hear that which you now see and hear, and they have not heard them"* (Luke 10:24).

The disciples are witnessing the Mystery of Ages, Christ, God the creator, is the man Jesus they are living with and watching. No greater privilege than this.

> *But now God makes known to us what is the riches of the glory of this MYSTERY: which is CHRIST IN YOU, the HOPE of glory. Whom we preach Paul says warning and teaching every-man in all wisdom; that we may present every man PERFECT in Christ JESUS.* (Col. 1:27, 28)

Paul declares we give thanks to GOD.

> *Since we heard of your Faith in Christ Jesus. Jesus, who hath delivered us from the power of dark-ness and hath translated us into the Kingdom of His Dear Son: In whom we have redemption through His blood, even the forgiveness of sins: He (Jesus) is the image of the invisible GOD… All things were created by Him. He is before ALL things, by Him all things consist He is the HEAD of the body that is the church: He is the beginning, the first born from the dead. That in all things He might have the preeminence For it pleased the Father that in Him should all the FULLNESS dwell. Having made peace through the BLOOD of His CROSS, He (Jesus) RECONCILED all things UNTO HIMSELF.* (Col. 1:4, 13–20)

And we follow Christ Jesus Our Lord, *"For in Him dwelleth all the fullness of the Godhead bodily And we are complete in Him who is the head of all principality and power"* (2:9–10).

Jesus's NAME above ALL NAMES. GLORIOUS NAME, EXALTED NAME, because it pleased the Father to allow the Son to go to the CROSS and reconcile the WORLD BACK TO HIMSELF. Thus, He set His NAME on high, high above all principalities and powers. There is VICTORY in the NAME OF JESUS. Jesus did it all; He wiped our sins away. He paid the debt.

> *Jesus Christ being the brightness of His Father's Glory, and the express image of His person, and upholding all things by the WORD of HIS POWER when He had by Himself purged our sins, sat down on the right hand of the MAJESTY ON HIGH. Being made so much better than the angels, as He hath by inheritance obtained a more EXCELLENT NAME than they.* (Heb. 1:3–4)
>
> *That through His death He might destroy him that had the power of death, that is the devil.* (2:14)
>
> *For verily he took not on him the nature of angels; but he took on him the seed of Abraham. Wherefore in all things it behoved him to be MADE LIKE UNTO HIS BRETHEREN, that he might be a merciful and faithful HIGH PRIEST in things pertaining to God, to make reconciliation for the SINS of the people.* (2:16–17)
>
> *Though HE were a Son, yet learned he obedience by the things which HE suffered; And being made perfect, Jesus became the AUTHOR OF ETERNAL SALVATION unto all them that obey him.* (5:8–9)

There is One Body,
One Spirit
even as ye are called
in One Hope
of your
calling

One Lord
One Faith
One Baptism

and Father of all
who is above all
and through all
and in you All

Ephesians
4:5

> *But these are written, that ye might believe that Jesus is the Christ, the Son of God; and that believing ye might have LIFE through HIS NAME.* (John 20:31)

From the beginning of creation, God has wanted to restore things as they were in the Garden of Eden, where He had fellowship with His creatures. He loved His creation and wanted to be with them. He was with us until the serpent being very subtle, beguiled Eve. They disobeyed and their SIN cut off their fellowship with their MAKER. God is so holy that He cannot be in the presence of sin. He had to cast them out of their perfect home, the Garden. His very NAME is HOLY, and how much more His presence. That is why He taught the Israelites in the desert, that they must be sanctified to have His presence come down and be with them in the Tabernacle. Everything around God must be holy, clean, without spot; for He says, *"Be ye Holy for I am Holy and be ye Perfect for I am perfect."* We and they were like God and He wanted to be with us and enjoy us. Listen to what God says.

> *And God said, Let us make man in our image, after our likeness... So God created man in HIS OWN IMAGE, in the image of God created HE him; male and female created HE them.* (Gen. 1:26–27)
>
> *Thou art worthy, O Lord, to receive glory and honour and power: for thou hast created all things, and for thy pleasure they are and were created.* (Rev. 4:11)
>
> *For the Lord's portion is his people; Jacob is the lot of His inheritance.* (Deut. 32:9)

We are made in God's very image. He created us for His pleasure, and He adores us and wants to be with us now and throughout eternity. He loved us so much He sent His ONLY SON who was cruelly treated and killed. He sent Him to redeem us back to Him, to put us back in fellowship with Him. Remember what Our wonderful and adorable (as Spurgeon would say) Savior said on the cross. *"Father forgive them for they know not what they do."* He wants us back folks, and He got us back at Calvary, if we believe in the NAME OF JESUS.

All the WORDS in the Holy Book are about Our GOD, One King. His NAME is JESUS from Genesis to Revelation; it is about the NAME of Jesus. Why? Because our GOD is ONE; we have ONE GOD, one faith, one baptism. And the Father saw it fitting to put all the fullness in and through King Jesus. Jesus, the Lamb of GOD, the Baptist says that taketh away the sins of the world. That's why His NAME is above every name. There is only ONE NAME we need to bother with; we go straight to Him. No go-betweens please. He did the cross; no one else, not even anyone else. So there is only ONE NAME that SAVES, and ONE NAME that holds power; even the demons testify to this. *"Paul we know, Jesus we know but who are you?"* If you want demons to tremble, just start using that NAME—Jesus, through prayer, praise, meditation, witnessing, study, discussions, maybe just chant that awesome NAME a bit and the devils will flee.

So are we done, or is there more? Yes, indeed. The Father has another hidden treasure: the second appearance on Earth of our LORD Jesus Christ. For no man knows the date or the hour. Please refer to Matthew 24 for details. He says the wise shall know. And HIS NAME will get bigger yet because the grand finale has not taken place yet. Oh, yes, oh yes, He's got a NAME, and He shall at the Father's appointed time, descend from heaven. And the fireworks will begin as He destroys His enemies and swoops up His saints and raises them to heaven far above this old sinful world. Wonder of wonders, the END or is it the beginning, which at last has arrived. Jesus with His angels and saints of heaven have arrived to do business. The day of His vengeance has come. He is the Just Judge and will take back all power and the kingdoms and nations of this world to Himself. He shall reign. He shall reign, and every knee shall bow. Oh yes, One

NAME is above all. Let us hear what Jesus Christ's beloved John has to say about his loving Lord in the last book of the Bible, Revelation.

> (Behold) *the time is at hand. He that over-cometh, the same shall be clothed in white raiment; and I will not blot out his name out of the BOOK OF LIFE, but I will confess his name before MY FATHER, and before His angels. He that hath an ear let him hear what the Spirit saith.* (1:3, 3:5)
>
> *And loud voices said Worthy is the LAMB that was slain to receive power and riches and wisdom and strength and honour and glory and blessing. For the Great Day of His Wrath is come; and who shall be able to stand?* (5:12, 6:17)
>
> *Behold, I come as a thief. Blessed is he that watcheth, and keepeth his garments.* (16:15)
>
> *The second woe is past; and, behold, the third woe cometh quickly. And the seventh angel sounded; and there were great voices in Heaven, saying, The Kingdoms of this World are become the kingdoms of Our Lord, and of His Christ; and He shall REIGN for ever and ever. And the four and twenty elders, which sat before God on their seats, fell upon their faces, and worshipped God, Saying, We give thee thanks, O Lord God Almighty, which art, and wast, and art to come; because thou hast taken to Thee Thy Great Power, and hast reigned.* (11:14–17)
>
> *And I saw as it were a sea of glass mingled with fire: and them that had gotten the victory over the beast, and over his image, and over his mark, and over the number of his NAME, stand on the sea of glass, having the harps of God. And they sing the song of Moses the servant of God, and the song of the Lamb, saying, Great and marvellous are thy works, Lord God Almighty; Just and true are Thy Ways, Thou King of saints.*

Thou art worthy, O Lord, to receive glory and honour and power: for thou hast created all things, and for thy pleasure they are and were created. (Rev. 4:11)

Who shall not fear thee, O Lord, and glorify THY NAME? for thou only art Holy: for all Nations shall come and worship before Thee; for Thy judgments are made manifest. (Rev. 15:2–4)

And I saw heaven opened, and behold a white horse; and he that sat upon him was called Faithful and True, and in righteousness he doth judge and make WAR. His eyes were as a FLAME OF FIRE, and on his head were many CROWNS; and HE had a NAME WRITTEN, that no man knew, but He Himself. And He was clothed with a vesture dipped in BLOOD: and HIS NAME is called THE WORD OF GOD. And the armies which were in heaven followed HIM upon white horses, clothed in fine linen, white and clean. And out of HIS mouth goeth a sharp sword, that with it He should smite the Nations: and He shall rule them with a rod of iron: and HE TREADETH THE WINEPRESS OF THE FIERCENESS AND WRATH OF ALMIGHTY GOD. And he hath on his vesture and on his thigh a NAME WRITTEN, King Of Kings, And Lord Of Lords... And whosoever was not FOUND WRITTEN in the BOOK OF LIFE was cast into the Lake of Fire. (19:11–16, 20:15)

And only those whose NAMES are written in the LAMB'S BOOK OF LIFE may enter through the gates of God's Holy city. And they shall see His Face; and HIS NAME shall be in their foreheads. (21:27, 22:4)

ONE NAME PEOPLE, ONE POWER. David always has the right WORDS when He said,

So foolish was I and ignorant: I was as a beast before Thee. Notwithstanding... Whom have I in

Heaven but Thee? And there is None upon Earth that I desire besides Thee. (Ps. 73:22, 25)

HIS NAME shall endure for ever: HIS NAME shall be continued as long as the sun: and men shall be blessed in him: all nations shall call him blessed. Blessed be the Lord God, the God of Israel, who only doeth wondrous things. And blessed be HIS GLORIOUS NAME for ever: and let the whole Earth be filled with His glory; Amen, and Amen. The prayers of David the son of Jesse are ended. (Ps. 72:17–20)

For thus saith the High and Lofty ONE that inhabited ETERNITY, whose NAME is HOLY. I dwell in the High and Holy Place with him that is...of a humble spirit. (Isa. 57:15)

And the LORD shall be KING over all the Earth: in that day shall there be One LORD, and HIS NAME ONE. (Zech. 14:9)

And the same John of Revelation sums it all up John says, *"These things have I written unto you that believe on the NAME of the SON of GOD: that ye may know that ye have ETERNAL LIFE and that ye may believe on the NAME of the SON of God, Jesus"* (1 John 5:13).

And whosoever calleth upon the NAME of the Lord shall be saved!

JESUS, SAVE ME, amen.

His Word

He sent HIS WORD, and healed them, and
delivered them from their destructions.

—Psalm 107:20

You can praise GOD all day long, you can sing to the high heavens, and you can worship His glorious name all you want. Yes, Jesus inhabits the praises of His people. But…but it is the WORD that heals.

It is the WORD that delivers.

It is the WORD that gives us FAITH.

It is the WORD that breaks up the fallow ground of our hearts.

And it is this faith that moves those mountains, kills those Goliaths, and puts to flight the enemy. It is by faith, if you will please, that we get to heaven. It is by faith that we learn to know that Jesus is who He says He is, and that He has conquered death, hell, and the grave for us by His ATONING BLOOD. And by faith, we must believe that Jesus will give us grace for this journey, this pilgrimage here below, and carry us all the way to the end, till we see his glorious face.

The WORD teaches us, consoles us, instructs, leads, guides, and comforts us and in all those aspects; the WORD is healing. It is the WORD that inspires us to worship and praise Him. The WORD reminds us of all His glory. The Holy Writ is an autobiography actually written by Him. Jesus is the author through His prophets, apostles, and disciples who were eyewitnesses of His glory. The disciples recorded as much of the WORD of Jesus as the Holy Spirit gave them recall of. The red letters and WORDS are straight from the infallible lips of the Father. Jesus's Words were heavenly, divine, and perfect purified seven times.

> *The WORD which ye hear is not MINE, but*
> *the Father's which sent me.* (John 14:24)
> *"I have given them THY WORD" Jesus says to*
> *his Father.* (John 17:14)

The Bible is God's WORD, all of it. He is the author of every WORD therein by the power of the Holy Spirit. *George Mueller* in *his autobiography* tells us that the most important thing for a Christian to do is to read and meditate in God's WORD. He states, *"It often astonishes me that I did not see the importance of meditation upon scripture earlier in my Christian life"* (p. 137).[1] I wished he said that I had learned this early on, to just read and enjoy GOD'S WORD; enjoy GOD. So often we hit God right out of the sheets with a prayer list that we can repeat for near memory every morning. No, to listen to GOD through His WORD is what matters most because Jesus is our BREAD of LIFE. He is our very life; it is more important to hear what the Father has to say to us. He speaks first and then we will know how to pray.

You know a man by his fruits. Mueller is a stellar example of the working of the Holy Word upon a man's heart. It is said he read the Bible through some two hundred times. And the fruit of his spiritual labor was not in vain. He established orphanages for the street children of England and led others all over the world to do the same. He never asked for a copper penny but asked only GOD to supply the needs for these baby children. He housed, trained, and taught the children from the Bible. Thousands of them were grounded in the truth through His WORD of LIFE ministries and schools that are still active today. The WORD of GOD is powerful.

Read the word of God first; don't accost GOD with two pages of prayer requests that is only a verbal run through, reminding God of thus, thus, and so. GOD already knows all that. He wants you to listen to Him and His WORDS that your soul and spirit may be blessed, and then your spirit will intercede on the behalf of all those requests. God wants us to feast at His table that our soul may be revived for another day of service to God and fellow man. It is way more important that we listen to GOD first. He is our teacher then we will know better what to pray for or talk to Him about. The soul must be fed. Like Mr. Mueller says, just as we feed the fleshly man, we must feed the spiritual man so he will have life; on page 137, he discusses this. If we do not feed our physical body, we will have no strength to work, so also the spiritual man must be fed spiritual food, which is the WORD of GOD.

Just as Matthew 4:4 states, *"Man shall not live by bread alone, but by every WORD that proceedeth out of the mouth of GOD."* Feed the man, and he will have strength to work; feed the spirit and he will have strength to work God's works. He will have instruction to know what to do. Remember Jesus said, *"Without ME ye can do nothing."* That is what he is meaning here. God must direct our course because the prince of the power of the air is strong and subtle and will lead us into many vain and useless paths and endeavors that only waste away our hours and days here, which are so fleeting. Yesterday, it was ten years ago, the day before, it was twenty years ago, and the day before that, it was thirty years ago and on and on. Our days are like a shadow that passes as the sun goes down. We do not realize until the end is upon us, and we say what have we done for Jesus, or did the cares of this life consume our days, and at the end our basket of offering for the Lord only has a very few things in it. "As you have done to the least of these, so ye have done to me."

Feed the hungry.
Clothe the naked.
Visit the sick.
Visit the imprisoned.
Visit the misfortunate.
Do all as unto the LORD.

Or are we working on our big pile of gold heaping it and heaping it for our children that are already rich and well able to care for themselves. While our neighbors are naked, hungry, and thirsty—and yes, our neighbors are our "third world misfortunates." And if it were not for the grace of God, there go I. You could easily have been born in the wrong country in a dry and thirsty land.

Early I will seek thee, oh, My LORD and Savior. I will spend my choice hours of the morning letting you talk to me through your HOLY WORD. Because *"Father knows best,"* and we know nothing at all. And just a little talk with Jesus lets us know how little we do know. If any man lack wisdom, let him ask of God who will give us liberally, generously, and will prune away the vanities that consume our precious, precious and few and short and fleeting days here.

If we, as Mr. Mueller says in so many words, do not cement our earliest morning thoughts in with Christ. You will soon see as the hours of the day pass, how worldly and discouraging the day will be without our early morning foundation upon the solid ROCK, CHRIST JESUS. Our archenemy is strong. Do not underestimate his skills at diverting our attention away from Jesus and misguiding us with the cares of this world that by next week will be forgotten and won't matter a tittle. The prince of the power of the air grows stronger by the day. His power is real, but no, no, not even a match for the weakest saint on his knees. This is his territory, and we are foreign invaders for our kingdom is God's kingdom—that heavenly kingdom we are just passing through here; this foreign land is not our home. Listen and perceive the strength of our enemy as Satan tempts our beautiful Savior.

"Again the devil taketh him (JESUS) *up into an exceeding high mountain, and showeth Jesus all the kingdoms of the world, and the glory of them. And saith unto Him, All these things will I give thee, if thou wilt fall down and worship me* [the devil] *"* (Matt. 4:8–9).

You see, we are in the devil's territory as he states here to Jesus. But Jesus simply said, "Be gone, Satan." And Jesus assures us of our victory with Him.

> *Be of good cheer; Jesus says I have overcome the world.* (John 16:33)
>
> *Peace I leave with you, MY Peace I give unto you: not as the world gives, Give I unto you. Let not your heart be troubled, neither let it be afraid.* (John 14:27)

> *Ye are of God, little children, and have over-*
> *come them; because greater is He that is in you, than*
> *he that is in the world.* (1 John 4:4)

Yes, indeed, the Holy Spirit whose temple we are is greater, *is greater*. Who is greater, God or the devil? So yes, this Jesus lives within us by the power of the Holy Spirit. If Jesus had not ascended back to the Father to ask Him to send us His Holy Spirit, we would be like those in the OT that had to get up each morning and sacrifice a lamb or a goat. No, no, Jesus was the one time sacrifice that did away with all that; now we have Him abiding in us and with us. You see, that is why the weakest Christian on his knees makes the DEVIL TREMBLE. Jesus is within us; we are the temple of the living GOD. So now, you can picture God's army versus Satan's. All us Christians versus all those very ugly and hopeless demons of hell. Light versus dark, and praise be to God that we have, own, and possess the victory every time we call or turn our EYES TO JESUS. Yes, the victory is ours.

That is why it is important to first thing acknowledge JESUS each waking day and take hold of him; "CLEAVE UNTO THY GOD," Moses says. CLEAVE to Him for He is thy life. So first thing we open that Holy Book and read and devour Jesus. He is our suste-nance. He is our bread. Our bread of life.

Father Knows Best

And He makes everything simple; it is us that makes it diffi-cult. Take the English language for example. Jesus spoke in common everyday terms, but the achieved writer wants others to perceive him as a man of intelligence so he contrives words of a higher order, which sometimes we have to check for their meaning. But Jesus, no, Jesus had fishermen disciples, and the crowds had to understand exactly at their level of communication. Jesus always keeps things simple and easy to understand. He loves us. He is crazy about you, friend. Crazy enough to live like a servant and minister of all. He is crazy in love with you, dear friend. Yes, you think, perhaps, "It is I that love Jesus."

You say, "I love you, Lord, as Peter said three times. Yes, LORD, you know I love you." But, friend, Jesus is astonishingly crazy in love with you—you, yes, you.

Jesus used His voice, His words, His garments, His time, all His time, and finally He used his very own blood to pour over our sick souls to heal them. Everything about Jesus is healing. His WORDS heal, His voice heals, His garments heal, everything He touched was healed. Let's ask the centurion who hunted Jesus down for his sick, tormented servant back home. Matthew records this well; hear him.

> *And when Jesus was entered into Capernaum, there came unto him a centurion, beseeching him, And saying, Lord, my servant lieth at home sick of the palsy, grievously tormented. And Jesus saith unto him, I will come and heal him. The centurion answered and said, Lord, I am not worthy that thou shouldest come under my roof: BUT SPEAK THE WORD ONLY, and my servant SHALL BE HEALED.* (8:5–8)

This centurion had faith in the WORD of GOD. For he declared, "Just speak your WORD, O, great physician" and he shall be healed. Just the WORD, just a WORD from Jesus, JUST A WORD will heal. And we have that same WORD today. The Gospels are full of Jesus's Words. Isaiah is full of Jesus's Words. Deuteronomy is full of Jesus's Words. Each and every book in the Bible is full of Jesus's Words. We have the same Words today that Jesus used with the crowds back two thousand years ago. The very same Words of healing are at our disposal, and when coupled with FAITH in GOD, they heal. They heal our sick bodies and souls and deliver us from our destructions or sins. The KEY is FAITH in GOD or FAITH in HIS WORDS. Jesus told us so, in verse 10 Jesus explains,

"Is not MY WORD like as a Fire? Saith the LORD; and like a Hammer that breaketh the Rock in pieces." (Jer. 23:29)

Verily I say unto you, I have not found so great faith, no, not in all Israel... (Verse 10)

And Jesus said to the centurion, Go thy way and as thou hast believed, so be it done unto thee. And the servant was healed that same hour. (Verse 13)

The scripture also says, *"Thou shalt decree a thing and it shall be so."*

He had faith and belief in Jesus, as you have believed Jesus said, so it shall be for you. Jesus says if you have faith and belief, nothing shall be impossible unto you.

The disciples asked Jesus, "Why could we not cast him out?" And Jesus said, "Because of your UNBELIEF: for verily I say unto you, if ye have faith as a grain of mustard seed, ye shall say unto this mountain, remove hence to yonder place and it shall remove; and nothing shall be impossible unto you." (Matt. 17:19–20)

Wow, that's a good WORD for the day.

Folks, we cannot underestimate the WORDS of God; they embody the power of heaven. As we sit or kneel and read and meditate, these WORDS of Jesus become our very life. For the WORD goes into our heart and breaks up the fallow ground of unbelief. Now, no ritual or tradition can do this; the WORD alone does this work.

This WORD when meditated upon is like a super tiller that plows up, breaks up, weeds out the ground that has been sitting dormant for too long, and perhaps maybe has never seen so much as a small hoe or shovel. The more we read and prayerfully digest this WORD, the richer the soil of our heart becomes. No, one does not just plow the row once, but you go over and over it, making it fine. Then the man takes a handful of soil and brazenly shows his neighbor saying, "See, this I shall have a great garden this year for my soil is well turned and plowed." And the sower knows it is the wonderfully rich topsoil that yields the best of the best fruit. This is our ultimate aim, to be a fruitful, profitable servant; thus is our Heavenly Father glorified with much fruit being born again into his Kingdom. The Father wants heaven to be packed out, full to overflowing; He has a lot to share and wants oodles of loving children to spend the rest of eternity with Him.

This breaking up of fallow ground is called, in big words, *regeneration*.

It is a washing and a cleansing from sin and the earthly cares, which then builds our zeal so we can take on the very mind of Christ. The mind of Christ as stated in the gospels is to do the Father's will. Jesus makes this clear and simple for He stated many times, "I come to do MY FATHER'S WILL." Jesus said, "I have come to SAVE the WORLD," and this must be our mission also. As disciples and followers of Jesus, we become His hands and feet; His ambassadors here on Earth. As the Our Father Prayer states, "Thy WILL be done, and that is us doing the will of God." When we are cleansed, our mind becomes clear and focused on the father's desires, that of being fruitful and bearing much fruit.

> *"Now ye are clean through the WORD which I have spoken unto you. Abide in me, and I in you. As the branch cannot bear fruit of itself, except it ABIDE in the VINE, no more can ye, except ye abide in ME"* (John 15:3–4).

It is the wise that winneth souls. It is the WORD that heals all men; all men without Christ are sick and need healing. You say, "How can I do this? I am in a mud hut in the middle of the jungle." My friend, where there is a will, there is a way. Look at that zealous preacher Brainerd, who, against all odds, won over villages of East Coast Indians for Christ. Not being himself able to speak the language he labored through a drunken, alcoholic interpreter and won them for Christ (page 47 from *E. M. Bounds on Prayer*). He knew that nothing was too difficult for the Master; he labored with prayers, fastings, and tears. The Indians saw the ardent love in his face and were baffled at his pressing anxiety over them. The Holy Spirit came and did the work and fell upon those Indians, and in days and hours, they were totally following Christ to the jot and tittle.

Against all odds, Brainerd remained steadfast and diligent awaiting the conversion of thousands. He in nothing wavered but believed GOD for what He had asked. Yet this young man was so eloquent, knowledgeable, and ministry capable that all the churches desired him for their pastor. In E. M. Bound's book, he quotes President Edwards as bearing testimony that Brainerd was *"[a] young man of distinguished talents had extraordinary knowledge of men and things, had rare conversational powers, excelled in his knowledge of theology and was truly for one so young, an extraordinary Divine…and he had extraordinary gifts for the pulpit"* (*E. M. Bounds on Prayer*, p. 468).[2]

This man exhibited the Mind of Christ as our great example the Apostle Paul and he says, *"Let a man so account of us, as of the ministers of Christ, and stewards of the mysteries of GOD"* (1 Cor. 4:1).

He was slavish in his duties for Christ. Brainerd could have had a pastorite in any of the biggest churches around, his excellence and holiness was well-renowned. No, he took the lower, most difficult, most humble seat. He was the people's preacher, devout and pious. He slept in the snow, in the woods with only a blanket and horse, trying to go from Indian village to Indian village. No comforts here, no comforts. He gave his life and all his energy in prayer and fasting before GOD alone, for lost souls. Truly Christ possessed this man, and he Christ. The mind of Christ is for lost souls.

> *"Knowing therefore the terror of the Lord, we*
> *persuade men"* (2 Cor. 5:11).

There is just too little *"fear of God"* today. We live as if we shall never give account to GOD and pretend He does not see anyway, and besides, who is keeping track? Woe, woe, woe. Paul says, "Woe is me for *necessity is laid upon me, yea, woe is unto me if I preach not the Gospel"* (1 Cor. 9:16). For a dispensation of grace was given unto him. His was a personal revelation of Jesus when he was knocked off his horse on the way to Damascus. Paul already had superior knowledge of the Old Testament, and through his encounter with Jesus, he came to the full knowledge of Christ as the Messiah the Savior of the World. Likewise, Brainerd rode his horse through the countryside, snow, rain, or cold; nothing was going to dampen his zeal toward the Indians, most certainly not a lack of faith. Job well done, brother. Can't wait to meet you.

This is a great example to follow, a true fellow laborer, born out of the WORD. He listened to Christ's WORDS and obeyed, thus bringing the healing of salvation to thousands who were aliens to Christ. These are the Christlike worth emulating. Paths they have trod, tested, and tried, the old paths are the good way.

> *I am the vine, you are the branches: He that abideth in ME, and I in him the same bringeth forth much fruit; for without ME ye can do nothing… If ye abide in ME and my WORDS abide in you, ye shall ask what ye will, and it shall be done for you. Herein is MY FATHER glorified, that ye bear much FRUIT, so shall ye be MY DISCIPLES.* (John 15:5, 7, 9)

David Brainard asked for souls and Jesus gave him thousands of souls—thousands, and that's a no-brainer.

What wait I for, we have the keys to the Kingdom! The mystery of ages has been revealed; we need only open our mouths and use our vocal cords for the highest commission set forth to man, and that is, *"Go therefore and preach to all NATIONS, repentance and remission of sins in the NAME of Jesus Christ"* (Matt. 28:19–20).

The easiest thing in the world to do, and we all the time want to complicate it. OPEN THY MOUTH, and Jesus will fill it. Do we want to see Messiah return? He is returning for a bride that is clean, washed, healed, clothed in grace and truth, without spot or wrinkle. His bride needs to be healed, saved from their very own destructions, SEND OUT THE WORD. Folks, do not, *do not* sit there and do nothing for God's kingdom; even a glass of cold water given will be rewarded. The servant that did nothing and went and hid the coins in the Earth was tossed by his MASTER into outer darkness. What pile of dirt are you hiding your coins and your talents under? What evil bank are you casting your treasure into when the Lord told in the parables over and over.

> *Jesus said unto him, "If thou wilt enter into LIFE ETERNAL, keep the commandments."* (Matt. 19:17)
> *If thou wilt be perfect, go and sell that thou hast, and give to the poor, and thou shalt have treasure in heaven: and COME and FOLLOW ME. But when the young man heard that saying, he went away sorrowful: for he had great possessions. Then said Jesus unto his disciples, Verily I say unto you, That a RICH MAN shall hardly enter into the kingdom of heaven.* (Matt. 19:21–23)

Moffatt's translation says it this way:

> *Then Jesus said to His disciples, "I tell you truly it will be difficult for a RICH MAN to get into the realm of Heaven. I tell you again it is easier for a camel to get through a needle's eye than for a RICH MAN to get into the Realm of GOD."* (23–24)

What wait I for, are the Master's instructions clear? Did He not say, "I planted a noble vineyard and now look at its weeds? Thorns are choking all the good seed. Cast off the filthy lucre of this world and get for yourselves the true RICHES of heaven that moth and rust cannot corrupt. Put your money into rich soil. The ministries that are helping, funding, clothing, and MOST OF ALL and BEST OF ALL giving forth the WORD of LIFE, with Bibles. And discipling those that have never heard the NAME of JESUS CHRIST to our SHAME.

Come on, people, help out; ministers are crying on the behalf of these needs. Do right with your funds, stop hoarding and building bigger barns when you can dig a well for a thirsty community. There is no distance with Jesus; just picture you and your bounty—yes, I say bounty, living right next door to a mud, straw hut without water, without a toilet, without lights. Jesus will require it of us. Don't be an ostrich that don't cut the mustard with JESUS. He has a heart meter He has put on every man and child. He reads your activities by the minute.

No, our own comforts are screaming at us. Just listen on Saturday and Sunday to the home improvement shows. They tell how to polish and line your nest with the softest of feathers so that you may retire in comfort and spend the rest of your days rocking yourself to sleep with the lies of justification—oh, but I earned it; I deserve it.

And what did David say? He said all that we have has been given to us and we are only returning it to you.

> *Now therefore, Our God, we thank Thee, and praise Thy glorious name. But who am I, and what is my people, that we should be able to offer so willingly after this sort? FOR ALL THINGS COME OF THEE, AND OF THINE OWN HAVE WE GIVEN THEE. For we are strangers BEFORE THEE, and sojourners as were all our Fathers. Our days on the Earth are as a shadow, and there is none abiding.* (1 Chron. 29:13–15)

We are returning it all back to you Jesus, or do you want to hoard it to your own condemnation? And what saith David about a house for GOD, all you home improvers? David said, "O Lord you do but live in a tent while I live in a palace, no I want a house for MY GOD a resting place." So yes, Mr. Putin, Mr. Zi, and all the rest of you. Build houses of worship please? Let them be as numerous as the banks or stores and supermarkets please. We want places of worship, not air bases of destruction in every country. Not nuclear plants, petroleum fields, and electronic bases, from which we plan to destroy one another either. "Open now thine eyes" and "Behold Jesus's nail-scarred hands." Please, please, Jesus pleads with you.

> *Then the people rejoiced, for they offered willingly, because with perfect heart they offered willingly to the LORD and David the KING rejoiced with great joy, and David blessed the LORD before all the congregation. David said Blessed be Thou, LORD GOD of Israel Our Father, forever and ever. Thine, O Lord, is the greatness And the power. And the glory, And the victory, And the majesty: For all that is in the Heaven and in the Earth is THINE: THINE is the Kingdom, O LORD, and Thou art exalted as head above all.* (29:9–11)
>
> *O Lord our God, all this store that we have prepared to build thee an HOUSE for thine HOLY NAME cometh of thine hand, and is ALL THINE OWN. I know also, my God, that thou triest the heart, and hast pleasure in uprightness. As for me, in the uprightness of mine heart I have WILLINGLY OFFERED all these things: and now have I seen with joy thy people, which are present here, to offer WILLINGLY unto thee. O Lord God of Abraham, Isaac, and of Israel, our fathers, keep this for ever in the imagination of the thoughts of the heart of thy people, AND PREPARE THEIR HEART UNTO THEE: And give unto Solomon my son a PERFECT HEART, to keep thy commandments, thy testimonies, and thy statutes, and to do all these things, and to BUILD THE PALACE, for the which I have made provision.* (29:16–19)

Friends, our Fathers Abraham, Isaac, and Jacob dwelt in tents. Why, why, why, do you think you need an entire Holiday Inn as thy abode? Wake up. Read again about the poor beggar Lazarus and the rich man, who only wanted the crumbs from the rich man's table, who ended up where? Lazarus went to heaven; the rich man cried out from hell. Wake up, the flames are right now biting your *ass*—yes, your *ass*!

The most important thing we can ever do is to give the WORD of LIFE to a dying soul. And yes, without Jesus, we are all good as dead men wandering this universe in hopeless circles of frustration. Jesus is life's only satisfaction. Ask St. Augustine who is best known for his verse of *hope*.

"For thou hast made us for Thyself and restless is our heart until it comes to rest in Thee" (The Confessions of St. Augustine, p. 5).[3]

And pray tell, to know THEE O GOD is the answer to everything. For Thou, O GOD, art the Healer, the Deliverer, all of our help, and all of our happiness. The best thing we can do for a man is to give him Jesus. The best thing to do for our nation and the countries of the world is to give them the WORD of GOD, which heals and delivers that we may usher in the Messiah and live in peace.

The great apostle says it best:

> *How then shall they call on HIM in whom they have not believed? And how shall they believe in Him of whom they have not heard? And how shall they hear without a preacher? And how shall they preach except they be sent? As it is written, How beautiful are the feet of them that preach the GOSPEL of PEACE, and bring glad tidings of good things!* (Rom. 10:14–15)

Yes, we must open our mouths for Jesus, OPEN THY MOUTH and Jesus will put the WORDS of delivery there. Have faith in GOD to do the work; do not rely upon yourself in all things ask for Jesus's guidance. He will do what we cannot. Rely on Him. Jesus is all in all. Now that you have met the best, you can forget the rest. Jesus only, Jesus only. Jesus is all in all; follow Him. Then with the sweet psalmist we will also declare, *"COME AND HEAR, ALL YE THAT FEAR GOD AND I WILL DECLARE WHAT HE HATH DONE FOR MY SOUL"* (Ps. 66:16).

Yes, when HIS WORD is sent, Jesus heals us and delivers us from our destructions.

Peter boldly declares, "LORD there is nowhere else to go." "Thou hast the WORDS of eternal life." It is by His WORDS of TRUTH that we are begotten through the GOSPEL. His WORDS are life; after all, HE is the WORD. Peter later tells us in his first epistle, *"Being born again not of corruptible seed, but of incorruptible BY THE WORD of GOD which liveth and abideth forever"* (1 Peter 1:23).

So yes, we can sit in our little hut and praise and sing all day. Praise is the way into the courts of heaven, but unless we put legs to our prayers, what advantage is it to our lost neighbor, who really, really needs to hear the TRUTH.

We will have all eternity to praise GOD; we will be praising HIM forever like the angels, so let's gather in the harvest now, so there will be lots of souls in heaven praising GOD throughout eternity. God is so great He really doesn't need us to tell Him; He needs us to work. "Show me your faith, and I will show you my faith with my works," James says in 2:18. Yes, but God inhabits the praise of his people, you say. I say I would much rather see the Savior inhabit the soul of another lost human being. So you see, we are to spread the GOOD NEWS: HE LIVES, JESUS LIVES, and you too through the WORD preached unto you can have this newness of life, everlasting life. The everlasting Gospel of Jesus Christ is the LIFE. (Live it.)

Jesus said, *"I AM THE WAY THE TRUTH THE LIFE."* We can build lofty choirs of hundreds of souls clothed in robes of white in buildings of crystal and marble, but if the whole city around you is on its way to HELL, what is its advantage on you? I would rather be down on the street corner showing some lost street person John 3:16 out of my little black book. One soul saved is worth more than all this world's gold. To each man his reward.

> *But when he saw the multitudes, he was moved*
> *with compassion on them, because they fainted, and*
> *were scattered abroad, as sheep having no shepherd.*
> *Then saith he unto his disciples, THE HARVEST*
> *truly is plenteous, but the labourers are FEW; Pray*

ye therefore the Lord of the HARVEST, that he will send forth labourers into HIS HARVEST. (Matt. 9:36–38)

It is the ALMIGHTY WORD that inspires, moves, molds, and creates men for the job at hand. We have been weighed in the balances too often and found wanting. The weight of the pendulum is tipped heavily in evil's court. The handwriting is on the wall.

"You do err not knowing the scriptures, nor the power of God" (Matt. 22:29).

We are fallen short telltale signs everywhere—evil abounding, no force of GOOD to counterbalance the upcoming STORM. Children are fainting in the way, and men are throwing in the towel. Hearts are heavy and nowhere to turn, or so it seems, because if there is a LIGHT around, it should be set on the table for all to see. Where is their HOPE, folks? Jesus said, "Seek and ye shall find," but HOPE is hidden; instead our children are offered a plate of immorality and rebellion. Jesus is the HOPE of all mankind, but the devil with the help of the evil ones have cloaked our world in veils of blackness and darkness tattooing their particular brands of evil everywhere. Keep it dark, the evil one says, just don't allow any light through; someone might see their phoniness and embrace the truth. I am reminded that:

> *When the enemy shall come in like a flood, the SPIRIT of the LORD shall lift up a standard against him. So shall they fear the NAME of the LORD from the West and His glory from the rising of the sun. And the Redeemer shall come to Zion and unto them that turn from transgression, saith the Lord.* (Isa. 59:19–2)
>
> *For as by one man's disobedience (ADAM) many were made sinners (US), so by the obedience of one (JESUS)shall many be made righteous. Moreover the law entered, that the offence might abound. But where sin abounded, GRACE*

did much more abound: That as SIN hath reigned unto death, even so might GRACE reign through righteousness unto ETERNAL LIFE BY JESUS CHRIST OUR LORD. (Rom. 5:19–21)

Every arrow and street sign should be pointed in the direction of HOPE. But no the arrows are pointed to hospitals, rehabs, bars, brothels, movie theaters, theme parks. Tell me is that all the HOPE our children and fellow man get. Tear the commandments down, turn out the lights, you're praying fetch the Gestapo. If there is a LIGHT around, let's put it where all can see. Yes, true revival begins with me. Or do we make the cross of Christ in vain? Did Jesus die for nothing, so you and I can shut up and keep quiet? Was Jesus quiet? We must take the limits off God and start believing and start having faith that, yes, Jesus is the conqueror; and He showed total victory at Calvary. Let's broadcast this precious HOPE till all men understand and believe. No, Jesus was not a quiet man, He went about shouting in the face of the enemy and crying out against evil, and His father *thundered* from heaven, "Hear ye Him *this is My Precious SON.*" Jesus and the disciples have shown us the road. They spent their days walking over dusty roads in sandals, going from city to city, carrying the good news with signs following to strengthen the less believing. If Jesus is the WAY, where is the LIGHT for all to see? Remember, we are the LIGHT. We, yes, us, we are the LIGHT of the WORLD. If Jesus is the TRUTH, let's proclaim it please! If Jesus is the Life, let's pick up the faint-hearted and show them a better *way.*

So why are you sitting there? Time is short. So let's redeem it; let's restore what the cankerworm hath eaten, what the moth and rust have destroyed. Not a minute to waste. The Master is high profile and demanding, expecting your all because He gave you HIS ALL. He bankrupted heaven and sent His SON JESUS for our ATONEMENT.

John continues with his most excellent instructions: *"If ye abide in ME, and MY WORDS abide in you, ye shall ask what ye will, and it shall be done unto you. Herein is MY Father glorified that you bear much fruit: so shall ye be my disciples"* (John 15:7–8).

We want the WORD out there for the LOST and Jesus says, *"ASK WHAT YE WILL"* so yes, we PRAY for

> more laborers
> for the harvest
> that is ripe
> and
> falling
> to
> the
> ground.

Each morning, we pray, "LORD, in Jesus's NAME, send laborers today into your harvest fields." That an abundance of fruit may be reaped. I alone am one person, but as we pray for more workers to help in the harvest, more will be done, and Jesus will be glorified. And best of all, those poor lost undone, hopeless souls will find their way to Jesus.

> *"Come unto ME, all ye that labour and are heavy laden, and I will give you rest. Take my yoke upon you and learn of ME; for I am meek and lowly in heart: and ye shall find rest unto your souls. For my yoke is easy and my burden is light"* (Matt. 11:28–30).

Yes, let's invite them into the Lord's path. His way is easy, His burden light. The devil's way is gruesome, oppressing, and taxing; but Jesus's way is easy.

> *"If the SON therefore shall make you free, ye shall be free indeed"* (John 8:36).

(Oh, blessed WORDS these are.)

No more heavy bondage of sin to carry around. The shackles are loosed, and we are free of the weight of sin, for sin is a heavy burden;

it is the weight of sin that makes man's way dark and hopeless. But Jesus, through His disciples, that's you and me, brings life and light and hope, and rescues the lost, and undone and sets them on the path of LIFE in Jesus. Thus, souls are born into the kingdom and…

> *"Herein is My Father glorified that you (should) bear much fruit. So shall ye be MY Disciples." Jesus* says to all *"Follow ME and I will make you fishers of men."* Paul says *"Follow me as I follow Christ."* (So as the WORD goes forth, souls are born into the kingdom. The WORD does not return void but accomplishes that which it was sent to do.) Because the *"WORD of GOD is quick and powerful and sharper than any two-edged sword, piercing even to the dividing of soul and spirit and is a discerner of the thoughts and intents of the heart."* (Heb. 4:12)
>
> The WORD is the precious seed of the sower that brings forth life in the heart of man. *"A sower went forth to sow and when he sowed some fell by the wayside and the fowls devoured it. Some fell upon stony ground* (and we know that does not work) *and some fell among thorns and got choked but others fell into good ground and brought forth fruit some a hundredfold, some sixtyfold and some thirtyfold. Who hath ears to hear let him hear!"* (Matt. 13:3–9)

Then the Lord proceeds with an expletive of his parable, and verse 22 says, *"He that received seed among the thornes is he that heareth the WORD and the CARES of this world and the deceitfulness of riches, choke the WORD and he becometh unfruitful."* You see, it is all about bearing fruit yet how many of us simply play church and then go about our cares until the next Sunday when we again occupy space in church. I ask you, is this bearing fruit? Okay, Jesus explains in verse 23, *"But he that received seed into the good ground is he that heareth the WORD and understandeth it"* [Is not this the key? Light on my path] *and which also bear fruit some a 100 and some 60 and some 30 fold."* And for the sake of those not listening let me repeat!

"And herein is My Father glorified that ye bear much fruit." It is all about being fruitful. If a tree doesn't bear fruit, you cut it down; it is good for nothing. The WORD is life. This dead world needs life; we have to give it to them, or they die and perish in their sins and go to a devil's hell. God says, "Warn them for me, warn them. Give them Christ's WORDS. The word is life. It is only the WORD that can quicken a man and revive him and bring him back to life." See, the hymn says, *"Send the light the precious Gospel light let it sound from shore to shore."*

What does Rousseau say? *"Men are born free but are everywhere in chains."* Yes, chains of darkness without the WORD of LIGHT. What is another NAME for Jesus that John makes plain for us in Revelations *"THE WORD."* Jesus said He is the truth, the WORD of Truth. God help you if your light is not showing for the Master said; shout it from the housetops, because if we withhold truth, every country will soon be as North Korea. Godless, miserable, and self-defeating. For see how the WORD says, *"And JUDGMENT is turned away backward, and Justice standeth afar off: for TRUTH is FALLEN IN THE STREET, and equity cannot enter. Yea TRUTH faileth; and he that departeth from evil maketh himself a prey: and the LORD saw it, and it DISPLEASED Him that there was no JUDGMENT"* (Isaiah's powerful WORDS, 59:14–15).

Yes, every country would soon be like North Korea without the WORD, without the LIGHT, WITHOUT GOD. And the epitome of no GOD is HELL, hell on Earth. The old Russian proverb says go GODWARD not hellward. Common sense, people, please. There is a God in heaven hello, hello, and we are His little creatures, hello, hello, and we must worship GOD; yes, He says so in the first and second commandments. Thou shalt love and worship the LORD THY GOD.

So God is not pleased with no fruit; it is all about being fruitful. This is what pleases the Father. Do you want to please or displease Him? Look at what He did for us, the CROSS, CALVARY, the GRAVE, beaten and despised and we cannot even open our mouths to others about His wonders? No we are too busy chatting up a storm about nothing and nowhere and nothing at all, or should I say about life, the world, and all its glories; it's time to CONSIDER.

"Love not the world," Jesus says, and God's wrath is for the disobedient. Consider what the LORD has done for you and stop putting your light under a bushel basket, but put your light on the table so all can see. The harvest is plenteous and the laborers are few. Many, many in the valley of decision, the fruit is ripe to harvest. Consider it, the LORD will REQUIRE IT. He will require this of us, so consider. Do it, just do it, go possess the LAND because

> *[f]or as the rain cometh down, and the snow from heaven, and returneth not thither, but watereth the earth, and maketh it bring forth and bud, that it may give seed to the sower, and bread to the eater: So shall MY WORD BE that goeth forth out of MY MOUTH: IT SHALL NOT RETURN UNTO ME VOID, but it shall ACCOMPLISH that which I please, and it shall PROSPER in the THING whereto I SENT IT."* (Isaiah's blessed WORD 55:10–11)

Now, Holy Father in Jesus's name, forgive us our sins and help our slackness, ease, and complacency concerning LOST SOULS and help us to spread the KNOWLEDGE of JESUS CHRIST wherever and however the Lord would inspire us. That we may be about the Father's business. We ask in the MOST HOLY BLESSED FOREVER NAME OF JESUS CHRIST our LORD and SAVIOR. Amen.

> *The eyes of the Lord are in every place beholding the evil and the good.* (Prov. 15:13)
> *His eyes are upon the ways of man, and he seeth all his goings.* (Job 34:21)
> *(Heaven and Earth shall pass away, but MY WORDS shall NOT EVER pass away.)* (Matt. 24:35)

Amen!

Softly and Tenderly

1 Soft-ly and ten-der-ly Je-sus is call-ing, Call-ing for you and for me;
See, on the portals He's waiting and watch-ing, Watching for you and for me.

2 Why should we tarry when Jesus is plead-ing, Pleading for you and for Me?
Why should we linger and heed not His mercies, Mer-cies for you and for me?

3 Time is now fleeting, the moments are passing, Passing from you and from me;
Shadows are gathering, (Jesus is) coming, Com-ing for you and for me.

4 Oh! For the won-der-ful love He has promised, Promised for you and for me;
Tho' we have sinned, He has mercy and pardon, Par-don for you and For me.

(chorus)

Come home...come home,... Ye who are wear-y, come home;...
Ear-nest-ly, ten-der-ly, Je-sus is call-ing, Call-ing, O sin-ner, come home! (Will L. Thompson)

Early

———— ⌘ ————

S eek the Lord while He may be found; seek ye Him evermore. Is not the dew upon the leaf a telltale sign of how to fly? Early will I seek Thee, when my heart is pure and my mind is a ready chalkboard for you Lord to write on. Early will I seek Thee before my mind and body become too heavy with the weight of the day. The dew is the garden's clock and our reminder to be wiser than the children of this world. The Garden of Eden was simply watered with a fine mist springing from the ground each morning. Everything is peaceful and orderly here in the garden, the early robin has not even arrived yet to survey her territory. Seek early while all is still quiet and peaceful for the enemy has not yet gathered his plans for the days destructions. Yes, early will I seek thee, O, Lord—early. Early so I can be one step ahead of the enemy. Early before the confusions of the day over-whelm us. Early just me and God. David says,

> *O God Thou art my God. Early will I seek Thee.* (Ps. 63:1)
> *O satisfy us early with Thy mercy that we may rejoice and be glad all our days. And teach us to number our days, that we may apply our hearts unto wisdom. We spend our years as a tale that is told. And a thousand years in Thy sight are but as yesterday when it is past, And as a watch in the night.* (Ps. 90:14, 12, 9, 4)

Let us follow David as he seeks God early. And let us be awed with the Lord's magnificence as Peter reiterates a thousand years,

"But beloved, be not ignorant of this one thing, that one day is with the Lord as a thousand years, and a thousand years as one day" (2 Peter 3:8).

Our perspectives change as we take on the reality of life in God's real time. So then, it has only been two days ago that Jesus was walking the Earth. And I believe we are on God's time, not our own time down here on Earth.

> *"My voice shalt Thou hear in the morning, O Lord; in the morning will I direct my prayer unto Thee, and will look up"* (Ps. 5:3).

Mornings are always refreshing; one more day it seems with a new lease on life granted us for another twenty-four hours. Jesus's compassions and mercies are new each morning; they fail not. Come into His presence, asking, pleading, believing in His mercy and gain strength for the day. Come early while the mind is clear, and thus we will have right priorities to guide us into Godly paths for God's glory, not our needs, but yes, our needs too.

Jesus is our great example; the Bible says that Jesus says, *"Follow Me,"* and His way is perfect. Jesus had an early schedule, no sleeping in for Him. He was in Holy Communion with the Father before a chirp could be heard. This is true love, to lay down your comforts and seek the face of the HOLY GOD. It was always early, and Jesus went by Himself to seek the one He loved. I and the Father are One and Jesus wanted only to please His Father.

> *"My meat is to do the will of Him that sent ME, and to finish His work"* (John 4:34).

Jesus had a work, a mission to accomplish and this was the driving force of His life. He said, *"I have a baptism to be baptized with and how am I straightened til it be accomplished"* (Luke 12:50, Moffatt).

His zeal for the Father's will drove Him into His arms, He needed this alone time with the Father before the crowds came looking for Him. He needed the early quiet hours when the rest of the world was still slumbering. This is the place where He was strengthened for the long day ahead of Him. Jesus said I seek not My own will but the will of Him that sent Me. Moffatt says it this way, *"I have a baptism* (Jesus says) *to undergo, what tension I suffer, til it is all over"* (Luke 12:50). *"And when Jesus had received the vinegar, He said, it is finished"* (John 19:30).

Jesus zeal accomplished His mission; now He is forever comforted with His Father.

Let us look to King David the man of God as another worthy example. A man after God's own heart the Lord says, he prepared His heart before the Lord. Seven times a day will I seek unto my God he says; no wonder he was the apple of God's eye. No wonder the communion there was so holy. David sought after his precious Savior with all his heart, and out of the heart are the issues of life. The Lord says with the heart man believeth unto salvation. David had a sure bond with the Lord, an everlasting covenant to establish his throne forever. David's kingdom would be forever. David found favor with God and man; David prayed and sought unto his God seven times a day. SEVEN TIMES A DAY.

Psalm 89 explains

> *I have made a covenant with My chosen, I have sworn unto David my servant. Thy seed will I establish forever, and build up thy throne to all generations. I have found David My servant, with my holy oil have I anointed him. With whom my hand shall be established mine arm also shall strengthen him. The enemy shall not exact upon him; nor the son of wickedness afflict him. Also I will make him my firstborn, higher than the kings of the Earth. My mercy will I keep for him for evermore, and my covenant shall stand fast with him. His seed also will I make to endure forever and his throne as the days of Heaven. My covenant will I not break nor alter the thing that has gone out of My lips. Once have I sworn by My holiness that I will not lie unto David. His seed shall endure forever, and his throne as the sun before me.* (Thus saith the Lord.)

It shall be established forever as the moon (thus saith the Lord) and as a faithful witness in Heaven. (Ps. 89:3, 4, 20–22, 27–29, 34–37)

And again in 2 Samuel chapter 7, we have more details of David's covenant with God.

> *And it came to pass in the night that the Word of the Lord came unto Nathan the prophet saying. Go tell my servant David, Thus saith the Lord of Hosts; I took thee from the sheep cote, from following the sheep, to be ruler over My people, over Israel; And I was with thee whithersoever thou wentest and have cut off all thine enemies out of thy sight, and have made thee a great name, like unto the names of the Great men that are in the Earth... Also the Lord telleth thee that He will make thee an House... And thine house and Thy kingdom shall be established forever before thee: Thy throne shall be established forever. According to all these WORDS and according to all this vision so did Nathan the prophet speak unto David.* (2 Samuel 7:4, 5, 8–9, 11, 16, 19)

Now what did praying and seeking unto his God seven times a day reap for David? Yes, an everlasting kingdom and throne. David is of the tribe of Judah and Jesus Christ descended from David's bloodlines. The throne of God is forever, and when Jesus Christ returns to the Mount of Olives the second time, He shall sit upon David's Throne and reign over the nations of the Earth. Favor, David won favor with God and man; he sought unto his God early on early in life, and God exalted him to be captain of His Host, Captain over all Israel.

> *The people whom God went to redeem for a people to Himself and to make thyself a name O God (by redeeming them from Egypt) And thou hast confirmed to thyself thy people Israel to be a people unto thee forever and thou Lord art become their God.* (2 Sam. 7:23–24)

David came to realize that all the Lord was doing through him was for the sake of His people, Israel. But, friend, you do not become God's chosen by being a sluggard. David was diligent and steadfast in serving his God and the rewards are apparent. His training with the sheep on the hills of Jerusalem served him well. King David, the sweet psalmist of Israel, his praise brought him right into the throne room of God and there he remained, as the sun and the moon with an everlasting covenant in heaven, signed and sure.

So early, early we will seek Him whom my soul loves and early secure the advantage. It is the sluggard that sleeps in harvest and is shameful, Proverbs says. We will have all of eternity to rest after we cross the finish line, so press on, press toward the mark of the high calling in Jesus. Psalm 119 says, *"I prevented the dawning of the morning, and cried; I hoped in Thy word. Mine eyes prevent the night watches, that I might meditate in Thy word"* (147, 148).

T. R. always said, *"I'd rather wear out then rust out."* The disciple is not above his master and Jesus said, "Come follow ME." My yoke is easy and my burden is light. Our priorities must be His priorities, redeeming the time because the days are evil. He is not willing that any should perish, but that all should come to the saving knowledge of Jesus Christ our Lord. It is a wise man that winneth souls. God is glorified most in the salvation of a soul.

Redeeming the time because the days are hopeless for all who have not yet entered the Captain's ship. And there is only one objective in this race against evil: to please and honor the Master. Jesus said I have come into the world that I might save the world. We are His hands extended, and He says come the fields are already white to harvest. And David says, *"My flesh trembleth for fear of thee; and I am afraid of thy judgments"* (119:120).

Why because David had already been there and done that. When he messed up, God came down on him, like the doors of hell swinging wide open. He paid heavily, heavily for his mistakes and that is why he said, "My flesh trembleth for fear of THEE, and I am afraid of thy judgments." Never a dull moment with King David, but he learned. And God is likewise asking us to fear for His judgments and tremble on the behalf of the unsaved. Those that are not yet sealed with the Holy spirit of God.

You know, every single living soul should want to meet this extraordinary God. Just out of curiosity, to see who He is, to touch Him, to know Him, to admire, and to find out more about Him. It blows me away to know that we are in His image in His likeness as the Father is also. Jesus said if you have seen me you have also seen the Father. Unfortunately, some will come short and miss the mark of meeting Him, if we are not about the Master's business of showing the lost the right road to take. The Great Apostle says, *"Wherefore we labour that whether present or absent we may be accepted of Him"* (2 Cor. 5:9).

This is all that is important or worthy of concern, to be accepted, to make it, and bring along as many others as possible, snatching them out of the fire, hating even the smell of smoke. Hosea says.

"He hath done all things well"

"His going forth is prepared as the morning" (6:3).

Jesus had this morning thing figured out, it was always early with Him. Early got it done. Truly the fear of the Lord will cause us to be the first student sitting at the feet of Jesus in the morning.

Give to Him the best hours of the day; give to Him your full attention—no distraction, no hurried appointments to cause you to rush with God. God is not rushed; He always is and will be. Don't rush God. Do not expect much if you set your clock and say, "I have one hour here before I go to work, no God wants every minute of your time—every ounce of your being. He created you, you are His, and He owns you. Does the piece of pottery say to the ceramicist, "I will do this or that"? No, the piece is subject unto its owner. We must submit to His will. *"If the Lord wills I will do this or that."* If the Lord wills. It is His will we seek to please not our own will. Get your ducks in a row, get your priorities right, as God would have it, friend.

Let's look at the fifth Gospel and hear what the man of God Isaiah has to say. This is Jesus's favorite Old Testament book.

> *But we are all as an unclean thing, and all our righteousnesses are as filthy rags; and we all do fade as a leaf; and our iniquities, like the wind, have taken us away. And there is none that calleth upon thy name, that stirreth up himself to take hold of thee: for Thou hast hid thy face from us, and hast consumed us, because of our iniquities. But now, O Lord, Thou art our Father; we are the clay and Thou our potter. And we all are the work of Thy hands.* [Be not angry forever, we pray Thee]... *for we are all Thy people."* "And it shall come to pass, that before they call, I will answer; and while they are yet speaking, I will hear. I am sought of them that asked not for me; I am found of them that sought me not.* (Isa. 64:6–9, 65:1, 24)

God is looking for a man after His own heart, one that will say not my will, but Thine. He is looking for the one who will empty himself of this world and be filled with His compassion. We owe Him everything, He has been so gracious unto us. We need stir ourselves to His cause, He is our example and mentor.

He found us when we weren't even looking for Him. He found us; we are His. He has ransomed us from the hands of the devil. And He is so gracious, He is one step ahead of you friend, He knows what you are thinking. And before you even call He has the answer there for you. Oh, our gracious God, He asks so little and gives so much. My yoke is easy and my burden is light. He says, Come follow me.

> *"But seek ye first the kingdom of God, and his righteousness; and all these things shall be added unto you. Take therefore no thought for the morrow: for the morrow shall take thought for the things of itself. Sufficient unto the day is the evil thereof"* (Matt. 6:33–34).

First, God first and then the rest falls out according to the good pleasure of his will. God said we cannot serve two masters, *"Ye cannot serve God and mammon."* Some people think these things are just for the nuns and priests, God forbids such a thought. God's words are for every living soul that professes Jesus Christ as Lord. Wait upon Thy God, watch and pray that you, too, would be counted worthy. Keeping the night watch, keeping the morning watch. If ye had known what hour the thief would come, ye would have watched. The devil is a thief and murderer, the devil does not sleep. He is a fallen angel he does not need sleep. We cannot afford to be a laissez faire Christian, that's as good as not being one at all. God told Ezekiel, "I have made thee a watchman unto the house of Israel." Does a watchman sleep? Is he slack with His duties? We are watchmen, my friend; we are to warn the lost or their blood will be required of us. Take the word of God seriously, or take it not at all. Nehemiah says as they rebuilt the wall of Jerusalem that the workmen had a hammer in one hand and a sword in the other (4:17); that is being watchful, ready, and able to take on the enemy. Isaiah 62:6 says, *"I have set watchmen upon thy walls O Jerusalem, which shall never hold their peace day nor night."* How much more important is our soul, and the souls of mankind. We are watchmen of souls, watchmen do not sleep on the job. I will rest my case with David,

> *O my soul, thou hast said unto the LORD, Thou art my LORD... Their sorrows shall be multiplied that hasten after another god... The Lord is the portion of mine inheritance and of my cup: Thou maintainest my lot. The lines are fallen unto me in pleasant places; yea I have a goodly heritage. I will bless the Lord, who hath given me counsel: my reins also instruct me in the night seasons. I have set the Lord always before ME: because He is at my right hand, I SHALL NOT BE MOVED. Therefore my heart is glad, and my glory rejoiceth: my flesh also shall rest in hope... Thou wilt show me the path of life: in THY presence is fullness of joy; at THY right hand there are pleasures forevermore.* (Ps. 16)

David, indeed, relished being in the presence of His God, waiting upon his God and listening at the feet of Jesus. Yes, the lines have fallen unto David in pleasant places because the LORD was his first and chief concern, and because he sought unto his God seven times a day.

Jesus calls early; when He dealt out His hand to Pharaoh through the man of God, Moses, it was an early wakeup call.

> *And the Lord said to Moses Rise up early in the morning, and stand before Pharaoh, and say unto him, Thus saith the Lord God of the Hebrews Let my people go, that they may serve me.* (Ex. 9:13)
> *For at this time I will send all my plagues upon thine heart and on thy people that thou mayest*

know that there is none like ME in all the earth." (Verse 14)

"But Pharaoh hardened his heart and sinned yet more." (Verse 34)

So the Lord repeated Moses's performance more than eight times of rising early in the morning and appearing before Pharaoh, but it was always early in the morning. There was an urgency now in the mission. God had heard the groaning of the Hebrew children in hard bondage under Pharaoh.

> *Wherefore say unto the children of Israel, I am the Lord, and I will bring you out from under the burdens of the Egyptians, and I will rid you out of their bondage, and I will redeem you with a stretched out arm, and with great judgments: And I will take you to ME for a people, and I will be to you a God: and ye shall know that I am the Lord your God, which bringeth you out from under the burdens of the Egyptians. And I will bring you in unto the land, concerning the which I did swear to give it to Abraham, to Isaac, and to Jacob; and I will give it you for an heritage: I am the Lord.* (Ex. 6:6–8)

God's business is always urgent; He had heard their cries and groanings. He wanted His surprise attack and blows to Pharaoh dealt early. In time of war, the enemy is usually dealt his blows and defeats early when the men are fresh and well-rested. Our earthly mission is also a war against evil and God wants us to armor up and put blows to Satan's kingdom early in the morning. Early before he has time to assemble all his troops and unbelievers for a counterattack.

The enemy to our soul is ever busy at the business of defeating mankind and bringing us into his hard bondage of deception and unbelief in our savior Jesus Christ. He works 24-7 going about as a roaring lion seeking to whom he may devour. We must exercise wisdom above the enemy to our soul and call on heaven before he makes a strong foothold for the day. God is showing us how to do business; all the battles of the day have been fought and won by 9:00 a.m.

And at midnight the Lord smote all the first-born in the land of Egypt. From the firstborn of Pharaoh, to the captive in the dungeon, and of all the cattle…and there was a great cry in Egypt…for every house was hit with dead. And Pharaoh called Moses by night and said Rise up and get you forth. The Egyptians were now urgent upon the Hebrew people to send them out of Egypt in haste for they said. WE BE ALL DEAD MEN. (Ex. 12:29–33)

You see, the Lord did all the work, did all the battle, the battle is not yours; it is the Lord's. And there is a battle raging, ignore it if you will, but we shall all stand before Christ and give account. Moses clung to His God and just listened to what God told him to do. God tells us and speaks His instructions to us in His sacred Word: the Bible. If you are weak, friend, ask God to make you strong. God wants warriors in this battle that are able to handle both sword and spear. Our battle is spiritual. God specializes in making the weak strong. He specializes in things thought impossible. God wants His kingdom established here on Earth by the power of the Holy Spirit. He wants Satan trampled under our feet for the glory of God.

Early, the Lord sent His warnings by the hands of the holy prophets. Everything had to be done early; they were in desert country and by 10:00 a.m. The sweltering heat can cook eggs on the rocks; it can be indecent for man or beast. Jeremiah says in chapter 7.

Since the day that your Fathers came forth out of the land of Egypt unto this day I have even sent unto you all my servants the prophets, daily rising up early and sending them. (Verse 25)

Thus saith the Lord the God of Israel amend your ways and your doings, and I will cause you to dwell in this place…in the land that I gave to your fathers forever and ever. (Verses 3, 7)

And now the Lord saith, I spoke unto you, rising up early and speaking, but ye heard not; and I called you but ye answered not... Also I set watch-men over you, saying hearken...but they said we will not hearken. (Verses 13, 6:17)

We will not hearken and do, so the LORD gave them over to destruction. He said, "Remove them from my sight" and His mercy utterly departed from them, so they were without a prayer and without pity. So He did to them after their own ways and their own doings; they reaped destruction.

If we are to live in peace until Jesus's return, we must seek His face, wait upon Him. Moses said, "Cleave unto Him, for He is your life." The world does not offer life, all life comes from Jesus. He is the creator of life and peace and joy, but if we turn our back on Him, He will turn His back on us. Our best time belongs in His hands, to wait on God is a lost art because this world teaches us only worldliness. We go to school for fifty years and learn nothing of God. GOD must be first on the agenda and God must be the whole agenda. God wants all of you, all the time. The great apostle says it best because he did it best.

> *I beseech you brethren by the mercies of God, that ye present your bodies a living sacrifice, holy, acceptable unto God, which is your reasonable service. And be not conformed to this world: but be ye transformed by the renewing of your mind, that ye may prove what is that good and acceptable and perfect, will of God.* (Rom. 12:1–2)
> *For of Him and through Him, and to Him are all things: To Him be glory for ever and ever.* (Rom. 11:36)

Jesus needs all of us, not some or a little or later maybe; esteem Christ lightly and you get the short end of the stick. God is all in all; He gave us all and delivered us from so great a death. He expects all. He it is who we will give account to, put yourself there now and imagine it; it can be a fearful thought. It should not be and cannot be if we are to live with Him in eternity. Christ said to prepare ourselves now; watch and pray. David said the Lord is always before ME. Christ our great example. He said there will be signs, but be ready, be watching, be praying. It is not enough to do a little. Jesus is the Master cup, the grand championship, the Heisman trophy, the Wimbledon Cup. Hello, hello out there. Paul said he counted himself not as apprehending yet. There's more to do for Christ. Can you honestly tell me how bold you will be in His presence on that day. Have we done all we possibly can for Christ?

Why spend so much time preserving your body with beauty, Botox, and organics when your very soul is in jeopardy, thou fool? The rich truth of Jesus's parable tells us that a certain rich man had a bumper crop with nowhere to store it.

> *And he said, this will I do: I will pull down my barns, and build greater ones. And there will I bestow all my fruits and my goods. And I will say to my soul, soul, thou hast much goods laid up for many years, take thine ease, eat, drink, and be merry. But God said unto him, Thou fool, this night thy soul shall be required of thee: then whose shall those things be...so is he that layeth up treasure for himself, and is not rich toward God.* (Luke 12:18–21)

This man was obviously not working in the Lord's vineyard but was building on his own pile of wealth without a thought for his soul. Unlike Job who

> *[w]as a perfect man and righteous, he feared God and detested evil... He had 7 sons and 3 daughters. His substance was so great...so that he was the greatest of all men of the East.* (Job 1:1–3)
> *When each week of feasting was over, Job sent for his children and had them purified, rising early and offering a burnt sacrifice for each of them, "It*

may be" said Job "that my sons have sinned by cursing God in their hearts." Thus did Job continually without fail. (Job 1:5–6 Moffatt)

The difference is night and day. Job was perfect in God's eyes, and He says so in verse 8. Job was concerned for his own soul and his children's souls also. He feared God and spent his wealth caring for all the poor around him. He worshipped his God by building an altar and doing animal sacrifices in proxy for his children, to make sure of their souls before God. And what does Jesus say?

But rather seek first the Kingdom of God; and all those things shall be added unto you. Fear not little flock, for it is your Father's good pleasure to give you the Kingdom. Sell that ye have and give alms provide yourself treasure in Heaven that faileth not, where thieves cannot break in and steal, and where moth and rust do not corrupt. For where your treasure is, there will your heart be also. (Luke 12:31–34)

It will be a sad day for some that do not understand Jesus Kingdom principles. The first being to love God with all your heart, mind, soul, and strength and the second is like it, love your neighbor as yourself. Seek God, His will, wait upon Him continually, knowing that your labor in the Lord is not in vain. We want His rewards in heaven, not here; that won't do us any good if we are in heaven. We want heavenly rewards, not earthly rewards that perish. Do everything for Christ as if your life depended on it. Who knows when the Father will roll up this old Earth as a scroll and say "It is done." I'm done, last scene, camera, action please. The world at this very moment is looking very perplexing and guaranteed nothing is solved by war, yet the Lord said there would be wars and rumors of wars. The Lord said, "Be not afraid but look up for our redemption is nigh." We know the signs, they are written of and recorded of Jesus in the Gospels. And they shall say, *"Peace and safety then sudden destruction."* Jesus has told it all to us before it comes to pass, if we are walking hand in hand with Jesus, it will be no surprise.

> *So likewise ye when ye see these things come to pass, know ye that the kingdom of God is nigh at hand. Take heed to yourselves lest at any time your hearts be overcharged with surfeiting, and drunkenness, and the CARES OF THIS LIFE, and so that day come upon you unaware. For as a snare shall it come on all them that dwell on the face of the whole earth. Watch ye therefore and pray always, that you may be accounted worthy to escape all these things that shall come to pass, and to stand before the son of man.* (Luke 21:31, 34–36)

These things that must shortly come to pass will be no surprise to those who wait on Jesus all the day long. He will be speaking to us and assuring us that His grace will be sufficient to carry us through anything. "Abide in Me," Jesus says. "I am the vine you are the branches." Paul says for me to live is Christ and I say, revive us again, O, God, that your favor and your blessings will be ours. Let the mind that is in Thee, O, God, be in us. Let us have the Father's heart that we might abide in His will and bring forth fruit unto eternal life. Then will we, like Ezekiel and John, take the roll of the WORD and eat it and find that it is sweeter than honey and the honeycomb.

> *"Man does not live by bread alone but by every WORD that proceedeth out of the mouth of God"* (Matt. 4:4).

This is Jesus's command and He says, *"Everyone that heareth these sayings of Mine, and doeth them not, shall be likened unto a FOOLISH MAN"* (Matt. 7:26).

No, I want to hear Jesus say, *"Well done thou good and faithful servant."* On that day, at the end of my earthly pilgrimage.

There must be a holy urgency about God's work and a calmness that allows God to take hold of our very soul. The love of God will compel us to fulfill His will therefore time spent with Jesus builds our faith and belief. God does not want unhappy servants that force themselves to do for Him, when the love of Jesus is not ruling their heart. That is like giving grudgingly and that does not please God. God's love must rule everything we do and then doing for God is a pleasure. To know Him is to love him. "Learn of Me," Jesus says, "for I am meek and lowly of heart and I will give rest unto your souls." There is no more profitable pastime than building up oneself in the most holy faith. It reaps heavenly rewards. Ten minutes with Jesus in His word can accomplish things with God that might have taken you six months of frustration to do. God has miracles for those that seek him out.

Let us be urgent in God's work. His work is most urgent and He pays well. If we lightly esteem Him and His things, He will esteem us lightly. He is always looking for laborers for His work, for His vineyard. God needs you in His harvest laboring and pressing back the forces of evil that we may gather in a few more faint ones and show them the Master's path. In the Lord's own words, He says in Luke, *"The harvest truly is great, but the labourers are few; pray ye therefore the Lord of the harvest, that He would send forth labourers into His harvest. Go your ways; behold I send you forth as lambs among wolves"* (Luke 10:2–3).

This prayer should be on our lips constantly. Jesus is saying beseech the Father in Jesus's name because God is most glorified in the salvation of souls. One soul saved is worth more than all this world's gold. What would you give in exchange for your soul and happiness with God for all eternity. No trade, no deal no way. God is everything and without Him is hell for all eternity. *"A wise man will hear and will increase learning"* says proverbs, and "The fear of the Lord is the beginning of knowledge" (1:5, 7) and will cause him to depart from evil. For *"the heart is deceitful above all things and desperately wicked, who can know it"* (Jer. 17:9). And therefore we do not plot our own path and say my heart will lead me, no we follow the WORD of God and His truth, because His WORD is perfect. His

WORD is pure and has been tried in the fire seven times. Seven is God's perfect number and God's WORD is perfect. He says, "Follow me and I will make you fishers of men." God's work is urgent, God is looking for good men.

> *"Seek the Lord and His strength seek His face evermore"* (Ps. 105:4).

Redeeming the time in the face of eternity, because time waits for no man saving for that one occasion when Joshua said, *"Sun stand still."* Then the sun obeyed his voice and held its course for twenty-four hours whilst they finished the battle. Oh, to have power with God, what a joy.

> *The Lord reigneth, He is clothed with majesty and strength, wherewith He hath girded himself.* (Ps. 93:1)
> *He shows forth His loving kindness in the morning and His faithfulness every night. A brutish man knoweth not neither doth a fool understand this. And the wicked... He shall destroy forever.* (Ps. 92:2, 6–7)

But the righteous do see and understand that time is a treasure from the most high, to be used for His glory and purpose. We shall soon enough be checking out of here and our bank account in heaven must be full. We must ever redeem His blessed time, and that means getting a hundred years out of every twenty-four hours. It means holy warfare, pushing darkness down and back to hell. It means snatching a few souls that were tottering on the fence of unbelief. It means regaining our territory, which is the whole Earth. If we are redeeming the time, then the blind shall see, and the lost will find their way to Jesus.

Since meeting Jesus, all I want to do now is to make it to heaven and take along as many of Satan's prisoners as I can. Snatching them from Satan's clutches with fear and trembling. What did Peter say? *"Save yourselves from this* untoward *generation and be baptized in the name of Jesus Christ for the remission of sins and ye shall receive the Holy Ghost"* (and be baptized with fire) (Acts 2:38, 40).

Isaiah boldly says, *"Have no fear of what they fear, never dread it. The danger lies with the Lord of Hosts; Tis He whom you should fear, tis he whom you should dread"* (8:12–13 Moffatt).

Because He has the power to throw both soul and body into hell. It is God we fear, it is God we dread because His wrath is against all sin. And at the end of days, He shall pour out His wrath against all unbelievers and sinners. Such wrath the Bible says as the Earth has never ever seen. That is why a pious Christian is and should be concerned for the lost and perishing that have not yet found God's paths. But to us that are saved in Jesus, God tells us, *"Be not afraid of sudden fear, neither of the desolation of the wicked when it cometh. For the Lord shall be thy* confidence *and shall keep thy foot from being taken"* (Prov. 3:23–26)

God's curse shall be on the house of the wicked, not on God's believers.

> *For there shall be* great tribulation, *such as was not since the beginning of the world to this time, no, nor ever shall be. And except those days should be shortened, there should no flesh be saved, but for the elect's sake those days shall be shortened.* (Matt. 24:21, 22)
>
> *Men's hearts failing them for* fear, *and for looking after those things which are* coming on the Earth: *for the powers of Heaven shall be shaken.* (Luke 21:26)
>
> *And at that time shall Michael stand up, the great prince which standeth for the children of thy people: and there shall be a time of trouble, such as never was since there was a nation even to that same time: and at that time thy people shall be* delivered, *every one that shall be* found written in the book. (Dan. 12:1)

The Lord is our *confidence* because we are in Him. Safety is of the Lord, always, only Jesus can keep us safe. He says watch and pray always because we know not the hour of our Lord's return. It could be morning, evening or at midnight. The Lord gave us many parables to this end, the parable of the faithful and unfaithful servants.

> *"Therefore be ye also ready: for in such an hour as you think not the son of man cometh"* (Matt. 24:44).

And again the parable of the ten virgins, five were foolish and five wise.

> *"And at midnight there was a cry heard, Behold, the bridegroom cometh; go ye out and meet Him." "Watch therefore, for ye know neither the day not the hour wherein the Son of Man cometh"* (Matt. 25:6, 13).

It could be morning, noon, or on a night watch therefore be ye ready.

Watchful, waiting upon God. *"They that wait upon the Lord shall renew their strength; they shall mount up with wings as Eagles; they shall run and not be weary, and they shall walk and not faint"* (Isa. 40:31).

You say, how does one wait on the Lord? How? By reading His Holy Word, the Bible. Back to Christianity 101; *"Man shall not live by bread alone but by every WORD that proceeds out of the mouth of God."* That's how it's done, that is how we are to live. Please do not frustrate the grace of God. If we are not to read, why then were all these words meticulously recorded by all God's saints, prophets and disciples. The Bible plainly instructs us to study. We are built up and strengthened and made strong when we feed on the bread of life. The heavenly mana, the Word of God. Wait, I say on the Lord, and be blessed.

And why call ye Me Lord and do not the things I say? Is the disciple above his Lord? The Lord has a to-do list and His commands are law. It is His show, He has the first and the last Word. *"Therefore whosoever heareth these sayings of mine and doeth them, I will liken unto a wise man which built his house upon the Rock."* The Rock is Christ Jesus. And again Jesus says, *"All things whatsoever ye would that men should do to you do ye even so to them: for this is all the law and the prophets"* (Matt. 7:24, 12).

All the law and the prophets is fulfilled in this tiny little verse. This is the meaning of all that I am teaching you Jesus says. He nailed it with this one, this is the sum total of all I am telling you. The golden rule to live by. And Jesus was even telling them to love their enemies, love all men good or evil. Such things had not been taught or required before now. Jesus's teachings were indeed new. His was a Gospel of love, for God is love. And our Father in heaven wants us to be like Him.

> *"Be ye therefore perfect, even as your Father which is in Heaven is perfect"* (Matt. 5:48).

And James again tells us to *"be ye doers of the WORD, and not hearers only deceiving your own selves"* (1:22). And this is not easy seeing that the spirit wars against the flesh, and the flesh against the spirit. But God can make all things easy and come to pass for us by prayer. Of ourselves we are vile creatures, serving our own lusts. But as the Great Apostle says, *"Thanks be to God which giveth us the victory through our Lord Jesus Christ"* (1 Cor. 15:57).

As the disciples said to Jesus, why do you teach in parables. And you might wonder why does she quote so many scriptures.

First off, I love and adore the WORD of God and want it glorified and exalted as the scripture says. He has exalted His word above His most Holy name.

Second pass, it is difficult to improve on the perfect. The Word of God is pure and perfect, purified seven times.

Third, the Words of Jesus are the Father's Words, the Words of the Holy prophets; they were given the words they spoke by God and the disciples were eyewitnesses and miracle workers.

I simply love to quote the word of God because it is quick and powerful. My words are nothing, so let God's Words be magnified. I listen to my teachers and mostly use their Words, Jesus' Words, the disciples' accounts, and the Holy Prophet's Words. And they all are really God and the Lord Jesus and the Holy Spirit's WORDS. Amen.

Jesus is our hero, He is our perfect example. He tells us Himself, *"For I have given you an example, that ye should do as I have done"* (John 13:15).

Now Jesus here was talking about His washing of the disciples feet, but I am sure, that I am sure, He is speaking of His entire life being an example. What else would *"Come follow Me"* mean, coming from Jesus's lips? Yes, follow everything I preached and did, I am your example. Also Paul says, *"Follow me as I follow Christ"* was Paul behind even the chiefest of the apostles; no, he is the one that delivered the Gospel to the Gentiles. That's us. Did he accomplish so much by sleeping in and taking it easy? No, he pressed toward the mark, by day and night watchings, prayer, and fastings. He said, *"I will very gladly spend and be spent for you; though the more abundantly I love you, the less I be loved"* (2 Cor. 12:15).

And Jesus said, "I lay down my life for you, should you not lay down your life for the brethren? And Jesus said, if any man come after me, let him deny himself. Yes, deny yourself all that sleep and slumber. As Proverbs says,

> *How long wilt thou sleep, O sluggard? When wilt thou arise out of thy sleep?* (6:9)
> *The enemy neither slumbers nor sleeps, we then should keep our post. "Lest coming suddenly he find you sleeping and what I say unto you I say unto all,* watch.*"* (Mark 13:36–37)

And Paul in Thessalonians writes,

> *But of the times and the seasons, brethren, ye have no need that I write unto you. For yourselves know perfectly that the day of the Lord so cometh as a thief in the night. For when they shall say, Peace and safety; then sudden destruction cometh upon*

them, as travail upon a woman with child; and they shall not escape. But ye, brethren, are not in darkness, that that day should overtake you as a thief. Ye are all the children of light, and the children of the day: we are not of the night, nor of darkness. Therefore let us not sleep, as do others; but let us watch and be sober. (5:1–6)

Folks, Jesus has been here, the God of all the Earth, the God that created the Earth has been here. *"And I saw* (says the Baptist) *and bear record that this is the Son of God"* (John 1:34). It blows me away to think on this. Jesus was born here and walked throughout the cities of Israel preaching and working miracles. And the Lord said to Thomas blessed is he who has not seen and yet believes. It's like this is the greatest thing ever and no one is talking about it. Tell me, is there anything besides Jesus, is there anything else; no, He is it. Jesus says learn of Me, come unto Me, and Peter says, *"There is nowhere else to turn Lord; you have the WORDS of ETERNAL LIFE." "Take my yoke upon you, learn of ME; for I am meek and lowly in heart: and ye shall find rest to your souls. For my yoke is easy and my burden is light. Come unto me all ye that labour and are heavy laden"* (Matt. 11:28–30). That's us we are all of us heavy laden and there is nowhere else to turn. "Come learn about Me," Jesus says. There's nothing else, folks; Jesus is the last stop before glory and He is glory.

> *Thus saith the Lord, Let not the wise man glory in his wisdom, neither let the mighty man glory in his might, let not the rich man glory in his riches: But let him that glorieth glory in this, that he understandeth and* knoweth me, *that I am the Lord which exercise lovingkindness, judgment, and righteousness, in the earth: for in these things I delight, saith the Lord.* (Jer. 9:23–24)

How well do you know Jesus?

Well then, what wait I for, if the Lord be God let us serve Him morning, noon and night, redeeming the time because the days are evil, and the night cometh when no man can work. And Jesus said, "I must go to yonder city to preach also because for this reason was I sent of the Father." For the people had constrained Him to remain with them. "No," Jesus said, "there is more work to be done. I must go, I must be about the Father's business." Early before daybreak, Jesus was already in the temple preaching to the early crowd.

Now Jesus is our example so *"go and do likewise."* We should be early about the Father's business of spreading the WORD. Jesus saves, heals, delivers. Jesus is the way, the truth, the life, and our hope of ETERNAL LIFE. We must walk hand in hand with the Master, walking even in His footsteps, having our mind saturated, our heart ploughed and our body hedged about with His saving Word. Catching early the straying sheep so that they might not be devoured by the *"Lion that goes to and fro throughout the Earth seeking to whom He may devour."* His time is short; he is now working overtime to deceive uniformed souls fainting by the way. We should be spinning circles around the enemy. Our goal should be red hot as we snatch the tormented souls from his fangs. God help us if we run and hide like Jonah.

> *"So the ship master came to him and said, what meanest thou, O sleeper? Arise, call upon Thy God, if so be that God will think upon us THAT WE PERISH NOT"* (1:6).

There's a message there, right? God help you, man. Wake up and WAKE UP EARLY ON.

At ease, ignoring God, asleep in the lusts of the flesh, while God's work suffers, do we really think God does not see? Was God watching Jonah? God told Jonah, *"Arise go to Nineveh, that great city, and cry against it for their wickedness is come up before Me."* No, Jonah ran and hid, and God followed him with a tempest. Bottom line we are holding power that we have not even tapped the surface of. We hold the keys to the kingdom. God told Jonah, "Go warn Nineveh that they perish not." God wants us to wake up; call upon Him so that we will not perish. Us, our neighbors, our nation, "Warn them, warn them for Me," the Lord says. "Why sleep ye in harvest?" Jesus is the key that opens the door of life, tell them for Me. The Apostle says and some have fallen asleep and made shipwreck.

Some write themselves off with excuses; others amuse themselves, realizing nothing of the power of leading a lost soul to Christ. They have not a clue that we are saved to work, not retire. Excuse ME please, you will have all eternity to relax and tour. All the riches and tarnished beauty of this world is soon to melt with a very fervent heat; therefore, what manner of men ought we to be Peter says. Most likely, we should be shaking in our boots fearing for the LOST because the Almighty's great wrath will soon be poured out on the unbelieving, the wayward and the rebellious, shaking for fear of falling short in our duties. If God has graciously unshackled you by someone's early call, should you not pass on the favor, the baton in the race of life or death, blessing, or cursing.

If the truth has made you free, you are free indeed. The TRUTH IS the WORD, and the WORD of God enlightens to freedom. Only use not your liberty as an occasion of the flesh, but by love, serve one another. Once we, too, were bound by the ignorance of darkness, and how did we get set free? Yes, someone cared and was obedient to the heavenly call whose light was shining for all to see. So pass the WORD along; Jesus saves. Have you met Jesus yet, etc.? "God bless you" works also. Pray ye therefore the Father, for laborers to be sent into His vineyard. Now the parable says some arrived early and worked all day while others kept being hired throughout the day, and the owner paid the same amount to all them at the end of the day. So is the love and generosity of the Father. Some meet Jesus early, some meet Jesus at noon and as the thief on the right, and some meet Jesus two minutes till midnight. To every man his reward. Know ye that your labor in the Lord is not in vain.

Send the light, the precious Gospel light. *"To the hungry soul every bitter thing is sweet."* So yes, a WORD spoken in due season how sweet it is. It is like a hammer and chisel splitting the rock and conquering the darkness for Jesus. Like letting the light into a dark place, someone's dark soul. Early He sent them, Moses was in Pharaoh's courts before he could wipe the sleep from his eyes. Early Jeremiah set about weeping over Jerusalem's destruction, before the sun shone. Early Elijah was footin' it through the waste howling wilderness, one step ahead of Jezebel's sword. Joshua rose up early in the morning and took five thousand of his most valiant warriors and set ambush for the city of Ai. Not a sluggard among these holy ones. John the Baptist was pouring the chilly waters of the Jordan over repentant souls to baptism before dawn. David the sweet psalmist of Israel had a wakeful eye and slew the lion caught stealing his sheep. Ah, God's watchmen, I think sleep with one eye open and their weapon in their hand. Early HE sent them.

Leaning On the Everlasting Arms

1 What a fel-low-ship, what a joy di-vine Leaning on the ev-er-last-ing arms;

2 What a bless-ed-ness, what a peace is mine, Leaning on the ev-er-last-ing arms.

3 Oh, how sweet to walk in this pilgrim way, Leaning on the ev-er-last-ing arms;

4 Oh, how bright the path grows from day to day, Leaning on the ev-er-last-ing arms.

5 What have I to dread, what have I to fear, Leaning on the ev-er-last-ing arms?

6 I have bless-ed peace with my Lord so near, Leaning on the ev-er-last-iong arms.

(chorus)

Lean-ing, lean-ing, Safe and se-cure from all a-larms;

Lean-ing, lean-ing, Lean-ing on the ev-er-last-ing arms. (E. A. Hoffman, A. J. Showalter)

"As the shadow of a great rock in
a weary LAND" (Isa. 32:2)

A Voice

What's All the Uproar

We hear a lot of voices out there. Is anybody really saying anything, or is it the same old rock 'n' roll? We need to hear a "still, small voice": *"And after the earthquake, a fire. But the LORD was not in the fire: and after the fire a still small Voice...and Elijah went out and stood in the entrance of the cave, and behold, there came a Voice unto him and said, WHAT DOEST THOU HEAR ELIJAH"* (1 Kings 19:12–13).

Great question! If we all had the answer to this we would have our feet firmly planted on the Highway of Holiness. Like Elijah who defied all four hundred of Jezebels prophets on Mt. Carmel and brought fire down from heaven, thus proving that the LORD GOD *ALMIGHTY* was the *ONE TRUE* GOD. By this one challenge against wickedness Elijah brought *all* Israel to their knees, vowing thus they would faithfully serve the GOD of heaven. We also need to roar against the enemy in whatever corner of the Earth we are in. Help us, LORD, to know, to see, to grasp. Help us to consider.

Isaiah tells us in excellent WORDS our plight:

> *Hear O heavens, and give ear, O Earth: for the LORD hath spoken, I have nourished and brought up children, and they have rebelled against ME. The OX knoweth his owner, and the ASS his masters crib: but Israel doth not know, MY PEOPLE*

doth not CONSIDER. Ah sinful Nation, a people Laden with iniquity, a seed of Evildoers, children that are Corrupters: they have forsaken the LORD, they have provoked the HOLY ONE of Israel unto anger, they are gone away backward…they are Revolters. (Isa. 1:2–5)

Look out over the horizon of our LAND. Look with the Holy Prophets' eyes. NOW consider this, friend, our heritage, our children are growing up in atheist schools, never hearing the NAME of the SAVIOR of all mankind—JESUS CHRIST the LAMB of GOD that takes away the sins of the world. And prayer, what is that they say, never heard of it. Communion with Our Father in heaven; nope, don't know religion. Oh yes, well, Islam is quite popular. Judaic Christianity, hm…not sure; is that one of Katy Perry's new releases? Oh no, that's the "ROAR" maybe the Voice, I'm not really sure. Maybe it is some old Orthodox stuff the Russians practice, *like the doxology.*

Again, let us CONSIDER tabula rasa; this is our children's mind, and we let society write on our children's blank slate whatever they please, so long as it is not about GOD, heaven, hell, and the True WAY, right? Amen. Let it be things albeit dicey, bordering evil, the practice of evil arts, anything almost as long as it is pure evil. Evil tinged with ignorance, glowing with rebellion, hates most everything, and does not consider but roams about blindly in the darkness and the murky sludge of this world.

Could the enemy be right that we have become the Great Satan, and ever so popular is the idea. While there are many fainting in the way, groping in darkness for a light that would shine something meaningful on their path, such as PEACE, HOPE, FAITH, or CHARITY. *"Thus saith the LORD of Hosts the God of Israel… Will ye not receive instruction to hearken to MY WORDS Saith the LORD. I have sent also unto you all My Servants the Prophets, rising early and sending Them, saying, Return ye now every man from his evil way, and amend your doings"* (Jer. 35:13–15). God has spoken; are we going to help the cause, or are we just going to stand by and watch the devil carry the world off to hell in his clutches. Help! I hear screams for help!

Hello? Is there a GOD out there that my mom or dad forgot to tell me about? Proverbs 22:6 says that *"if we train up a child in the way he should go, when he is old he will not depart from it."* And the commands of the LORD GOD we have known from a child. Which are explicitly stated in Deuteronomy, the Book of the LAW…

> *Hear, O Israel: The LORD our GOD is one LORD:*
> *And thou shalt love the LORD thy GOD with all thine heart, and with all thy soul, and with all thy might. And these WORDS which I command thee this day shall be in thine heart: And thou shalt teach them diligently unto thy children and shall talk of them when thou sittest in thine house and when thou walkest by the way and when thou liest down and when thou risest up.* (Deut. 6:4–7)
> *Beware lest thou forget the LORD, when thy houses are full of good things and when thou hast eaten and are full.*
> *"Thou shalt fear the LORD thy God and serve Him. And thou shalt do that which is right and good in the sight of the LORD: that it may be well with thee"* (Deut. 6)

God's commands are not grievous; they are to help us live an orderly and peaceful life, God's two golden commandments are the sum of all the rest; to LOVE GOD and to love our neighbor as our self. *"Therefore all things whatsoever you would that men should do to you, do ye even so to them: For this is the LAW and the Prophets"* (Matthew 7:12) All the LAW is fulfilled in LOVE; love God, and love your neighbor. Why does God make it so simple? Simple yet profound. God's ways are easy, remember. He is our nursing Father that watches over us and makes it easy for us.

"Fear not little children for it is your Father's good pleasure to give you the Kingdom" (Luke 12:32). The Kingdom is life with Jesus our Savior who gives us abundant life, happiness, and hope, here

and now, and in the next life, we shall be with Him in His Home, in heaven, the Paradise of GOD. God is not slack concerning His promises, what He says He does, and His Home is like a gorgeous palace where there is no pain or sorrow forever more. He is the Great King, the Great GOD of all, and He does all His pleasure, for He created all things and reigns supreme over all dominions and powers now and throughout eternity.

Now our God, the all-wise GOD, knowing aforetime of our fall from GRACE, created a plan of redemption for us, to save us from our sins. A plan that would bring us back into favor with Him. The old Prophet Isaiah had a hotline with GOD ALMIGHTY and 56:1 says, *"Thus saith the LORD, keep judgement and do justice for MY Salvation is near to come, and MY Righteousness to be revealed."*

Again The LORD says,

> *Hearken diligently unto ME, and eat ye that which is good, and let your soul delight itself in fatness. Incline your ear,* (the LORD says) *and come unto ME: hear and your soul shall live: and I will make an everlasting covenant with you, even the sure mercies of David.* (Isa. 55:2–3)

And Isaiah further states,

> *Seek ye the LORD while He may be found, call ye upon Him while He is near: Let the wicked forsake his way and the unrighteous man his thoughts: and let him return unto the LORD, and He will have mercy upon him: and to our GOD, for He will abundantly pardon. For My thoughts are not your thoughts neither are your ways My ways, saith the LORD. For as the heavens are higher than the Earth, so are My WAYS higher than your ways, and MY THOUGHTS than your thoughts.* (Isa. 55:6–9)

For thousands of years, mankind did without a personal GOD and hoped that someday soon, the Messiah would come and show them a better way. The prophets foretold of a coming Messiah, which they all, the Holy Ones waited for. Isaiah foretold this in chapter 53, all of fifty-three. Verse 6 says, *"All we like sheep have gone astray we have turned everyone to his own way: and the LORD hath laid on Him the iniquity of us all… He is brought as a lamb to the slaughter"* (verse 7). The Father put Him to grief when *"He made His soul an offering for sin"* (verse 10). So they always had this Messianic hope in their hearts. Matthew 1:21 tells us, *"And she shall bring forth a SON and thou shalt call His NAME JESUS for He shall save His people from their SINS."* Truly, the LORD in His faithfulness and love of mankind did just that. Yes, JESUS CHRIST is the Savior and soul healer, born 2020 years ago in that manger in Bethlehem. He and He ALONE is the ticket you need to ride this train, you have to have a ticket with your name on it to get through the Pearly Gates. The Jesus ticket, your NAME written down in the LAMB'S BOOK of LIFE; that's right. Written right there in ink. *"And they Said believe on the LORD JESUS CHRIST, and thou shalt be saved, and thy house"* (Acts 16:31). The Apostle Paul is telling his jailor how to be saved; it is really that simple: BELIEVE. No, we do not work our way to heaven; it is not by works. It is the free gift of GOD's SON on the CROSS. They tried it by works in the Old Testament. All those animal sacrifices were their works. That was not what the Father needed. He needed His Son to die and atone for our Sins. And the glorious, adorable Jesus did that for us. A free gift from GOD for us. We must see it all by FAITH and BELIEVE. The free gift is eternal life, our ticket to heaven, if we follow Him, if we surrender our lives to Him.

Believe on Him; it is really that simple. Only the fool hath said in His heart "There is no GOD." Proverbs say. JOHN 3:16. You have seen it on T-shirts, billboards, license plates. Why? Because it is the sum of the total.

> *For God* so loved *the World, that He gave His ONLY BEGOTTEN SON, that whosoever believeth in Him should not perish, but have* (WHAT, WHAT?) *EVERLASTING LIFE!* (John 3:16)

But let's keep going (John 3:17):

> *For God sent not His Son into the World to condemn the World.* (no, no) *but that the World through HIM might be SAVED! "He that believeth on Him is not condemned: but he that believeth NOT is condemned already* [why] *because he hath not believed in the NAME of the ONLY BEGOTTEN SON of GOD."* Sad so sad, that some won't make it. For Verse 19 says, *"And this is the condemnation that LIGHT is come into the World, and men loved darkness rather than Light, because their deeds were evil."*

Yes, Jesus stated often and plainly that He, He was and is the LIGHT of the WORLD. And He stated plainly that He was not willing that any should perish, but that all men should come to the LIGHT.

Jesus was born to SAVE!

He is the remedy for SIN, we are born into sin every living soul except CHRIST, the Pure One, the Holy One, the Spotless Lamb of God that takes away the sins of the world. Yep, He's our ticket. Just one touch from Jesus and demons flee; we are cleansed and then stand perfect in the sight of GOD.

No more fainting by the way.

No more futile detours.

No other WAY, only ONE WAY.

Only ONE LIFE.

Only ONE TRUTH.

Yep, Jesus takes care of things in a hurry when we come to Him and ask. Just look at what He did for us and you too will be calling Him Adorable and the All-Glorious Jesus.

The Epistle to the Colossians says,

> *And you that were sometimes alienated and enemies in your mind by wicked works, yet now*

hath He reconciled. In the body of His flesh through death, to present, you holy and un-blameable and unreproveable in His Sight. (You are, you are reconciled back with Him.) (1:21, 22)

And ye are complete in Him, which is the head of ALL principality and power. (2:10)

Buried with Him in baptism wherein also ye are risen with Him through the faith of the operation of GOD, who hath raised Him up from the dead. (Our old sinful man is buried, we are a new man; born again, we are a new person.) (2:12)

And you, being dead in your sins...hath He quickened (made alive) together with Him having forgiven you ALL trespasses." (Do you get this?) (2:13)

Blotting out the handwriting of ordinance that was against us, which was contrary to us, and took it out of the WAY, NAILING IT TO THE CROSS." (Your sins are gone, gone, gone!) (2:14)

And having spoiled principalities and powers, He made a show of them openly triumphing over them in it." (The cross was an open show of triumph, do you get all this?) (2:15)

Satan got his ass kicked as the King's blood spilled from the cross and covered the earth with HIS grace. Yes, this open show for all mankind defeated Satan, how hardly would he have known that the King's death would spell VICTORY over sin, hell, and the grave. Christ bought our freedom from the Shackles of sin, and oh what a price He paid. For this, all our love we owe HIM!

Ephesians says, *"But GOD who is RICH in mercy for His great love where with He loved us. Even when we were dead in sins, hath quickened us together with Christ* [for by grace ye are saved],...*and has made us sit together in heavenly places in Christ Jesus"* (2:4–6).

Who would have known there is genuine help after all? All we have to do is ASK. ASK, He says, and ye shall receive. He turns no one away. He then pours out His abundant grace on our oh so empty and meaningless lives. He says, "FOLLOW ME," and His advice is the only way to fly.

How is it that I have missed all this? Where have I been? I have never heard this GOOD NEWS before. JESUS SAVES; JESUS HEALS. Let's shout this from the housetops please. As Jeremiah, the weeping prophet says, *"O EARTH, EARTH, EARTH, Hear the WORD of the LORD" "Cry aloud spare not lift up thy VOICE like a trumpet"* (Isa. 58:1).

Why did not our moms and dads tell us? Why didn't the schools teach this? Why isn't everyone talking about this? This is it. I need look no further; Jesus is all in all, and I am complete in Him, amazing! Why this is all we need. Jesus, just a good dose of Jesus. Just more and more of Jesus. The Prophet Samuel says to the children of Israel, *"I will teach you the good and the Right way: Only fear the LORD and serve Him in truth with* all your heart*: for* consider *how great things He hath done for you"* (12:23, 24). Amen!

Really every television station should be airing this, every radio station should be proclaiming it. Christ the LORD REIGNS; HE is king. Where have I been? Pinch me, let's see if I'm dreaming maybe. There is nothing else to talk about that holds a candle to this. Nothing else important; all of a sudden, nothing else matters. Jesus is alive on the nearly late great planet Earth. WOW! Little did we know, little did we consider. As the song lyrics say, "He lives, He lives." Christ Jesus lives today, and because He lives, I live also. I think this is all we should talk about nothing else and to think I was just that close to missing the *mark*.

What saith that old Holy Prophet Jeremiah, the weeping mother, the mother of all prophets. Like St. Augustine's mother. He saith, "Return your whorish heart back to the old paths, the tried and true paths of those like Enoch and that hairy man Elijah." Where did their paths lead. Yes, straight into the arms of Jesus? They so pleased God Almighty that one day their feet just lifted off the ground and they were elevated to higher ground. God's blazing chariot with that beautiful team of heavenly horses drove by and said, "WELL

DONE. All aboard, the Master and all heaven anxiously *awaits you.* Oh GLORY, GLORY, GLORY, GLORY!"

I bet you didn't know that God has teams of horses in heaven. Well King Solomon had all those beautiful Arabian mares out of Egypt, and so many that he built cities just for his horses. And what saith the Scripture O, foolish one. "A greater than Solomon is here." If Solomon had cities of stalls, what do you think King Jesus must have. And Jesus saith in LUKE 11:31, *"The Queen of the South shall rise up in the judgement with the men of this generation, and condemn them: for she came from the utmost parts of the Earth to hear the wisdom of Solomon; and, behold, a greater than Solomon is here."* Jesus's very own red letter words. And in verse 20, Jesus says, *"But if I with the finger of GOD cast out devils, no doubt the Kingdom of GOD is come upon you."* Why did Solomon cast out devils, heal leprosy, raise the dead, make the blind to see, not even? And yet all the Earth came and flocked and brought presents of gold (without measure) just to have audience and hear Solomon's wisdom. And again, Jesus said a greater than Solomon is here, walking the Earth, standing on the same dirt you are standing on. Wake up, folks. Queen Sheba came to see Solomon, and she gasped in horror, could not catch her next breath, fainted, and said, "The half, the half was not told me. I had to come and see for myself and what I see far exceeds anything I was told." And again Jesus said, *"A greater than Solomon is here."* Shall we wake up now or later, much later? When it is too late, and Jesus is passing out the crowns and says, "And who are you?"

Why didn't anyone tell us that Jesus is

THE WAY
THE TRUTH
THE LIFE?

And man shall not live by bread alone but by every WORD of GOD. This is why it is so much fun to read the WORD of GOD daily and let Him breathe into us His LIFE. Then we have strength, we can get up and do our work. Then we can run and not be weary.

LOOK around, folks, the world is like hamsters in a cage. Around and around they go, and oh, how weary they are. But God's children need not be weary because Jesus's mercy is new every morning. Each and every morning, new mercies we see and the way grows clearer; the path gets brighter because His WORD shines light and strength on our path. What does the Psalm say? All the paths of the LORD are MERCY and Truth; teach Me thy WAY, O, LORD. Give me a burning love for you, Jesus, I want to make heaven my home.

Why didn't anyone tell us? It has been preached, broadcasted, heralded from the beginning of time that a redeemer was coming into the world called the Messiah. But we need those anointed ears that Jesus talked about and those anointed eyes to see the TRUTH. It is a FAITH THING. Jesus is the INVISIBLE ONE, the INVISIBLE GOD. He was sent to Earth by His Father 2,020 years ago in a body. He was and is the incarnate real GOD, robed in the body of an earthly man. He is both God and man. Jesus told doubting Thomas, "Blessed is he that does not see and yet believes." Thomas said, I will not believe Jesus rose from the dead until I see Him. And Jesus also said, "Bring me some bread and fish" and Jesus ate them, proving He is man, and then Jesus vanished again from them, proving He was GOD. The GOD ALMIGHTY that had just gotten VICTORY over Satan and abolished his evil works. The Epistle of Jesus's beloved John 3:8 says, *"For this purpose the Son of GOD was manifested that He might destroy the works of the devil."* Oh yes, Satan still kicks around and tries to make us believe he has the victory, but no. As Bunyan says, *"He is a toothless lion,"*[1] just a mirage. Oh, he still has a few punches in him, but Jesus DEFEATED him at the CROSS. That old devil that still prowls the Earth, taking the unbelieving as his prisoners, but Jesus has one final scene with him that is yet to unfold and then he shall be chained in everlasting torment for eternity.

So the apostles were eyewitnesses of Jesus's glory, life, and triumph. The beloved John was the apostle that leaned on Jesus's breast. I see him as the baby of the apostles, a tender young man maybe twenty years old, and Jesus did love him in a special way. We can see this in John's Gospel his three epistles and his book of Revelation.

He talks incessantly about God's LOVE that "GOD is LOVE." Let's explore this in 1 John 4:9–15,

> *In this was manifested the love of GOD toward us in that GOD sent His Only Begotten SON into the world, that we might live through Him."* Herein is love; not that we loved GOD, but that He loved us, and sent His SON to be the propitiation for our sins. Beloved if God so loved us, we ought also to love one another. No man hath seen GOD at any time. If we love one another, GOD dwelleth in us, and His love is perfected in us. Hereby know we that we dwell in Him, and He in us, because He hath given us of His Spirit. And we have seen and do testify that the Father sent the SON to be the Saviour of the World.* "Whosoever shall confess that Jesus is the Son of God, GOD dwelleth in Him and He in GOD.

And John further writes 5:1, 4, 7, 11, 12, 13, *"Whosoever believeth that Jesus is the Christ is born of GOD."* (This is what we mean by *"born again."*)

> *And whosoever is born of GOD overcometh the World, and this is the victory that overcometh the World, even our FAITH." "For there are three that bear record in Heaven, the Father, the Word, and the Holy Ghost: these three are one.* [Notice He, JESUS, is called the WORD.]
> *And this is the Record that GOD hath given to us eternal life, and this life is in His SON.* He that hath the Son hath life. *He that hath not the Son of God hath* not *life.* These things have I written unto you that believe on the Name of the Son of God that *ye may know that ye have eternal life."*

And John concludes the first epistle, by repeating himself a lot because he wants us to know the facts for sure. As 5:19 says,

> *"And we know that we are of GOD and the whole world lieth in wickedness."* Why? Because the god of this world; the devil and Satan has their eyes and hearts blinded from the light of the truth. But John says we are His witnesses we saw it all, we touched Him we lived with Him, He is God incarnate.

Verse 20 says,

> *And we know that the Son of God is come, and hath given us an understanding, that we may know Him that is TRUE and we are in Him that is true even in His Son Jesus Christ. This is the true God and Eternal Life." "And Now little children,* abide *in Him, that when He shall appear we may have confidence, and not be ashamed before Him at His COMING."* (1 John 2:28)

Yes, Jesus came to Earth 2,020 years ago, He came to His own and His own recognized Him not. But I say, Don't fear to you that missed Jesus the first time. He is coming again to the Earth to the Mount of Olives from where He left us at His Ascension to the Father. He says in Matthew 24, *"We should learn the Parable of the fig tree; When his branch is yet tender, and putteth forth leaves, Ye know that summer is nigh. So likewise, when ye shall see all these things know that it is near even at the door"* (Matt. 24:32–33).

The Lord says, *"Watch therefore: for ye know not what hour your Lord doth Return"* (verse 42). This is what all the buzz is about, everyone is getting ready and knows that it is soon by how the Lord describes the state of our affairs in the world in chapter 24. It is even at the door (verse 25). Jesus says, *"Behold I have told you before"* (it all happens). And in verse 35, He assures us of the truth of His coming back saying, *"Heaven and Earth will pass away, but MY WORDS will not pass away."* How hardly can they, Jesus is the WORD, and all scripture must be fulfilled. Jesus is THE WORD. Did you hear me? Jesus is THE WORD!

The Lord is returning like a thief in the night. We must watch and be ready. Jesus assures His believers it will not overtake us because we will be watching and daily expecting and be ready. But the unbeliever will not have a clue because they have not read the scripture and are unaware of how the future is to unfold. God's children, however, will know perfectly well and will understand as the events of God's kingdom play out.

Verse 44 warns us, *"Therefore be ye also ready: for in such an hour as ye think not the SON of MAN cometh."* But it is the Father's command performance, He is the director and Jesus says, *"But of that day and hour knoweth no man, no, not the angels of Heaven, but My Father only"* (verse 36).

Well, this is great; all I want to talk about now is Jesus and His soon return. I bet all God's children feel the same way. Missing heaven and ending up in hell would be tragic—no, insane—and it strikes the "fear of God" into my very soul. Hell is really meant for the devil, the wicked, the unbelieving, and all such antichrists. GOD wants us all to be with Him. Indeed He has said that He is not willing that any perish but that all come to the knowledge of His saving grace, which is in Christ Jesus Our Lord. Joel 3:16 says, *"The LORD also shall ROAR out of ZION and utter His VOICE from Jerusalem, and the Heavens and the Earth shall shake: but the LORD will be the Hope of His people."* So comforting the LORD is, the GOD of all comfort; like a mother, He does not overlook any areas of assurance.

In Revelation, He is also the "Great Voice." John says if we have ears to hear Him, Jesus gives an invitation to all:

> *Behold I stand at the door and knock: if any man hear My VOICE and open the door, I will come in to Him and will dine with him and he with ME" "To him that overcometh will I grant to sit with ME in MY THRONE, even as I also over-*

came, and am set down with MY FATHER in His Throne. (3:20–21)

"Behold I come quickly: hold that fast which thou hast, that no man take thy crown." Again very important… "He that overcometh the same shall be clothed in white raiment; and I will not blot out his NAME out of the Book of LIFE, but I will confess his NAME before My Father, and before his angels." *Is your NAME on the Father's lips? On Jesus' lips? "He that hath an ear let him hear what the Spirit saith."* (3:11, 5–6)

The LORD's VOICE is the ONE we want to hear, no other voice for Jesus said, "My sheep hear My VOICE and another they will not hear." There are many voices, all declaring they are the way (these be false religions). Jesus says, "I am the WAY, and My sheep hear My VOICE." For He is our Good Shepherd and the Good Shepherd lays down His Life for His sheep.

His VOICE is very unique; it has power. I don't think we can mistake it for any other. In the days of Moses, His VOICE thundered and shook the Earth. In Jesus's day, His VOICE bellowed out of heaven saying, *"This is My Beloved Son, hear ye Him."* Peter says, *"Jesus received from GOD the Father honour and glory, when there came such a VOICE to Him from the excellent glory* [saying] *"THIS IS MY BELOVED SON, IN WHOM I AM WELL PLEASED. And this VOICE which came from Heaven we heard when we were in the Holy Mount"* (2 Peter 17–18). The apostles and the crowds also heard the Father's VOICE out of heaven many times. They were eye witnesses to these events. Eyewitnesses to this GLORY. Yes, the twelve apostles lived and preached with Jesus for three and a half years; that is a long time in training. John lovingly says, *"That which was from the beginning, which we have heard, which we have seen with our eyes, which we have looked upon and our hands have handled, of the WORD of LIFE"* (1 John 1:1).

THAT'S JESUS, THE WORD of LIFE.

> *Now Jesus hath promised "Yet once more I shake not the Earth only but heaven also...that those things which cannot be shaken may remain" Wherefore we receiving a* Kingdom *which cannot be* moved, *let us have grace, whereby we may serve GOD Acceptably with Reverence and godly fear: For our GOD is a consuming fire."* (Heb. 12:27–29)

Wow, that says it beautifully. It's difficult trying to improve on the great apostle's writings. Because Jesus so gifted Him with Revelation that I think the pens burnt up as he wrote, for indeed the WORD is powerful. The LORD says, *"Is not MY WORD like as a FIRE? And like a hammer that breaketh the rock in pieces"* (Jer. 23:29) Certainly powerful enough to break up the ground in the stoniest, hardest heart. So powerful is His WORD, LIKE HIS VOICE when He will shake the Earth again. Then only the good things of GOD will remain. So next time someone asks you what's shaking, you can think on the LORD's big shake, soon to come. SOON TO COME!

> *The Eternal will ROAR from on HIGH, from His SACRED ABODE He will utter a cry, thundering at His own homestead, shouting at all dwellers upon Earth, as men shout loudly at the vintage. The noise shall come even to the ends of the Earth; for the LORD hath a controversy with the NATIONS, He will plead with all flesh.* (Jer. 25:30, 31 Moffatt)

The LORD's VOICE will be heard. Better sooner than later. If we take heed now, we will save ourselves a lot of gloom and doom. His VOICE is saying, "Hear my warning and repent." *"Howl ye shepherds and cry and wallow yourselves in ashes."* If we humble ourselves now, He will exalt us later. But if we exalt (or are at ease now), He will humble us later. For the fierce anger of the LORD is against all haughtiness and pride and the wicked shall find no place at all. He shall burn up His enemies.

Raise your VOICE strong and clear to your maker on high. Make a joyful noise before Him. Come into His courts with praise, sing unto the LORD with a loud VOICE! Proclaim His glory, exalt your maker like King David. Instead I am afraid we waste our time and breath exalting one another. Get Him in your court friend; He's all that counts. He is a friend that sticketh closer than a brother. He is closer to you than your wife or your girlfriend, and in the day of GOD's wrath; neither gold or power will save you. Get into His ship now, and be ye saved all ye ends of the Earth. Come on, folks, anyone can sing the blues, just ask BB.

> *Moreover I will take from them the VOICE of Mirth, and; the VOICE of gladness, the VOICE of the bridegroom, the Sound of the millstones and the LIGHT of the candle. And I will bring upon that land all MY WORDS which I have pronounced against it.* (Jer. 25:10, 13)

Yes, you have a VOICE. Use it to GOD's GLORY. Let your VOICE be heard. Sing for GOD's glory. He gave you a VOICE and a MOUTH. Use it now for GOD PLEASE.

> *"Today if ye will hear His VOICE. Harden not your hearts as in the provocation, in the day of temptation in the Wilderness."* (tempt ME not saith the LORD tempt ME not*) "For we are made partakers of Christ if we hold the beginning of our confidence steadfast unto the END; While it is said, Today if ye will hear HIS VOICE, harden not hour hearts. As in the provocation."* (Heb. 3:7–8, 14–15)

We had better get this figured out and fast. For we must all appear before the JUDGEMENT SEAT OF CHRIST. Today, we have to hear His VOICE; today we must listen to His warnings. As a kindly parent Jesus warns us. The warnings get more intense the parent then resorts to more drastic measures and says, "Okay, next time you will get a spanking," or as the Bible says, the rod of correction. GOD'S voice is loud and clear. He demands obedience to His WORDS, how will we know His WORDs if we do not read His WORD? Hello, hello, try say, just Proverbs out for size. Listen to what she says in Proverbs 8:

> *Doth not WISDOM CRY? And UNDERSTANDING put forth her VOICE? She crieth at the gates of the city. Unto you, O men, I call; and MY VOICE is to the sons of man. O ye simple understand WISDOM: and ye fools, be ye of an understanding heart. Receive instruction and not gold; For Wisdom is better than rubies; and all things that may be desired are not to be COMPAIRED TO IT. The Fear OF THE LORD is the beginning of WISDOM The Fear of THE LORD is to HATE EVIL PRIDE ARROGANCY and the EVIL WAY and the FROWARD MOUTH DO I HATE (SAITH the LORD) Counsel is Mine, and sound WISDOM: I am UNDERSTANDING; I have STRENGTH. By me Kings Reign and Princes decree justice. By me Princes Rule, and Nobles even all the Judges of the Earth. I love them that love ME; and those that seek Me early shall find ME. Riches and honour are with ME... My fruit is better than gold... The LORD possessed ME in the beginning of His Way, before His works of old...or ever the Earth was. While as yet He had not made the Earth... I was there... When He pre-pared the Heavens, I was there... Then I was by Him, as one brought up with Him: I was daily His delight, Rejoicing always before Him;... Hearken unto ME O ye children... Hear instruction and be*

wise. Blessed is the man that Heareth ME Watching daily at My gates; waiting at the posts of My doors. For whosoever findeth ME findeth LIFE, and shall obtain favour of the LORD.

The FEAR of THE LORD is WISDOM. Now that's a good taste of Proverbs. But I highly recommend all thirty-one be read.

Time is flying, folks. Our days are as a shadow, or as the dew of the morning, Father time waits for no man. Let us flee youthful lusts and redeem the time. Oh, but you want to spend your best years serenading the women, walking the red carpet, and getting accolades from man. Eyes wide open please, because God is not amused with folks that waste time. And waste their lives reeling in millions, only at the last to be some miserable dope, some old fool that did it all wrong.

"I did it my way." Oh, yuck. Build your house on the rock on the SOLID ROCK, not on shifting sand, that will soon disappoint you. You are knocking yourself out and without a cause. If you are slaving, I mean slaving for that big house, fine dining, and impeccable threads, GOD help you, man. You are truly a rebel without a cause. You are truly most miserable. This house of cards shall soon come crashing down because Jesus Christ is not your foundation and chief cornerstone, and great shall be the crash of it. Remember King David's challenge with Goliath. He said, *"Is not there a cause here."* When God is your cause, your victory is in the bag. David did not hesitate though he was just a teen and Goliath a giant, fifteen feet tall and a seasoned warrior. David ran up to the Philistine Goliath and said,

Thou comest to me with a sword, spear and shield: but I come to thee in the NAME OF THE LORD OF HOSTS, the GOD of the armies of Israel, whom thou an uncircumcised heathen hast defied. This day will the LORD deliver thee into mine hand: and I will smite thee and take off thy head from thee and I will give the carcases of the host of the Philistines this day unto the fowls of the air, and the wild beasts of the Earth; THAT ALL THE EARTH MAY KNOW THAT THERE IS A GOD IN ISRAEL! And all this assembly shall know that the LORD saveth not with sword and spear: FOR THE BATTLE IS THE LORD's and He will give you into our hands. Then David hasted and ran toward the GIANT and David put his hand in his bag and took thence a stone, and slang it, and smote the Philistine in the forehead, that the stone sunk into his forehead; and he fell upon his face to the Earth. So David prevailed with a sling and a stone and he slew the Philistine with his own sword. (1 Sam. 17:45–50)

IS THERE A CAUSE? IS THERE A CAUSE?

Yes, Jesus Christ, our LORD and SAVIOR is being tossed from our midst, taken from our schools, and replaced with atheism. Most of our major cities have become eyesores with dirty filthy and sick, homeless people cluttering everywhere looking like refugees from a third world country. Other cities are now modeled after Las Vegas. Nudist colonies and sanctuary cities everywhere. Our beloved monuments and CROSSES are being torn down; our hard-won constitution is disregarded. The communist party runs full reign in our midst. The Democratic party has more communists than Carter has pills. Riots, vagrancy, and prostitution and murder is in our streets.

I would say THERE IS A CAUSE.
GOD's HONOR is at stake.
Choose ye this day whom ye would serve
GOD or filthy mammon (money).
I put before you life and death; choose LIFE.
CHOOSE JESUS.

"Come follow me," Jesus kindly says. "It is for your benefit. COME FOLLOW ME, and I will make you fishers of men." Now, that's smart, wisdom of the ancients; don't wait until you are an old fool and still on stage pelting out rock 'n' roll. Like, how stupid is that? Redeem the time; we don't have much of it. Christ is all and all; I want the King's plate, not the swine's corn. I pray you do also.

> *Be not deceived. GOD is not mocked: for whatsoever a man soweth, that shall he also reap. For he that soweth to his flesh shall of the flesh reap corruption; but he that soweth to the Spirit shall of the Spirit reap life Everlasting. And let us not be weary in well doing for in due season we shall reap, if we faint not. As we have therefore opportunity let us do good unto ALL men, especially unto them who are of the household of FAITH.* [This scripture is one I think to be highly overlooked along with verse 2.] *"Bear ye one another's burdens and so fulfill the LAW of CHRIST.* (Gal. 6:7–10 and 2)

On this verse 2 hangs the LAW and the prophets because if you love God you will also love others as yourself. Just think how smooth the machinery of humanity would run if we were doing all the above. No need for social services at this rate; throw them out the window. A perfect example of this command of love is fulfilled in the parable of the Good Samaritan (LUKE 10:30–37). Please read. What all did the Good Samaritan do? He had mercy and compassion, he did not evade the issue because it would take time and money. We are all pressed for time and money, but this man had a knowledge of the MOST HIGH, knowing it was first his responsibility and second that whatever any good thing a man doeth; the same shall he be rewarded of the LORD. He did not say, "It is none of my concern." The man most likely owed a debt and so was justly beaten half to death and robbed. No, no, he had the compassion of Jesus; he bound up his wounds and took him to the inn and took care of him. And when he had to depart the next day, he gave money to the host and said, "Take care of him, and whatever else I will owe you I will repay you the next time I am by this way." This is the Gospel of Jesus in action: "Be ye not just a hearer of the WORD but a doer." Let us see what the Perfect Law of Liberty says in JAMES 2:8–20:

> *If ye fulfill the Royal Law according to the Scripture, Thou shalt love thy neighbor as thyself, ye do well.* (Verse 8)
> *For he shall have judgement without MERCY, that hath showed No MERCY; and MERCY Rejoiceth against judgement. What doth it profit, my brethren, though a man say he hath Faith and have no works, can Faith save him?* (Verse 13–14)
> *Even so Faith, if it hath not works, is dead, being alone.* (Verse 17)
> *Thou believest that there is one God; thou doest well: the DEVILS also believe and tremble But wilt thou know. O vain man, that FAITH without works is dead?!* (Verses 19–20)

So then, we must have works we must serve the LORD. The Scripture saith, "How can we say we love God who we can't see and we do not love our brother who we can see. In that ye have done it unto the least of these, ye have done it unto ME saith the LORD."

Every calling has a work. The men of old that were called used their VOICE for GOD. We are all called Jesus says, "*COME FOLLOW ME* and I will make you Fishers of MEN." There is no higher calling no greater career, than to work for Jesus. Jesus is our great example. Jesus raised His VOICE against evil and shouted, "*REPENT for the Kingdom of Heaven is at hand. And Jesus walking by the Sea of Galilee saw Peter and Andrew… And said come "Follow ME and I will make you fishers of men"* (Matt. 4:17–19).

How did John the Baptist use his voice for God? He also came preaching in the wilderness and warning, *"Repent for the Kingdom of Heaven is at hand… Who hath warned you to flee from the wrath to come? Bring forth therefore fruits meet for repentance"* (Matt. 3:2, 7–8). Knowing God is serious business, we are called to service; He is looking for VOICES to fulfill His Great Commission: *"Go ye into all the world and preach the Gospel to every creature."* This is how all four gospels end and then Jesus ascends back to His Father in heaven. These are Jesus's very last Earthly WORDS: "Go use your VOICE and preach MY KINGDOM's Good News." Second Chronicles 16:9 says, *"For the eyes of the LORD RUN TO AND FRO throughout the whole Earth, to show Himself strong in the behalf of them whose heart is perfect toward Him."* What do the Marines say? "We are looking for a few good men," but The LORD is looking for YOU. Man up, friend.

"And I sought for a man among them, that should make up the hedge, and stand in the gap before ME for the LAND that I should not destroy it: BUT I FOUND NONE" (Ezek. 22:30).

God needs a few good men with a clear, strong VOICE to proclaim His message; be a VOICE for heaven. Jesus is calling, calling for you and for me. What wait I for, not my will LORD but thy will be done through my life, right? One soul saved is worth all this world's gold. As Jeremiah tells his scribe Baruch, *"Seekest thou great things for thyself? Seek them not: for behold, I will bring evil upon all flesh, saith the LORD"* (Jer. 45:5).

It is the last hour, friends, the Bridegroom is soon, very soon coming for His Bride (the church). God says, "Warn them, warn them for ME." Let thy VOICE echo through the LAND; that His coming is near, prepare ye the way of the LORD, make His paths straight. What did the LORD tell our beloved Prophet Ezekiel?

> *Son of man, I have made thee a Watchman unto the house of Israel; therefore hear the WORDS at MY MOUTH and give them warning from ME. When I say unto the wicked, Thou shalt surely die. And thou givest him not warning, nor speakest to warn the wicked man from his wicked way, to save his life; the same wicked man Shall die in his iniquity; but his blood will I require at thine hand.* (3:17–18)

And verse 27,

> *And when I speak with thee, I will open thy mouth, and thou shalt say unto them THUS SAITH THE LORD GOD He that heareth, let him hear; and he that forbeareth let him forbear: for they are a Rebellious house."* Folks if you are saved, you are saved to Service, not to sit and warm a pew. God calls us to serve, you friend are that WATCHMAN. A WATCHMAN of souls; God requires it of us. If we love our fellow man we will WARN them for God. We will shout His message far and wide, if the LOVE of CHRIST floods our soul, it will be as JEREMIAH says; A FIRE PENT UP IN MY BONES.
>
> *Then I said, I will not make mention of HIM, nor speak any more in HIS NAME. But His WORD was in mine heart as a burning fire shut up in my bones, and I was weary with forbearing, and I could not stay.* (20:9)

As the LORD says, "I wish you were either cold or hot but since you are lukewarm I will spew you out." But I know that I know we are all fired up about Jesus, because we love Him so, and His Holy Spirit is being poured out at this last hour to revive us.

> *And if our Gospel be hid, it is hid to them that are LOST: In whom the god of this world hath blinded the minds of them which believe not, lest the LIGHT of the Glorious Gospel of Christ, who is the image of GOD, should shine unto them. For we preach Christ Jesus the LORD… And God who commanded the LIGHT to shine out of darkness. Hath shined in our hearts to give the LIGHT of the Knowledge of the glory of GOD IN THE FACE OF JESUS CHRIST.* (2 Cor. 4:3–6)

And knowing therefore the Terror of the LORD, we persuade men. (Verse 11)

For the LOVE OF CHRIST CONSTRAINETH US…that they which live should not henceforth live unto themselves, but unto Him which died for them, and rose again. (Verse 14, 15)

Go into all the world and preach the Gospel.

LORD, forgive us of all our sins, and save us from Thy great wrath. Keep us in Thy mercies and let the knowledge of THEE cover the Earth in Jesus Holy NAME.

I Love the LORD because He Hath heard my VOICE. (Ps. 116:1)

LORD HEAR MY VOICE. (Ps. 130:2)

What a Friend

1 What a Friend we have in Je-sus, All our sins and griefs to bear! What a priv-i-lege to carry Ev-'ry-thing to God in prayer! O what peace we often for-feit, O what need-less pain we bear, All be-cause we do not car-ry Ev-'ry-thing to God in prayer!

2 Have we tri-als and temp-ta-tions? Is there troub-le an-y-where? We should nev-er be dis-cour-aged, Take it to the Lord in prayer. Can we find a friend so faith-ful Who will all our sor-rows share? Je-sus knows our ev-'ry weak-ness, take it to the Lord in prayer.

3 Are we weak and heav-y-la-den, Cumbered with a load of care?—Pre-cious Savior, still our ref-uge,—Take it to the Lord in Prayer. Do thy friends despise, for-sake thee? Take it to the Lord in prayer; In His arms He'll take and shield thee, Thou will find a sol-ace there. (Joseph Scriven and Charles C. Converse)

"Neither is there Salvation in any other for there is NONE other NAME under heaven given among men, whereby we must be SAVED" (Acts 4:12).

Making God Great Again

⸻

I f by now, friend, you are not raptured by the love of Jesus, if you are not gloriously swept off your feet, you have indeed missed the mark and are yet in no-man's-land. If you are not mesmerized by His lovely WORDS, your religion is vain. As St. Augustine says, "I want to enjoy my God and revel in His presence, just dreaming about my heavenly home, that is all bliss." It's like this Earth is messed up, and I am glad the LORD is making a clean, brand-new one for us. If Jesus does not excite you, if your heart does not groan and travail with passionate love of the Savior, then you have been short-changed in your experience. Because the LORD is fresh and glowing, more than I dreamed, and He becomes more beautiful each day. Oh, glorious, adorable Jesus. His heavenly mercies fall fresh each dawning morn. How lovely is that NAME of NAMES. At the mention of JESUS of Nazareth, the demons take leave; depressed and undone they back off. Oh my Savior, oh my Savior, my adorable, suffering GOD MAN. He came, He worked, He left; He stayed, oh Glorious Savior of the Earth.

My Jesus, my Jesus, the WORDS are on FIRE, my page is aflame, oh, heavenly Jesus. My pen writes for me, His love, too, is for the Redeemer of all creation. Everything that is, was and will be has its existence in Him, oh, lovely GOD on High. Adore HIM, adore Him, for He is in heaven and we are still prisoners on Earth. All nature and creation groans for His release; how long oh, LORD, how long?

My King of kings,
My LORD of lords,

My Master of masters,

How long, oh, LORD, till you undo these heavy shackles and let the prisoners of Earth escape. Our perplexity overwhelms; we groan beneath its shame and wonder. How long, my LORD, until you set the prisoners free. The little birdie on the sill has a strain so fair, yet I know that I know her little heart beats beneath those feathers saying, "How long, my LORD, how long?"

Jesus, my Maker, my Savior, the gentle man that walked Galilee's hills walks still among us, in our bodies of flesh. He dwells in this old body of flesh; yes, by His Holy Spirit, He dwells in me. Oh, the Mystery of our salvation, oh, the Great God of heaven dwells within this body of CLAY. Remember that name: Clay—what a name, what a name; how true it is. He our Redeemer dwells in these bodies of clay. What did Jesus tell His disciples? "Tarry here at Jerusalem until I send the gift of MY HOLY SPIRIT TO EARTH." Pentecost—that lovely day that Jesus breathed His Spirit into the Earth, starting with those in the upper room that tarried there. Then they, in turn, went out and laid their Holy Hands on all those that would believe in Jesus, and it spread and spread over the Earth. All Jesus believers being filled with His Spirit, and down through the ages, the holy men kept laying their hands on new believers who received the gift of Jesus own—His very own Spirit. And so it is today, to this very hour, new believers are still being endowed with Jesus Holy Spirit. His Spirit is in the world, in us, the Comforter that will lead you into all TRUTH. For it is the Precious Holy Spirit of God that lightens the mind and gives us understanding of the WORD of Jesus. The Apostle says, "You have no need of a teacher, for the Holy Spirit will teach you." What did Jesus say to the Samaritan woman at Jacob's well (John 4:21–24)?

> *Jesus saith unto her, Woman, believe ME, the
> hour cometh, when ye shall neither in this mountain,
> nor yet at Jerusalem, worship the Father. Ye worship
> ye know not what: We know what we worship: For
> SALVATION is of the Jews. But the hour cometh,*

and now is, when the true worshipers shall worship the Father in Spirit and in Truth: for the Father seeketh such to worship Him. GOD IS A SPIRIT and THEY THAT WORSHIP HIM MUST WORSHIP HIM in SPIRIT and in TRUTH.

Jesus is a God-man, the God robed in human flesh. The Father is a Spirit and totally, totally out of sight.

The Holy Spirit is GOD's Spirit—sent here to do Jesus's work. These three give themselves equal importance. The Father is glorified in the SON, and the Son is glorified by the Holy Spirit and the Father.

John 14:24, 26 declares it this way, Jesus says, *"The WORD which ye hear is not MINE, but the Father's which sent ME"* (verse 24).

And the Comforter *which is the HOLY GHOST, whom the Father will send in MY NAME, HE shall teach you all things, and bring all things to your remembrance whatsoever I have said unto you. Now I go unto the Father: and MY FATHER is greater than I.* (Verse 28)

Here John talks about the gift of the Holy Ghost as an Unction and an anointing.

In 1 John 2:20, 27, He says, *"But ye have an Unction from the HOLY ONE, and ye know all things."* And again, *"The anointing which ye have received of Him abideth in you, and ye need not that any man teach you: but as the same anointing teacheth you of all things, and is truth, and is no lie, and even as it hath taught, ye shall abide in Him"* (in who, in Jesus Christ).

And Hebrews admonishes us that we should learn, relearn, and learn again and keep on learning, because the devil is quick to snatch away those things of our memory which produces godliness.

"Wherefore (as the Holy ghost saith), today if ye will hear His Voice, harden not your hearts as they did in the wilderness, 40 years" (Heb. 3:7–8). It is the Holy Ghost that causes us to hear His Voice, causes

us to understand His WORDS, quickens them to our heart and mind. But 5:12 exhorts, *"For when for the time ye ought to be teachers, ye have need that one teach you again which be the first principles of the oracles of GOD: and are become such as have need of milk, and not of strong meat."*

And we know that Hebrews 4:12 says, *"The WORD of GOD is quick and powerful and sharper than any two edged sword, piercing even to the dividing asunder of Soul and Spirit, and of the joints and marrow, and is a discerner of the thoughts and intents of the heart."*

So the WORD of GOD is real and true and by the Holy Ghost becomes understandable! It works up the fallow ground of our heart and makes us useful instruments to the Master's glory and honor. Just as Jesus walked about teaching these same WORDS, so the Holy Ghost teaches us the WORDS of Scripture written down and recorded of Jesus in His Gospels by the disciples. The WORDS of Jesus Gospel are to those that perish foolishness, but to us that believe, they are the power of God. A force to be reckoned with, powerful and full of *Majesty*.

Let's finish Paul's chapter 4 to the Hebrews (verse 13). *"Neither is there any creature that is not manifest in His sight: but all things are naked and open unto the eyes of Him with Whom we have to do."* *"For the eyes of the LORD run to and fro throughout the whole Earth, to show Himself strong in the behalf of them whose heart is perfect toward Him"* (2 Chron. 16:9).

Let us strive to be aware of his presence and strive to be in His presence. And Paul says in verse 14, *"Seeing then that we have a great High Priest that is passed into the Heavens JESUS the SON OF GOD let us hold fast our profession. For we have not an High Priest which cannot be touched with the feeling of out infirmities; but was in all points tempted like as we are, yet without* sin.*"*

Folks, Jesus is our High Priest; Jesus is our Priest. Verses 14 and 15 explain that it is Jesus we have for a Priest. He is the only priest you will ever need. He is the Priest we go to; it's His door we knock on. He's the Priest we need, so with this Priest verse 16 tells us. With Jesus as our High Priest.

"Let us therefore come boldly unto the THRONE of GRACE, that we may obtain mercy, and find GRACE to help in time of need." And that we may at His Throne find forgiveness of all our sins, daily sins and otherwise. Come to His Throne; it is He that listens and is the intercessor to the Father for us and it is Jesus who forgives our sins. Jesus is our Priest; all the priest we will ever need. Come boldly to His Throne.

> Job says, *"I would seek unto God, and unto God would I commit my cause: Which doeth great things and unsearchable; marvelous things without number."* (5:8, 9)
> *Can that which is unsavoury be eaten without salt? Or is there any taste in the white of an egg?* (6:6)

It is Jesus who forgives sin, the Gospel says. Jesus is our Priest the Epistle of Hebrews says. It is God that is the forgiver of sins—that is a no-brainer, so it is to His Throne I will come for forgiveness. He is our Priest.

> *"Lo this. We have searched it, so it is; Hear it. And know thou it for thy good"* (Job 5:27).

Signed, sealed, and delivered.

In Thee, O God, is forgiveness of sins, and that is why we Fear Him. Micah says,

> *Who is a GOD like unto Thee, that pardoneth iniquity, and passeth by the transgression of the remnant of His Heritage? He retaineth not His anger for ever, because He Delighteth in MERCY.* (7:18)

What saith the mighty Prophet Ezekiel,

> *Therefore I will judge you, O house of Israel, everyone according to his ways, saith the LORD GOD, REPENT and turn yourselves from all your transgressions; SO INIQUITY SHALL NOT BE YOUR RUIN.* (18:30)

You really got to love this WORD; it is so right on!

Sin reigned from Adam to Moses, and with Moses came the LAW by which their sins could be forgiven through burnt animal sacrifices. For without the shedding of blood, there is no remission of sins. But the law was imperfect. They deforested that part of the world, trying to burn enough sacrifices for their sins. The cedars of Lebanon are all but gone. And the LORD punished all sin when the children did not keep the LAW. As Daniel says,

> *To Thee O LORD our God belong mercies and forgiveness.* (9:9)
> *As it is written in the LAW of Moses, all this evil is come upon us: yet made we not our prayer before THEE LORD OUR GOD, that we might turn from our iniquities and understand thy truth.* (9:13)

And in Paul's studies, he concludes in Romans 3:10, *"As it is written, there is* none *righteous no not one"* and furthermore *"under the law: every mouth shall be stopped and all the world shall become guilty before GOD"* (3:19). Jesus was manifested to solve the problem of the LAW. Jesus was manifested to take away the sins of the WORLD. Paul continues to the Romans,

> *But now the righteousness of God without the law is manifested… Even the righteousness of GOD which is by* Faith *in Jesus Christ unto all and upon ALL them that believe… For ALL have sinned and*

come short of the glory of GOD; Being justified freely by His grace through the REDEMPTION that is in Christ Jesus: Whom God hath set forth to be the propitiation through FAITH in His BLOOD. (3:21–25)

Where the LAW fell short, Jesus Christ took over and made a new covenant in His blood, the remission of sins through His blood. Christ was manifest to take away our sins. And what saith John 1:29, "Behold the LAMB of GOD which taketh away the Sin of the world." This LAMB, Jesus is the LAMB. He would replace the animal sacrifices required by Moses to forgive sins.

What, people, do we think Easter is all about? Jesus is Easter; He is the LAMB sacrificed for our sins. Do we get this? A no-brainer please; Jesus the bloody sacrifice, the LAMB SLAIN, is our WAY, is our Door into heaven.

So forgiveness of sins is by a priest, yes, Jesus is that Priest. Jesus went about preaching and forgiving sins. Jesus is still that same preacher only now He is in heaven where He is more powerful, but still that preacher that forgives our sins. The Scripture saith that He is the *mediator* between God and man. THE ONE AND ONLY MEDIATOR!

> *And Jesus said unto her, thy sins are forgiven… Thy FAITH hath saved thee; go in peace.* (Luke 7:48, 50)
>
> Jesus alone has the power to forgive sins. *"He hath delivered us from the power of darkness, and hath translated us into the kingdom of His Dear SON: In whom we have Redemption through His Blood. Even the forgiveness of sins." "And you being dead in your sins… He hath quickened together with Him, having forgiven you all trespasses; Blotting out the handwriting of ordinances that was against us, which was* contrary *to us, and*

took it out of the way nailing it to the cross." (Col. 1:13–14, 2:13–14)

So your sins are forgiven, little children, by the power of Jesus's Cross; you are blood bought. You are his possession. He has redeemed you from the curse of the LAW. Jesus has fulfilled the LAW for you; our debt is to Jesus. We are His purchase; He owns us. We are His precious, blood-washed possession. We have an inheritance set in heaven through His blood-bought sacrifice. You know the center of the Universe truly is Jesus, look what He did. *"And by Him all that believe are justified from* all *things, from which ye could not be justified by the* LAW *of* MOSES *"* (Acts 13:39).

Again Acts 13:41 says, *"Behold ye despisers, regard and wonder marvelously: I work a work in your days, a work which ye shall in no wise believe, though a man declare it unto you."* Who would have known that God would come to Earth and take a human body. And be born of the seed of King David, and that David would be his lineage. David did not even know that although the LORD did tell David, He would establish his Throne forever, forever. Also 1 Chronicles 29:23 says, *"Then Solomon sat on the throne* of the LORD *as king instead of David his father, and prospered and all Israel obeyed him."* The throne is called *the throne of the LORD*, and Scripture tells us when Jesus comes back He will sit in David's Throne. The wonders do not stop, God's work never ends. I think we have only seen the tip of the iceberg; it has really only just begun.

It starts and ends with Jesus 33 BC or 33 AD. A thousand years are as ONE DAY to the LORD, and one day as a thousand years. So according to God's calendar, it has only been two days since Jesus was here. You see, there is no time in heaven; imagine that. Time was created for us peons down here, so we could sit around saying yep Wednesday hump day and only noon, still three hours to go. If we only knew, folks, we are in a Salvador Dali movie, and we don't comprehend. There is no time in heaven, and fairly soon, the Almighty is going to take time from this Earth, *"and time shall be no more."* Check it out, Revelation.

I told you so, it's begun; oh yes, in Earth's time, it is over with—done, the end. Jesus is about to switch scenes; this one is old, and He is bored with it. Camera, action! Please, on with it. Oh yeesss, hail King Jesus. I am wondering if that "Heil Hitler" meant "Hail Hitler." God help Him if it did. His place in hell will be the WORST. No, there is only one NAME we honor, the Father says, and that is the Holy NAME of His Son Jesus Christ. Wake up, hello. Who died for you, friend?

"No greater LOVE than that a Man lay down His life for His brother." NO GREATER LOVE.

I repeat, there is ONLY ONE NAME WE MUST HONOR; THAT IS THE NAME OF JESUS CHRIST, END OF CONVERSATION! I am not going to say what I want to say here, so leave it at that. ONE, ONE NAME ONLY upon our lips, folks, the NAME OF JESUS CHRIST of NAZARETH that shed His blood for me.

The LOVER OF MY SOUL.

All that being said—let us visit the old man on the isle of Patmos. He is the longest reigning of the twelve on Earth, and I think Jesus kept his tender love around because he expressed Jesus's sentiments perfectly. GOD IS LOVE. Jesus wanted his testimony to go forth till the last possible minute, that his Earthly temple could tolerate this ungodly and perverse world. John was the boy of the group and Jesus's special friend, like David and Jonathan's friendship. GOD IS LOVE, he says, and when Jesus's Spirit is evacuated from this Earth due to the unfolding and sequence of what must still take place, according to Holy Scriptures in the Book of Revelation and Daniel, all that will be left is HATE. No goodness, no GOD, no grace, no holiness will remain, only hatred and all of hell's angels will remain. John knew all this for GOD IS LOVE; LOVE only exists in GOD and with His Holy Spirit. When this leaves, only hell remains. Jesus Christ gave John the great visions in the Book of Revelation to show him things that should shortly come to pass. I think Catholics call it the Book of the Apocalypse, which is the last book in your Bible.

There is a special blessing to those that read this book. I will admit at first the book scared me because I did not fully understand the prophesies, but now, I love it because the time is short and bad things only happen to bad people. John says, "*Blessed is he that readeth*, and they that hear the WORDS of this *prophesy…*for the time is at hand" (1:3).

> *From Jesus Christ…the first begotten of the dead, and the Prince of the kings of the Earth, unto Him that loved us and washed us from our sins in His Own Blood. And hath made us kings and priests unto GOD and His Father.* (1:5–6)
>
> *I John, was in the Spirit on the LORD'S DAY and I heard a great VOICE like a trumpet saying, I am Alpha and Omega, the First and the Last: What thou seest write in a book.* (Verses 10–11)
>
> *And I turned to see the Voice…and I saw 7 golden candlesticks and…one like unto the Son of Man in the midst.* (Verses 12–13)
>
> He laid His hand upon me and said, "Fear not… I am He that liveth and was dead and behold I am alive for evermore, Amen and I have the keys to Hell and Death. "Write,…these things John. (Verses 17–19)
>
> He that hath an ear, hear what the Spirit saith… (2:7)
>
> I have somewhat against thee because thou hast left thy *first love.*
>
> *Remember from whence thou art fallen and REPENT, and do thy first works, or else I will come unto thee quickly, and will remove thy candlestick… except thou REPENT.* (2:4–5)
>
> *I know thy works that thou art neither COLD nor HOT: I would thou wert COLD or HOT. So then because thou art lukewarm, and neither cold nor hot, I will spue thee out of My Mouth. I counsel thee to buy of Me gold tried in the fire, that thou mayest be rich: and white raiment that thou mayest*

be clothed... As many as I love, I rebuke and chasten, be zealous therefore, and REPENT. (3:15–19)

Behold I stand at the door and knock: if any man hear My Voice, and open the door, I will come in to him, and will dine with him, and he with ME. *To him that overcometh will I grant to sit with ME in MY THRONE, even as I also overcame, and am set down with MY FATHER in HIS THRONE. He that hath an ear let him hear what the Spirit saith.* (3:20–22)

Okay, I said all that to say this; folks, we ought to be hot and zealous for our first love, Jesus Christ. Looking at all He has done for us; He washed us in His precious blood and made us clean and fit for His Kingdom. We are begotten of Him through His WORD and His *blood*, we did not have to do a thing; only believe and accept Him as our LORD and Savior. Behold what manner of love the Father hath that He has made us His SONS, and if SONS then heirs of all the Father has. We cannot just be lukewarm when we consider all He has done. We do not want to just make heaven by the skin of our teeth. His desire is toward us. He wants us to realize the greatness of His gift of Sonship so that we reciprocate His great love. Moses said cleave unto your God. *CLEAVE* means that every breath of your body is shouting praise, adoration, worship, and thanksgiving to Him who gave His life for you. Because without Jesus's ultimate sacrifice, there would be no throne or crown for me and you. Jesus paid it all, all to Him I owe! Bow down, bend the knees, and worship. He wants our love for Him hot and real, like at the first when you first met Him.

What did King David say, *"So foolish was I, and ignorant: I was as a beast before Thee"* (Ps. 73:22). Job said, *"Behold, I am vile"* (Prov. 40:4). God told Moses, take off your sandals, you are on holy ground. Do the math, make the comparisons. Jesus said the Father is greater than I. Wow, imagine that.

"For we know in part... But when that which is perfect is come, then that which is in part shall be done away with" (1 Cor. 13:9–10). *"Then shall we know if we follow on to know the LORD"* (Hosea 6:3).

And again Philippians 3:21, *"Who shall change our vile body, that it may be fashioned like unto His glorious body."* Corruption shall not inherit incorruption. Philippians 2:5–8 also says,

> *Let this mind be in you which was also in Christ Jesus: Who being in the form of GOD… made Himself of no reputation and took upon Himself the form of a servant, and was made in the likeness of men. And being found in fashion as a man, He humbled Himself and became obedient unto death, even the death of the cross.*

Do the math again, make the comparisons. Here is the Almighty, creator of heaven and Earth, who has always existed and forever will. The all-powerful one, all-perfect, no blemish, all Holy One, becoming a man, made out of clay. Who would have thought it friend, not even the devil himself could have imagined this one. What did he keep saying, *"If you are the Son of God turn these stones into bread. If you are the Son of God come off that cross and save yourself."* If, if, if! So many if's; it should have made a normal man doubt. *"For now we see through a glass darkly; but then FACE to FACE: now I know in part; but then shall I know even as also I am known"* (1 Cor. 13:12).

Line upon line, folks, here a little there a little. *"O the depth of the riches both of the wisdom and knowledge of GOD! How unsearchable are His judgements, and His ways past finding out! For who hath known the mind of the LORD?"* (Rom. 11:33, 34).

The thought of GOD making Himself human is beyond comprehension. And going to the depths of depravity and being shamefully treated, mocked and spit on, cruelly treated, and then slaughtered worse than any animal; who is suddenly put out of His misery. NO, Jesus's agony cannot be measured or known, one minute would have been too much for you and me, but hours and hours that seemed like eternity, too very much. O, the LOVE of God, my friend—no greater LOVE than a man lay down His Life. The shepherd gave His life for His sheep. "And the glory of the LORD shall be revealed, and all flesh shall see it" (Isa. 40:5).

Do you see it?

> *He humbled Himself and became obedient unto death, even the death of the cross. Wherefore GOD also hath highly* exalted *Him, and given Him a* NAME *which is above every name: That at the* NAME *of Jesus every knee should bow, of things in Heaven and things in Earth, and things under the Earth; And that every tongue should confess that Jesus Christ is* LORD, *to the GLORY OF GOD THE FATHER.* (Phil. 2:8–11)

Jesus was the Lamb of God from before the foundations of the Earth. We really will only know the whole story in the LIGHT of heaven because there is so much more about GOD that we know so little here. One thing we do know is that the Father has exalted Jesus, and He is above ALL; every single thing is under His feet. There is no Higher; he is the MOST HIGH GOD. He is exalted and glorified. Every time John sees Jesus on His Throne, He is being exalted. At His trial, Jesus said to Pilate, "From henceforth you shall see the Son of God seated at the right hand of the Father with all the angels of heaven."

> *And I beheld and I heard the voice of many angels round about the throne…ten thousands times ten thousands… Saying with a loud voice Worthy is the LAMB that was slain to receive power, riches, wisdom, strength, honour, glory and blessing.* (Rev. 5:11–12)

His eyes were as a flame of FIRE, and on His HEAD were many crowns. (Rev. 19:12)

Again,

> *There were great voices in Heaven, saying, The kingdoms of this world are become the kingdoms of our LORD, and of His Christ and He shall REIGN FOREVER and ever. And the 24 elders which sat before GOD, fell upon their faces and worshipped GOD saying, We give Thee thanks, O LORD GOD Almighty which art, and wast and art to come; because Thou hast taken to Thee THY GREAT POWER, and DOST REIGN.* (Rev. 11:15–17)

And all the people of heaven cried,

> *Alleluia; Salvation and glory, and honour and power, unto the LORD our God: For true and righteous are His judgments." "And a Voice came out of the Throne saying, Praise Our GOD, all ye servants, and ye that fear Him, both small and great" "And a great multitude thundered with a mighty Voice saying, Alleluia: for the LORD GOD omnipotent REIGNETH.* (Rev. 19:1, 5–6)

Now all these verses are no mistake for heaven has received her KING. The LORD JESUS CHRIST KING of the UNIVERSE is being installed to His rightful THRONE. This great ceremony is taking place in heaven in John's vision. Jesus Christ is being anointed King of heaven and Earth with and by the praises and adulations of all His subjects, the saints, and angels of God. All heaven is rejoicing for the LAMB, for His great judgments, which are righteous. This is the greatest LOVE STORY of all time, the greatest love affair in the world. That the King of Glory would willingly submit Himself to being created and transformed into a man, then teach and heal for three and a half years before willingly submitting Himself to the horrors of Calvary for me. No greater love, no none, no greater love. I am surprised the birds didn't fall out of the trees, and the animals faint and the angels fall out of heaven to see such a sight, and to witness all these events of their Creator. The Earth is still reeling from Christ's visit to Earth. We all groan and travail, waiting for all this pageantry to take place. And now John sees, the culmination of the great *love* story. The bride (the church) has made herself ready, and there will be an astronomical marriage feast.

> *Let us be glad and rejoice and give honour to Him for the Marriage of the Lamb is come, and His wife hath made Herself* [that's us] *ready…arrayed in fine linen, clean and white.* (Rev. 19:7–8) [Be sure you are born again friend so you won't miss this.]
>
> *Blessed are they which are called to the Marriage Supper of the LAMB. And I saw heaven opened and behold a white horse: and He that sat on him was called Faithful and True, And in Righteousness does He judge and make war. His eyes were as a flame of fire and on His Head were many Crowns… His vesture was dipped in* blood: *and His Name is called The WORD of GOD and the armies of Heaven followed…and He shall smite the Nations and Rule them with a Rod of Iron: and He treadeth the wine press of the fierceness and wrath of Almighty God, And He hath on His vesture and thigh a Name written KING OF KINGS and LORD of LORDS.* (Rev. 19:9, 11–16)

This is that very same Jesus who walked in the cities of Israel and thereabout. This same exalted King is Jesus of Nazareth, the lowly servant, that is now enthroned and exalted at the Right Hand. The King who left His Throne and His Glory because He loved me and came to give His life's blood a ransom for my sins so that I could one day be with Him in His Throne. So that I could be like Him, glorified by His great love wherewith He loved me. The greatest love story, the greatest love affair, and the Father kept saying, *"This is My Beloved Son in Whom I am well pleased." "Hear O Israel the LORD*

Our GOD is ONE LORD." "He hath done everything WELL." Yes, the greatest love story of all time!

He wants our love hot, a blazing flame of passion if you will. A torrid zealous passion with the LOVE of Christ burning in your heart for ALL that He has done and will do. He wants us anxiously waiting and watching at the door on the precipice of eternity. Christ all in all. If you are not there, something is wrong with you. No worry, you cannot change a hair to white or gray, so you only need ask Him. LORD make me hot, not cold, not lukewarm even, but hot, very hot. He will do it for you, only ask. *"Come out of her, My People, that ye be not partakers of her sins, and that ye receive not of her* plagues. *For her* sins *have reached unto Heaven"* (Rev. 18:4–5). Woe, woe, woe, folks, wake up. Wake from your slumber.

This King of kings, King Jesus is coming back soon. He is making ready His Church, His Bride, now. He is stirring revival in the midst of His people and all those that are His see it. As the song goes, *"Everyday with Jesus is sweeter than the day before"*; maybe that is because we are getting just that much closer to seeing Him. So get worked up, folks; encourage yourself in the LORD because He is on the way back here.

But of all the excitement that Jesus Our LORD stirs, it is still difficult to comprehend, in an overwhelming way, that the King of Creation once lived here among us. He was here, all three, the Father, the Son, and the Holy Spirit, were here, dwelling among us and we knew it not because Jesus said, *"I and My Father are ONE"* (John 10:30). If the Father and Son are ONE, then all three were here, the entire Godhead—Father, Son, and Holy Spirit were here, dwelling among their own creation. I can think of nothing more exciting than *God with us.* God living with us and being our Earthly King, and He will live with us again on this very Earth. Jesus also said since you have seen Me, you have also seen the Father and know Him too. This is our real family, folks: Jesus, the Father and the Holy Spirit are the for-real family you have always dreamed about. The Perfect Father, Son, and us will be perfected and our dwelling with Him will be in Our Majesty's own perfect Home, His Kingdom, the Paradise of GOD. Listen here as His beloved John records Jesus's WORDS for us. Our own words fall so short of what the heart sings of, so let

Jesus's WORDS talk to us. This is a long quote please read it softly and tenderly as Jesus gave it to us, Gospel of *St. John chapter 14*:

> *Let not your heart be troubled: ye believe in GOD, believe also in ME. In My Father's house are many mansions: if it were not so, I would have told you. I go to prepare a place for you. And if I go and prepare a place for you, I will come again, and receive you unto MYSELF; THAT WHERE I AM, THERE YE MAY BE ALSO. And whither I go ye know, and the WAY ye know. Thomas saith, "LORD we know not whither Thou goest; and HOW CAN WE KNOW THE WAY?* [This is important friend, so read it again and again until you also know the way, you must know what Thomas is asking, this is the way you enter into heaven; it is through Jesus Himself.] *Jesus saith unto Thomas* [you know, doubting Thomas] *I AM THE WAY,* [Thomas] *I AM THE TRUTH,* [how? His Words are truth] *I AM THE LIFE:* [Jesus's WORDS are life.] *NO MAN, none, no one, NO MAN COMETH UNTO THE FATHER, BUT BY ME"* [By JESUS CHRIST]. (John 14:1–6)

Through Jesus Christ for He *alone* is the door.

Friends, the Catholics must understand that it is a personal relationship with Jesus that is the deciding factor for eternal life. One may sit in a Church every Sunday and still not have that personal relationship with Christ Jesus our LORD. It must be a burning reality of the heart. You must know for sure that the Holy Spirit is in you and with you. You must know His presence and feel the reality of Jesus being closer than a brother to you. He must be real to you, and the one way to do this is to meditate by reading His Gospels and then Jesus's Spirit comes all over you and you realize, yes, Jesus is more real to me than any person on Earth. He is now your REALITY. You possess Him, and He possesses you. You are His, sealed by the Holy spirit. The Holy Spirit is the witness to you that you are a believer, and on the right road to heaven, *"O taste and see that the LORD is good,"* or real. Let's continue with verse 7 as this will explain.

> *If ye had known ME, ye should have known MY FATHER also: and from henceforth ye know HIM, and have SEEN HIM. Philip says, LORD show us the Father Jesus says to him, Have I been so long with you, and yet hast thou not known ME, Philip? He that hath seen ME hath seen the FATHER; and how sayest thou then, Show us the Father? Believest thou not that I am in the Father, and the Father in ME? The WORDS that I speak unto you I speak not of Myself: but the Father that dwelleth in ME, He doeth the works.* (John 14:7–10)

And Colossians 1:15 tells us that *"Jesus is the image of the invisible GOD,"* another Words they look alike, and we look like them. He created us to be His family and His children; we are GOD's family. And the Son is in the Father and the Father in the Son, and He abides with us now through His Holy Spirit, which is a Real Entity. He the Holy Spirit is a reality. Jesus did not leave us or His disciples alone, for the devil to beat up and trash. No, He sent us His Holy Spirit to be in us to protect us from Satan and the World. John says, "Greater is He that is in you than He that is in the World." GOD is greater, the Holy Spirit of GOD, is greater, and this is the victory that overcomes the world, even our "faith." We are victorious in Jesus Christ.

Are you getting excited about Jesus yet?

It is not in man to direct his own path. We must lean on the Savior, asking Him to direct us continually. But when the waters are stirred, it is time to move, and the Spirit is stirring in the world right now. When you feel a little excitement, make a note of it and press in; do not pass your opportunity by. Remember please, "Draw nigh to GOD and he will draw nigh to you" (James 4:8).

Seize your opportunity, even the smallest, and be inspired in the presence of GOD. King David often used this theme of encouraging himself in the LORD. He came into the Master's presence by way of song and praise. Many of us are not musical, so we come into His presence through meditation of His WORD, which usually gives way to praise and thanksgiving because of the truths which stir our Spirit. The Spirit is moving, folks, yield to Its calling.

> *Now there is at Jerusalem by the sheep market a pool which is called in the Hebrew tongue Bethesda, having five porches. In these lay a great multitude of impotent folk, of blind, halt, withered, WAITING FOR THE MOVING OF THE WATER. For an angel went down at a certain season into the pool, and troubled the water: whosoever then first after the troubling of the water stepped in was made whole of whatsoever disease he had.* (John 5:2–4)

It's like the old preacher says, when the waters are stirred, expect a miracle; move out in the Spirit and expect great things. *"Prove ME saith the LORD of Hosts, if I will not open the windows of Heaven, and pour you out a blessing, that there shall not be room enough to receive it"* (Mal. 3:10).

According to your faith, be it unto you.

"Return unto ME and I will return unto you saith the LORD of Hosts" (Mal. 3:7). You plus God, friend, equal all the power of heaven, and nothing shall be impossible unto you. All heaven is at your disposal just because you know the King of kings.

> *Call unto me, and I will answer thee, and show thee great and mighty things, which thou knowest not.* (Jer. 33:3)
>
> There's always more than we can expect with GOD, even more than we can fathom, because His thoughts are higher than ours, much higher. Relax and take the limits off of the MOST

HIGH GOD, trust in Him to do you good. *For the foolishness of GOD is wiser than men, and the weakness of GOD is stronger than men.* (1 Cor. 1:25)

Delight thyself also in the LORD; and He shall give thee the desires of thine heart. Commit thy way unto the LORD; TRUST also in HIM; and He shall bring it to pass. And He shall bring forth thy righteousness as the LIGHT, and thy judgement as the noonday. Rest in the LORD, and wait patiently for HIM: FRET NOT THYSELF… Mark the perfect man, and behold the upright: for the end of that man is PEACE. And the LORD shall help the righteous and deliver them:…and SAVE them, because they trust in HIM. (Ps. 37:4–7, 37, 40)

GOD is not slack concerning His promises of which we have too many to count and numerous reasons for loving and adoring Him. Christ has <u>poured</u> Himself out for us, He has held nothing back. As a generous LOVER He has given His all. As James says, *"Every good gift and every perfect gift is from ABOVE, and cometh down from the Father of Lights, with whom is no variableness, neither shadow of turning. Of His own will begat He us with the WORD of Truth."* (1:17–18)

Everything is of, to, through and for the LORD, He is all and all. He has slain all our enemies for us, Death, hell and the Grave and soon will bind and chain Satan eternally. *"And having spoiled principalities and powers, He made a show of them openly triumphing over them in it"* (Col. 2:15) *"And ye are complete in HIM, which is the head of all principality and power, for in Him dwelleth all the fullness of the Godhead bodily"* (Col. 2:9–10) And being a good loving husband He has picked up the tab, the entire tab. And as a jealous groom He wants all our love and adoration. And as for me it is a done deal, signed, sealed and delivered. Hosea paints the perfect picture: *"Yet I am the LORD thy GOD from the Land of Egypt, and thou shalt know no god but ME: for there is no Saviour besides ME." O Israel, thou destroyed thyself; but in ME is thine help.* (Hos. 13:4, 9)

O Israel, return unto the LORD thy GOD; for thou hast fallen by thine iniquity And I will heal their backslidings, I will LOVE them freely: For Mine anger is turned away from him. (Hos. 14:1, 4)

Hosea is a supreme example of God's jealous LOVE for His sinful, backsliding, unthankful, and sometimes unholy children. But His all-encompassing love overpowers their insensibilities and he cries return, "Return unto ME O MY beloved; for in ME is thine help."

And I will close with these beautiful WORDS.

And I will betroth thee unto ME Forever, yea, I will betroth thee unto ME in Righteousness, and in judgment, and in loving kindness, and in mercies. I will sow her unto ME in the Earth; and I will have mercy upon her that hath not obtained mercy; and I will say to them which were not MY PEOPLE, Thou art MY PEOPLE, and they shall say, Thou art MY GOD. (Hosea 2:19–23)

Amen and amen.
(Even so, come quickly LORD JESUS.)

And they brought the colt to Jesus...and set Him thereon...

And when Jesus was come nigh, at the descent of the Mount of Olives, the whole multitude... Rejoiced and praised GOD with a loud voice for all the mighty works they had seen;

Saying BLESSED BE THE KING. (Luke 19:35–38)

Hell

———— ∅ ————

No story would be complete without presenting both sides. God is a god of justice, and God has created both good and evil in hopes that we would choose good. David says, *"He hath prepared His throne for judgment, and again… Righteousness and judgement are the habitation of His throne"* (Ps. 9:7, 91:2).

And we all know there will be a judgment, a reckoning day; this is common knowledge. *"And as it is appointed unto men once to die, but after this the judgment"* (Heb. 9:27). The big "J."

So yes, there is a judgment, and *hell* is real! But the powers of darkness would keep you and I oblivious to this fact. That yes, most certainly, there is a hot burning hell into which Christ Jesus the Lord our Judge is going to cast all His enemies and nonbelievers alike. He makes all this clear in His teachings in the Gospels. Here in Matthew 13:30 is a picture of the world today. Jesus says, *"Let both grow together until the harvest: and in the time of harvest I will say to the reapers, Gather ye together first the tares, and bind them in bundles to burn them: but gather the wheat into my barn."* Both will grow together that is both good and evil people. The harvest is the end of the world and Judgment day, which looks to be rather close at hand. Jesus explains further to His disciples saying the tares burned in the fire are the children of the wicked one, those that found no pleasure in following God. And so it shall be in the *end of the world.*

> *"The Son of Man (GOD) shall send forth his angels, and they shall gather out of his kingdom all things that offend, and them which do iniquity; And*

shall cast them into a furnace of fire: there shall be wailing and gnashing of teeth" (Matt. 13:41–42).

Now God in His wisdom and justice is not pushy, and He has given us our freedom. For what kind of a kingdom would mandatory love be. He wants to know for real that we love Him and will choose Him over everything else. *"For God hath not appointed us to wrath, but to obtain salvation by Our Lord Jesus Christ who died for us…that we should live together with Him"* (1 Thess. 5:9). Jesus showed us how much He loved us; enough to die for us. Greater love, greater love hath no man than this that He lay down His life for His friend. And again Jesus said I am the GOOD SHEPHERD. "I lay down My life for My sheep that they may have life." Jesus is the perfect example of love, and He expects this kind of love in return. Remember the Holy Spirit of God is a perfect gentleman… He is not pushy.

God in His righteousness will not force His way of His love upon us, He gives us the choice, but the alternative is a fact. Joshua says,

> *CHOOSE YOU THIS DAY WHOM YE WILL SERVE… BUT AS FOR ME AND MY HOUSE, WE SERVE THE LORD."* *"If you for-sake the Lord, and serve strange gods, then He will turn and do you hurt and consume you, after that He hath done you good… Ye cannot serve the lord (and idols too) for He is a Holy God. He is a JEALOUS GOD.* (Josh. 24:15, 20, 19)

It is clear as light versus darkness, and as evil versus good. There is the straight and narrow that leads to life everlasting with our Lord and Savior, or there is the broad way, filled with the pleasures and corruption of this world. Now,

> *Ye do err not knowing the Holy Scripture. "And judgment is turned away backward, and justice standeth afar off: for TRUTH is fallen in the street and equity cannot enter."* (Isa. 59:14)

But to this man will I look, even to him that is poor and of a contrite spirit, and that trembleth at MY WORD. (66:2)

The key here is trembleth, because he that has such a fear of God is aware of His righteous judgments and FEARS, FEARS the living God and His judgments. Every man will give account of himself to GOD.

Jesus thus commands us, *"Enter ye in at the strait gate: for wide is the gate, and broad is the way, that leadeth to destruction, and many there be which go in thereat: Because strait is the gate, and narrow is the way, which leadeth unto life, and few there be that find it"* (Matt. 7:13–14).

Few that is; eight people in the days of Noah were saved and that is out of an entire world full of people. And GOD again tells us that as in the days of Noah so shall it be in the days when the Son of Man returneth. They were eating, drinking, and marrying until the flood came and took them all away. Because of their sins and delusions they did not know, though they were warned, and it overcame them as a snare, as a trap set by the fowler for the bird. Poof, and it was upon them, and it was too late; the flood carried them away. Therefore, the LORD admonishes us betimes in His Gospels to watch and pray and have oil in your lamp as the five wise virgins waiting for their bridegroom. The oil is the wisdom and grace of GOD that results from reading HIS WORD. And at midnight, a voice of the bridegroom was heard, and the five wise virgins went out to meet Him. Jesus is that bridegroom of His Church, and we are His bride, His church, and we are awaiting His soon return.

"Be vigilant," the LORD says.

"Not everyone that saith unto me, LORD, LORD shall enter into His kingdom of Heaven; but he that doeth the will of MY FATHER which is in Heaven" (Matt. 7:24).

And what is this will of the Father, simply this, *"Therefore all things whatsoever ye would that men should do to you, do ye even so to them: for this is All the LAW and the PROPHETS"* (Matt. 7:12).

This is it—love; that is, the Father's will that we love one another even as we love ourselves. And all the law is fulfilled by this. LOVE, laying down our lives for the brethren. Now here we can all bewail ourselves, that God would help us to fulfill His will in treating others better than ourselves. Have faith; all things are possible through Jesus Christ our LORD. GOD can help us do this, for LOVE is a fulfilling of the LAW.

God is not a hard task master; the devil is, and he takes men at their will. We can see by the state of the world that hell hath enlarged itself and opened wide its mouth for the unbelievers and disobedient. Have mercy on us, LORD; show us the way in Jesus's Name. We want to make heaven our home. Jesus used another parable to illustrate heaven and hell, the rich man and the beggar Lazarus. Jesus paints His pictures in neon hues of red and yellow deserving of His righteous judgments. So we see the rich man that fared well in this life and a poor beggar that had his sights set on an afterlife.

> *There was a certain rich man, which was clothed in purple and fine linen, and fared sumptuously every day: and there was a certain beggar named Lazarus, which was laid at his gate, full of sores, and desiring to be fed with the crumbs which fell from the rich man's table: moreover the dogs came and licked his sores. And it came to pass, that the beggar died, and was carried by the angels into Abraham's bosom: the rich man also died, and was buried; and in hell he lift up his eyes, being in torments, and seeth Abraham afar off, and Lazarus in his bosom.* (Luke 16:19–23).

Jesus is giving us an illustration of hell and heaven and the rich man is no happy camper at this place. But Lazarus, which was poor and despised is now faring well. Most everything Jesus taught reminds us that, yes, evil is rewarded with hell and good with heaven. What a man sows that shall he reap. Jesus teaches the good versus evil theme over and over. What do you think? Maybe He has a point to make and He wants us to really, really consider. He does not want us to diminish any part of this sermon. He wants us to realize that hell is a most miserable abode, and with all our efforts and energy, we must avoid it, escape from its grasps and from the city of destruction—hell. Let's continue our story.

> *And he cried and said, Father Abraham, have mercy on me, and send Lazarus, that he may dip the tip of his finger in water, and cool my tongue; for I am tormented in this* flame. *But Abraham said, Son, remember that thou in thy lifetime receivedst thy good things, and likewise Lazarus evil things: but now he is comforted, and thou art tormented"* [in this FLAME]. (Luke 16:24–25)

In this what, *flame*, yes, *flames*—sounds like *hell* to me. And notice also that he was buried and went straight to hell versus Lazarus who went straight away on angel's wings to *heaven.* Oh, friend, life is too short, and too frustrating to spend it on ourselves. Why? It only takes on meaning and gets easier when we give it all to Jesus. It is such a mess here, and the world wants to candy-coat it, so as to convince themselves that everything will be all right, just keep calm and carry on. No, no, and no, without God as the focus of your life, it is a most treacherous and meaningless ritual of nothingness. You end up traversing this rocky road in circles and your poor little soul gets sicker and emptier by the day. This is where most faint and grab for the medications that numb the mind into limbo, and when you wake up, that limbo will be a seat in HELL.

Only God, only God brings joy and happiness for us. It is God's spirit in this world, in His children that make life even tolerable.

For the HOLY WORD exclaims, "*Thou wilt show me the path of life; in Thy* PRESENCE *is fullness of joy; at Thy right hand there are pleasures forevermore." David continues, "I have set the LORD always before me: because He is at my right hand, I shall not be moved"* (Ps. 16:11, 8).

David knew the presence of God and He longed to be there often. He knew it was a place of healing because of his encounter with Saul, who made him his harp player because it drove away the evil spirit that beset him. David knew well the luxury of the presence of God. He said in Psalm 95, *"Let us come into His presence with thanksgiving and make a joyful noise unto Him... For the LORD is a great GOD and a great King above all Gods. Oh come, let us worship and bow down: let us kneel before the LORD our MAKER"* (verses 2, 3, 6).

David knew the balm of Gilead, and his life testifies of a man who walked hand in hand with his LORD and Maker. His own lips testify, yes, oh, yes. *"The lines are fallen out to me in pleasant places; yea, I have a goodly heritage."* From shepherd boy, to king in the palace, also from his bloodlines came his Maker, Jesus the Christ, the Messiah. Only God, if He does not direct your paths, you have missed the mark entirely, you, my friend, are still lost, without Jesus as your Captain.

For those still in denial of a HELL, it has been talked about, and acclaimed by all men of great learning and wisdom since time in memorial. Again, David can give us an apt picture of this ungodly of ungodly places.

> *So foolish was I, and ignorant: I was as a beast before THEE. For I was envious at the foolish, when I saw the prosperity of the wicked. Until I went into the sanctuary of GOD; then understood I their end. Surely Thou didst set them in slippery places; Thou castedst them down into DESTRUCTION. How are they brought into DESOLATION, as in a moment! They are utterly consumed with terrors... Thou shalt despise their image.* (Ps. 73:22, 3, 17–20)

And Job has given us his description of the wicked in chapter 21. He says to his friends,

> *Suffer me that I may speak; and after that I have spoken mock on. Ye say where is the house of the Evil? And where are the dwelling places of the wicked? God shall reward him, and he shall know it. For he shall drink of the wrath of the Almighty. Know ye that the WICKED is reserved to the day of DESTRUCTION? They shall be brought forth to the day of Wrath.* (Job 21:3, 28, 19, 20, 30)

Hell hath enlarged herself; she is naked before GOD and is NEVER FULL. We know of a certainty that God's throne was created for judgment and the evil are promised a place of destruction. God is omniscient, perfect in wisdom and understanding. He alone has the program planned and ready to deliver. Rest assured He is all just and declares *"that vengeance is mine I will repay saith the LORD."* Have confidence in your God, as the song says, "Put your hand in the hand of the man that stilled the waters and calmed the sea," our beloved Jesus. And the scripture says, "He hath done all things well," so hold onto your confidence, trust Jesus.

Now the devil's aim is to keep us out of heaven and distract us from the truths of God found in his WORD. The devil dangles some glitzy temptation over yonder and we go running; meanwhile the Bible gets buried in the back closet. We keep burying this book of TRUTH, till we don't even realize it's gone, someone has walked out the door with it. Then twenty years later, you are wondering like Pilate. *"What is TRUTH?"* You have lost sight of GOD and His promises because the WORD, the Bible, the TRUTH is gone.

Jesus said,

I AM THE WAY,
The TRUTH, and
THE LIFE.

Without the light, we go stumbling along in darkness, taking all those nasty detours off the straight and narrow like John *Bunyan's* pilgrim.[1] But God, by His mercy, kept sending messengers to help pilgrim find his way back, and resume his journey toward heaven. Our favorite man Isaiah explains how it is so,

> *For thus saith the high and lofty one that inhabiteth eternity, whose name is HOLY, I dwell in the high and holy place with him also that is of a contrite and humble spirit, to revive the spirit of the humble and to revive the heart of the contrite ones. I will not afflict forever. I will not be always wroth; for then man's spirit would give way before ME… Their sins have made ME angry for a while, I struck them in My wrath and turned away; and they went on, willful and rebellious. I marked them; the Eternal says. But now I heal them…and will recompense them with all consolation.* (57:15–18 Moffatt)

God is ever ready for us. He's there before your eyes gaze heavenward. Like the Prodigal's Father, arms wide open, out in the road waiting for His son, who he could barely make out in the distance, his visage was so small. Take that first step and fall into His loving arms. *"Draw nigh to God and HE will draw nigh to you."* One must wonder how all these thoughts assail me. Yes, it is about hell and the most important idea about our subject is how to stay out of it. And the easiest way to stay on the path to GOD is to keep the LIGHT shining bright to show us the way. Remember, Jesus is the LIGHT and the WORD is LIGHT and Jesus is the WORD incarnate. *Read the WORD.*

> *"Thy WORD is a lamp unto my feet, and a light unto my path"* (119:105).

And again, John 1:1 says, *"In the beginning was the WORD and the WORD was with GOD and the WORD was GOD."* (He that is the WORD is seated at the right hand of the Father right now.)

> *"Heaven and Earth shall pass away, but My WORDS shall not pass away."* Why do His WORDS not pass away; because Jesus is the WORD and the WORD is with GOD in Heaven. How do we clean up our act before GOD and become presentable before the throne. Again our instructor is the WORD of GOD.
> *"Wherewithal shall a young man cleanse his way? By taking heed thereto according to Thy WORD. With my whole heart have I sought THEE: O let me not wander from thee. Thy WORD have I hid in my heart, that I might not sin against Thee.* (119:9–11)

We have heard the phrase *"It's the economy stupid,"* but I have one upmanship here. *"It's the WORD fool,"* and the beginning of wisdom is the Fear of the LORD." The WORD, the WORD is all in all, should I repeat that, the WORD is ALL in ALL. Some small advice, give it a break and try Jesus, friend, and see how you pick up the pace. The Lord tells us that He will not pull a fast one on us. He does not do things in secret, but He warns us aforetime of His plans. But it is His creation and He will do as He pleases. David says, *"Our GOD is in the heavens: He hath done whatsoever He hath pleased in Heaven and in Earth"* (115:3).

"And when (the blind man) heard that it was JESUS OF NAZARETH, he began to cry out, and say, JESUS THOU SON OF DAVID, have mercy on me.

And many charged him that he should hold his peace: but he cried the more a great deal, THOU SON OF DAVID, HAVE MERCY ON ME." (Mark 10:47–48)

Paul tells us how the Master does as He pleases in Romans, *"Oh the goodness and severity of GOD: on them which fell severity, but toward thee goodness. If thou continue in His goodness. Otherwise thou also shalt be cut off"* (11:22).

And John the Baptist railed on the crowd saying, *"O generation of vipers, who hath warned you to flee from the WRATH to come? Bring forth therefore fruits worthy of repentance. And now also the axe is laid unto the root of the trees: every tree therefore which bringeth not forth good fruit is cast into the FIRE"* (Luke 3:7, 9).

These are God's warnings and standards. He wrote the rule book. Yes, Mr. Obama, Jesus Christ of Nazareth wrote the rule book. It sounds like mathematical equations with all these "thus, saith the LORD'S" and therefores, it is absolutely simple math (A = you + B = do good = C, heaven); and this all adds up to being doers of the WORD, not hearers only. For he that doeth the will of GOD shall inherit heaven, not the hearers; the doers. And this is my favorite mathematical equation. From Jesus, *"But seek ye first the Kingdom of God and his righteousness; and all these things shall be added unto you. Take therefore no thought for tomorrow, for tomorrow shall take thought for the things of itself. Sufficient unto the day is the evil thereof"* (Matt. 6:33, 34).

Oh yes, and Jesus does all kinds of math; He multiplied the fishes and loaves.

Next in verse 17, the Baptist says, *"Jesus fan is in His hand, and He will thoroughly purge His floor, and will gather the wheat into His garner, but the chaff, He will burn with FIRE UNQUENCHABLE."* Sounds like hell to me. Be not mistaken. God Almighty is of all things a just and righteous Judge. He is not willing that any should perish, but that all men should come to the TRUTH, which is in Christ Jesus Our LORD. Hell was originally created for the devil not for us.

But His throne was created for judgment and judge He will do. His throne is an everlasting throne and we shall sit in that very throne with Him judging the world. He shall rule and reign and we shall rule and reign with Him as overcomers.

> *The LORD reigneth... Righteousness and*
> *Judgment are the habitation of His Throne.* (Ps.
> 97:1–2)
> *The LORD shall endure forever: He hath pre-*
> *pared His throne for judgment. And He shall judge*
> *the world in righteousness, He shall minister judg-*
> *ment to the people in uprightness.* (Ps. 45:6–7)

It is apparent that God's love, mercy, and justice maintains His throne. He will not send a man to hell without sufficient mercy peppering His decision. But really, it is our decision and choice to choose heaven or hell. Jesus is the all just JUDGE; the real JUDGE. Every man will know and accept the judgment God passes on to him. For there will be an all-prevailing knowledge of the LORD with every living being that stands before Him, and they will know that Jesus Christ their maker and judge is the LORD GOD of all mercies. Fear the judge, fear the Almighty judge; it is He to whom we will give account and we must and shall all stand before Him.

> *"And fear not them which kill the body, but*
> *are not able to kill the soul: but rather fear Him*
> *which is able to destroy both soul and body in*
> *HELL"* (Matt. 10:28)
> Isaiah says, *"Neither fear ye their fear, nor be*
> *afraid. But sanctify the Lord of Hosts Himself; and*
> *let Him be your fear, and let Him be your dread"*
> (8:12–13).

And that is why there will be wailing and sorrow and pain untold for those that miss the mark. Those that wrote Jesus off as something invisible, and so felt that they did not have to deal with it. Wrong, wrong; it is God's kingdom and if He has made it invisible to us right now, so be it. He only asks that we believe, and if we don't believe, we are condemned to perish. Let us not be like the wicked King Belteshazzar who during a night of drunken debauchery and blasphemy, read his judgment on the castle wall, written by the hand of God. It read, *"THOU ART WEIGHED IN THE BALANCES AND ART FOUND WANTING"* (Dan. 5:27).

The next day, his kingdom was ripped from him and he died. Romans says, *"The wrath of God is revealed from Heaven against all ungodliness"* (1:18).

If you are out-of-the-way friend, it is time to consider and acquaint now thyself with Him and be at peace. He is the merciful and loving Bishop of your soul ready to pardon to the uttermost all that come to Him.

"Oh, sinner man, where you going to run to on, on, that day?" Behold now is the acceptable time; now is the day. Later on, then it will be too late; now is the time to acknowledge there is a God in heaven, who you will never regret knowing. So make your move, turn your gaze heavenward. And *"know therefore that God exacteth of thee less than thine iniquities deserveth"* (good old Job 11:6).

> *And Jesus said, so shall it be at the end of the world: the angels shall come forth, and sever the wicked from among the just, And shall cast them into the furnace of fire: there shall be wailing and gnashing of teeth. Jesus saith unto them, Have ye understood all these things?* (Matt. 13:49–51)
>
> And David says, *"Our days are as a shadow that passeth away."* (144:4)

Now, call upon thy God today, today is the right time.

But the wrath and vengeance of God is sure. He will with the full force of His holiness and righteous indignation pour out the vials of His WRATH that have been reserved unto the GREAT DAY OF THE LORD. His WRATH is waiting in the side wings of the Father's command. *"Soon and very soon, we shall see the King."* The saints under the throne cry night and day, "How long LORD until our blood is avenged on the wicked?" I tell you soon, soon, and sooner than you think, God is not asleep. He is not slack concerning His promises; He says speedily, speedily, I tell you He will delay no longer. Zephaniah paints the picture for us with neon reds and torch-hot blues.

> *I will utterly destroy and consume all things... Them that are turned back from the LORD, and those that have not sought the LORD, nor enquired for Him. I will punish their violence and deceit... For the Great Day of the LORD is near, it is near and hasteth greatly... the mighty man shall cry bitterly. That DAY is a DAY of wrath, A Day of trouble and distress, A Day of wasteness and desolation, A Day of darkness and gloominess, A Day of clouds and THICK DARKNESS A Day of trumpet and alarm... And I will bring distress upon men, that they shall walk like blind men, because they have sinned against the LORD: and their blood shall be poured out as DUST, and their flesh as DUNG. Neither their silver nor their gold shall be able to deliver them in the DAY of the Lord's wrath. But the whole land shall be devoured by the FIRE OF HIS JEALOUSY; for it shall make even a speedy riddance of all them that dwell in the LAND.* (Zeph. 1:2, 6, 9, 14–18)

Just thought you would like to know the facts, friend, because way back when I was in Catholic schools, I was never told any of this, but it is a signed and sure deal, for the Lord hath determined it. It is His DETERMINATION just as He destroyed the whole Earth in the days of Noah, just as! And the admonition as always is,

PRAY THAT YE MIGHT ESCAPE.

You cannot say you were not told. I tell you now and warn you this day, the Almighty fury of His justice is on the way, even at the door. I always said it would be in my lifetime. Why fury and wrath, you ask? Because God hates sin and evil, and they are to be abolished from His kingdom. It is His kingdom and He is about to clean it up; He cleans with FIRE. He has given us many examples of His WRATH against sin. Jude tells us, verse 7, *"Even as Sodom and Gomorrah…giving themselves over to fornication, and going after stranger flesh are set forth for an EXAMPLE, suffering the vengeance of ETERNAL FIRE."* Father Abraham tried to bargain with God for them but the outcry against them was great before the LORD (Gen. 19:3). Their sin vexed the LORD so much that He

> *"Rained upon Sodom and Gomorrah brimstone and fire from the LORD out of Heaven. And He overthrew those cities and all the plain, and all the inhabitants and all which grew upon the ground"* (24–25).

The Lord so utterly destroyed them, that they have literally disappeared off the face of the Earth.

> *I am the LORD, I change not.* (Mal. 3:6)
> *Jesus Christ the same yesterday, TODAY and forever.* (Heb. 13:8)

God's ruin is complete. The LORD says I will punish according to a man's doings and according to his ways. God could not find one righteous man in those cities, not one. The fear of the LORD is to depart from EVIL, that is how we save ourselves with GOD; we fear Him, the MAN with the power.

> *"Therefore turn thou to thy GOD: Keep mercy and judgment, and wait upon thy GOD continually"* Woe to those that corrupt themselves with not an ounce of Godly fear. *"Raging…and foaming out their shame,…to whom is reserved the blackness of darkness forever"* (Jude 13).

And Jude nails it with these two verses about Enoch, now Enoch is hot with GOD so listen…

> *And Enoch also, the seventh from Adam prophesied of these evil ones saying, Behold the LORD cometh with 10,000's of His saints, to execute JUDGMENT upon ALL, and to CONVINCE ALL that are UNGODLY among them of ALL their UNGODLY DEEDS which they have UNGODLY committed, and of ALL their HARD SPEECHES which UNGODLY sinners have UNGODLY spoken against HIM.* (Jude 14–15)

And over in the FAITH chapter, Hebrews 11, Paul says, *"By FAITH Enoch was translated that he should not see death; and was not found, because God had translated him: for before his translation he had this testimony, THAT HE PLEASED GOD."*

Yes, so how hot is that? Jesus said I would you were either hot or cold (never lukewarm)! There have only been two people besides Jesus Himself on the earth ever that have been translated clean outta here. Enoch and Elijah. So tell me, how do you do that again? Oh yes, *"HE PLEASED GOD."* What then should be our cry to GOD? Yes, LORD, LET ME PLEASE YOU EVERMORE. All the time, Jesus day or night and everywhere.

And I have said all that to say this, Enoch earned such high merits with the Master that he was given a flying red carpet to heaven. And it isn't likely that his prophecy is anything short of the mind of Christ. He said all these ungodly that have been so ungodly in all their ungodly sinning have totally and justly reaped the wages of sin and have earned the complete wrath and FURY OF HELLFIRE. God is all just, all-merciful, the angels and saints applaud His just judgments. We reap what we sow. GOD is not mocked nor pleased with our ease and slackness in Zion. The fear of the LORD is to depart from evil. Fight a good fight against evil, be strong in the Lord. He is your captain, report into Him immediately.

> *Put on the whole armour of God, that ye may be able to stand against the wiles of the devil. For we wrestle not against flesh and blood, but against principalities, against powers, against the rulers of the darkness of this world, against spiritual wickedness in high places. Wherefore take unto you the whole armour of God, that ye may be able to withstand in the evil day, and having done all, to stand. Stand therefore, having your loins girt about with truth, and having on the breastplate of righteousness; And your feet shod with the preparation of the gospel of peace; Above all, taking the shield of faith, wherewith ye shall be able to quench all the fiery darts of the wicked. And take the helmet of salvation, and the sword of the Spirit, which is the WORD OF GOD.* (Eph. 6:11–17)

Our archenemy is seeking company for himself in hell. Misery likes company. So don't be at ease, don't take this salvation lightly. Be on guard; he seeks to take you out and the devil does not sleep, he prowls about.

"Lift up thy voice like a trumpet, cry aloud, spare not, show my people their transgression and sin" (Isaiah 58:1) and no one comes out hitting harder than Ezekiel, whom GOD appointed as a WATCHMAN to His people. "Warn them from ME, give the people My warning," God says. But who is warning anyone today? We are all giving each other drugs until the day dawns, and we wake up in hell and no one knows what happened.

Meanwhile, the doctor has his pad and pencil ready to give you six to ten new drugs and up the ante on the ones you are already taking. Like Mr. *Spurgeon* says, *"You do violence to common sense people."*[2] Where is the Godly man among us? With the likes of the Apostle Paul, the great Josephus, George Muller, Billy Sunday, John the Baptist, John Wesley, the list goes on, but not enough. We cannot be complacent against sin, no matter how cunning, sly, and deceiving it is. We must all have God's message and a reason of the HOPE that dwells within us ready on demand. God, again I say, told Ezekiel to warn them from Me. Hell is hot, uncomfortable, and painful; repent for the Kingdom of GOD is near.

In our long list of godly men belongs our German brother Dietrich.[3] He was with utter brilliance weaving a web of repentance and encouraging the believers to take a stand and pull down the powers of enveloping darkness, death, gloom, anguish, and depression. The kind of darkness that Pharaoh experienced; it was thick and could be felt as a cloak of HELL.

I believe as Bonhoffer did that Hitler and his Gestapo war machine was the antichrist because everything that is against Christ is anti. Paul says even now there are many antichrists. Paul dealt with Nero, his antichrist of all insanity. Also insane Antiochus later who poured swine's blood on the temple altar, thus desecrating its holiness. And we have had a modern-day antichrist in Hitler.

Yes, Hitler made himself out as an idol, a king to be worshipped and praised. A dictator who believed GOD would smile on his genocide and insane torture of the JEWISH PEOPLE. Hitler was well on his way to ruling the world, and without the constraints of the Holy Spirit, he may well have succeeded. We must all pray the Our Father prayer and pray continually many prayers all in Jesus's name and unite our efforts worldwide in constraining the next antichrist spirit from reigning over the world. For that will be Jacob's trouble as Jesus tells us, and trouble that will make the Holocaust look like a Roman holiday. David said, "Let not an evil speaker be established in the Earth LORD GOD." The Apostle Paul has insight on this man of sin to come, and on God's just punishments for wickedness. He says,

> *Seeing it is a righteous thing with God to recompense tribulation to them that trouble you; And to you who are troubled rest with us, when the Lord Jesus shall be revealed from heaven with his mighty angels, In flaming fire taking vengeance on them*

that know not God, and that obey not the gospel of our Lord Jesus Christ: Who shall be punished with everlasting destruction from the presence of the Lord, and from the glory of his power; When he shall come to be glorified in his saints, and to be admired by all them that believe (because our testimony among you was believed) in that day. (2 Thess. 1:6–10)

Let no man deceive you by any means: for that day shall not come, except there come a falling away first, and that man of sin be revealed, the son of perdition; Who opposeth and exalteth himself above all that is called God, or that is worshipped; so that he as God sitteth in the temple of God, shewing himself that he is God. (2:3–4)

Well done, Dietrich; as a Prince, thou hast prevailed with GOD and man and hast succeeded in warding off the death angel from enveloping your homeland and the entire world. We wanted you here, but Jesus LORD and Savior wanted His faithful servant more. He knew you had finished your work here as a prince among man, and that you were weary and worn. So the LORD took your work mantle and exchanged it for your kingly robes. Good job, brother, can't wait to meet you.

And may Hitler know God's fullest retribution in hell; as David says, take him down quickly Lord God, for all his very ungodly deeds that he very ungodly committed. Such atrocities against the human RACE in shedding and causing to be shed the blood of millions and thousands of innocent men, women, and children deserve God's full wrath and may he have it forever. Hell welcomes you with open arms.

"And now your wicked troubling is ceased…
as you go down to the bars of the pit" (Job 17:16).

One note further, I believe as Dietrich was marching through the yard to the scaffold, that Job's words were on his lips, in his mind and upon the table of his heart.

> *"Naked came I out of my mother's womb, and naked shall I return thither; The Lord gave and the Lord hath taken away; Blessed be the name of the LORD"* (Job 1:21).

I bet there was not a dry eye to anyone that knew him. Blessed be the very remembrance of you.

Okay, we have examples of Godly and ungodly. What did the Almighty tell us in the book of Ezekiel? And what did He tell us about Sodom and Gomorrah? Did He not say these are set forth as examples? So does the LORD write His books in vain and for naught? Are we not made unto our GOD kings and priests? Are we not filled with the Holy SPIRIT and commanded to go into all the world and preach? And what did Jesus preach? *"Repent and be baptized for the remission of your sins"*? What did the Baptist come preaching and warning. *"Repent and bring forth fruit worthy of repentance."* Likewise, it is with the book of Ezekiel; he said repent and turn, so let it be our text book of instruction. *"And the WORD of the Lord came to Ezekiel again saying Son of Man I have made thee a WATCHMAN unto the house of Israel: therefore hear the WORDS at MY MOUTH and give them WARNING from ME"* (Ezek. 3:17).

Now the harsh truth here is that if we warn them not, then their blood will God require of us. They will receive God's wrath because they have not repented of their sins and we will be guilty for not giving them warning. And as Romans 3:19 says, *"That every mouth may be stopped, and all the world may become guilty before God."* Truly we are so guilty, friend, we are not doing the Master's business but our own and precious souls are being neglected. The Great Apostle says I have not ceased to warn you night and day with tears and fastings and prayers. He had to run for his life from many cities he preached in, yet he also had tens of thousands of converts and believers. So it is with some. The WORDS of LIFE fall on deaf ears and hardened hearts, but we are instructed, *"warn them for ME,"* as the Lord told Ezekiel. We are all little Ezekiels. We are watchmen to every house, to the house of the LOST. WARN THEM, WARN THEM FOR ME!

Jesus is our chief example, and what did He do for three and a half years? He came preaching and teaching and warning about God's impending wrath to come. His wrath is now very overdue against sin and oppression. Here. it is taught us in Ezekiel's book, listen to more, *"The time is come, the day of trouble is near…now will I shortly pour out my fury upon thee and will accomplish Mine anger upon thee. And I will judge thee according to thy ways… My eye shall not spare, neither will I have pity…and ye shall know that I am the LORD that smiteth thee"* (Ezek. 7:8–9).

God told Israel betimes. I am betrothed to thee, and it is the same today; we are His possession.

> *The Lord says… I am broken with their whor-ish heart which hath departed from ME and with their eyes which go a whoring after their idols.* (6:9)
> *Moreover I will make thee waste. Thus shall Mine anger be accomplished and I will cause My fury to rest upon them.* (5:13–14)

Think about it, He is our lover, we do not ignore Him without severe recompense.

> *"Now is the END come upon thee, and I will send MINE anger upon thee, and will judge thee according to thy ways, and will recompense upon thee all thine abominations"* (7:3).

THINK ABOUT IT!

> *"Destruction cometh and they shall seek peace and there shall be none"* (7:25).

It cometh, folks, it cometh. *"Jesus Christ the same yesterday, today, and forever"*; thus shall be the lot of all those that have not been BORN AGAIN and have not received Jesus Christ as their Lord and Savior.

Once again, the handwriting is on the wall, and we have been weighed in the balance and found wanting. Ezekiel tells us what is coming down the pike and very rapidly I must say. Because as Sodom and Gomorrah, the outcry against their sin entered in before God; so it is with us today. Abominations fill our LAND, and no one is speaking against them; rather, a chill attitude prevails, allowing for all kinds of sin and rebellion; as you do your thing, and I'll do mine. No, no, and again no, God says warn them to repent and bring forth fruit worthy of repentance, that the hand of God might be stayed. The hand of God is always stayed by righteous action. As in the case of Phineas, God put an everlasting blessing on his heritage and stayed the death angel in the Israeli camp because of his righteous action in slaying the couple fornicating on the altar. Thousands had already died, but God's hand of wrath was halted by Phineas's action. Praise God for mercy.

So it is with all sin, we must all turn from our sins and back to God to avoid the fury and righteous anger of God. We must abandon our abominations and turn back to the living God to avoid total destruction. How does Zephaniah instruct us?

> *Gather yourselves together, yea, gather together, O Nation not desired; Before the decree bring forth, before the day pass as the chaff, before the fierce anger of the Lord come upon you, before the DAY of the Lord's anger come upon you. Seek ye the Lord, all ye meek of the earth, which have wrought His judgment; seek righteousness, seek meekness: it may be ye shall be HID IN THE DAY OF THE LORD'S ANGER.* (Zeph. 2:1–3)

We must not be at ease; God hates ease. We must be daily before the LORD, watching and waiting. Asking, "LORD, what will you have me do? Lord guide me in thy truth." Thy WORD is TRUTH. For surely, man does no live by bread alone but by every WORD that proceeds from the mouth of GOD. That's an easy one Jesus said it many times in Matthew 4:4. Easy memorization, you need to. "Warn them for ME," the LORD says.

It is not enough for us to have our own salvation in the bag and allow our neighbor to descend into the pits of HELL because we did not have the courage or concern to speak up. If you purpose it in your heart and then pray about it, Jesus will make a way. God will surely require our complacency at His hand. Beware and fear God. What did little boy Samuel say, *"Speak LORD for thy servant heareth, here am I."* SO, LORD, speak to us and let us hear that we would not fall short. We want to walk worthy of our calling and election and be like Jesus our great example who said to His Heavenly Father, *"I HAVE DECLARED UNTO THEM THY NAME"* (John 17:26).

So let us love our neighbor as ourselves.

We have heard from Ezekiel the watchman. Now let us hear from John the Revelator.

> *I know thy works, that thou art neither cold nor hot: I would thou wert cold or hot. So then because thou art lukewarm, and neither cold nor hot, I will spue thee out of my mouth. Because thou sayest, I am rich, and increased with goods, and have need of nothing; and knowest not that thou art wretched, and miserable, and poor, and blind, and naked: I counsel thee to buy of me gold tried in the fire, that thou mayest be rich; and white raiment, that thou mayest be clothed, and that the shame of thy nakedness do not appear; and anoint thine eyes with eyesalve, that thou mayest see. As many as I love, I rebuke and chasten: be zealous therefore, and repent.* (Rev. 3:15–19)

God wants us to have a red HOT ZEAL for Him that surpasses and buries all our idols. It is fascinating to see that John as a younger man wrote that God is love and had much to say about GOD AS LOVE. Then he gets exiled to Patmos, and you see the full-blown picture of Christ JESUS as the GOD of WRATH. Not until he was old and persecuted for His testimony did he see the two sides of the coin, a God of tender love and a God of extreme WRATH. Amazing the wisdom one hundred years can bring, now the once tender young John is the oldest living Apostle of Jesus, aged and full of wisdom.

God is a God of love and justice who will recompense to His enemies a due amount of wrath. He is the Great King that doeth all things well. He is the LORD GOD that ruleth and reigneth over all the kingdoms of the Earth. The Israelites at the Red Sea witnessed the Almighty wrath upon His enemy. Pharaoh and all his chariots. Exodus 15 shows how God triumphed gloriously:

> *The horse and the rider hath been thrown into the sea… The LORD is a man of war: the LORD is His NAME… Thy right hand, O Lord, is become glorious in power: thy right hand, O Lord, hath dashed in pieces the enemy. And in the greatness of thine excellency Thou has overthrown them that rose up against thee. Thou sendest forth Thy wrath, which consumed them as stubble…*(And all the people said) *O Lord, who is like Thee, glorious in holiness, fearful in praises, doing wonders?* (Exod. 15:1, 3, 6–7)

And Isaiah adds, *"Therefore as the fire devoureth the stubble, and the flame consumeth the chaff, so their root shall be as rottenness and their blossom shall go up as dust: because they have cast away the LAW of the Lord of Hosts and despised the WORD of the HOLY ONE OF ISRAEL"* (Isa. 5:24).

God told Pharaoh I am the LORD, and there is none besides ME, but Pharaoh cast the WORDS of the Lord aside as nothing. And then the Lord said enough is enough, and the Lord totally destroyed Egypt—its people, its land, its Pharaoh, and its army, and to this day they have not been restored as a world leader. God says, "Listen to

My words and obey ME." Pharaoh listened not but mocked God so he reaped the wages of sin.

God's wrath is certain Isaiah says, "*Woe to the rebellious children saith the LORD… Behold the NAME of the LORD cometh from far, burning with His ANGER and the burden thereof is heavy: His lips are full of indignation, and His tongue is as a devouring FIRE*" (Isa. 30:27).

His tongue alone holds His wrath, how much more the full force of His being applied to our sins. The wickedness of man shall see God's wrath. His wrath is hell. For they add sin upon sin and know no shame, how hardly will God keep tolerating this. God wants us hot or cold, never complacent. Warn them for ME.

> "*Tell ye your children of it, and let your children tell their children and their children another generation*" (Joel 1:3).

What on Earth has happened to our Christian nation; our textbook used to be the Bible. Religion and the theologian were chief. How have the mighty fallen; truth is fallen in the street. No need to go to a third-world country; we have become that third-world country. There is no TRUTH only FRAUD and lies everywhere.

> *Alas for the DAY! For the DAY of the LORD is at hand, and as a destruction from the Almighty shall it come.* (Joel 1:15)
> *Multitudes, multitudes in the valley of decision for the Day of the Lord is near in the valley of decision… Put ye in the sickle, for the harvest is ripe…the press is full, the fats overflow, for their wickedness is great.* (Joel 3:14, 13)

How is it great? It is great because we have forgotten our Maker have forsaken our GOD and gone awhoring after our idols of silver and gold, mainly jobs, houses, properties, and investments. Yet God extends the olive branch and says, "Return unto me and seek My face." Then I will be your God and ye shall be my people. Amos says,

"The eyes of the Lord God are upon the sinful kingdom and I will destroy it from off the face of the Earth" (9:8).

We have heard that already, let us not let a crisis go to waste. What does Matthew 24 our favorite chapter on prophecy say from Jesus's own lips,

> *Nation shall rise against Nation, Kingdom against Kingdom. And there shall be Famines, and yes PESTILENCES, And earthquakes in diverse places. All these are the BEGINNING OF SORROWS.* (7–8)
>
> *Now learn a parable of the fig tree; When his branch is yet tender, and putteth forth leaves, ye know that summer is nigh: So likewise ye, when ye shall see all these things, know that it is NEAR, EVEN AT THE DOORS.* (32–33)

Now pretend you do not see the handwriting on the wall. Right now our predicament is self-evident, so while lies and confusion have free course in our LAND, let us put forth the TRUTH. Let us give all that are thirsty the LIVING WATER and all that are hungry the BREAD of LIFE that cometh down from the Father of LIGHT, *"Come now let us reason together though our sins be as scarlet they shall be white as snow."* Now is the time, now is the Day of SALVATION. There are lost sheep crying for help. Let us not waste a crisis, for the hearts are tender and the lost are famished for TRUTH.

> *And of some have compassion, making a difference and others save with fear pulling them out of the fire hating even the garment spotted by the flesh.* (Jude :22,:23)
>
> The Lord says, *"I will seek that which was lost, and bring again that which was driven away, and will bind up that which was broken, and strengthen that which was sick."* (Ezek. 34:16)

Hell, my friend, is in essence God's retribution to the unthankful, unholy, and ungodly sinnerman, who will not look to Him. So let us that are of the day and of the LIGHT press toward that mark of the high calling of GOD in Christ Jesus.

> *And being justified by His BLOOD we shall be SAVED FROM WRATH through HIM.* (Rom. 5:9)
> *Now unto Him that is able to keep you from falling and to present you faultless before the PRESENCE OF HIS GLORY with exceeding JOY, To the only WISE GOD OUR SAVIOUR, Be GLORY and MAJESTY DOMINION and POWER, both now and forever Amen.* (Jude :24,:25)
> *I will take the cup of salvation and call upon the Name of the Lord.* (Ps. 116:13)

LORD Jesus we call unto you to save us, save us and we shall be saved. Amen.

> *I will praise Thee, O Lord my God; with all my heart: and I will glorify THY NAME for evermore. For great is Thy mercy toward me: and Thou hast delivered my soul from the LOWEST HELL!* (Ps. 86:12–13)

When the Roll Is Called Up Yonder

1 When the trumpet of the Lord shall sound, and time shall be no more,
And the morning breaks, e-ter-nal, bright and fair; When the saved of earth shall gather o-ver on the oth-er shore, And the roll is called up yonder, I'll be there.

2 On that bright and cloudless morning when the dead in Christ shall rise, And the glo-ry of His res-ur-rec-tion share; When His cho-sen ones shall gather to their home beyond the skies, And the roll is called up yonder, I'll be there.

3 Let us labor for the Master from the dawn till set-ting sun, Let us talk of all His wondrous love and care; Then when all of life is o-ver and our work on earth is done, And the roll is called up yonder, I'll be there.

(chorus)

When the roll is called up yonder, When the roll is called up yonder,
When the roll is called up yonder, I'll be there. (J. M. Black)

The Exalted Word

He hath exalted His WORD above His great Name. Are you clueless, my friend? What should this tell us? Clueless, oh clueless generation that run to and fro from coast to coast and up and down in the LAND. What look ye for what search ye out. Is there honey in the rock my brother?

> *Surely there is a vein for the silver and a place for gold where they refine it… But where shall WISDOM be found? Man knoweth not the price thereof…neither is it found in the LAND of the Living… It cannot be gotten for gold… The price of WISDOM is above rubies.* (Job 21:1, 12, 13, 15, 18)

Furthermore, the wisest man ever to live concludes his wisdom this way, Solomon says,

> *The words of the wise are as goads and as nails fastened by the masters of assemblies, which are given from one shepherd.* (Eccles. 12:11)
> *A wise man's words…and collected sayings are like nails driven home, they put the MIND OF ONE MAN into many a life.* (Moffatt)

What does this remind you of, the Word of Life. The WORD OF GOD perhaps!?! Yes. Solomon had the wisdom of God but many a wife caused him to grow cold in his soul. Who is this wise man of the Gospels, of the WORD that Solomon is talking about? Who is this wise man? It is Jesus of course. His WORDS, His anointed WORDS, given by the Father Jesus says. These WORDS are not MINE but the Father that sent ME gave them to ME. Do we doubt? God forbid. God is not a man that He can lie. His WORDS are as good as nails driven home, the WORDS OF THE MASTER. The WORDS of the one and only shepherd of mankind. When we take up His Word, we are taking on the MIND of Christ, the Master of assemblies. And His WORDS are as nails fastened in our minds and hearts, we become ONE with Christ through his HOLY WORDS. Jesus, God the Father, the Holy Spirit are ONE GOD all breathe the same breath of salvation. Remember, GOD IS ONE.

Jesus collected sayings, have been put together by His holy disciples and apostles into the books of the gospels and epistles. But Jesus's WORDS are not confined to the NEW TESTAMENT; remember the old is fulfilled in the NEW and the NEW in the OLD TESTAMENT. God is ONE. He is the author of eternal salvation; He was there in the beginning before ever the Earth was. Second Timothy says, *All scripture is given by inspiration of GOD and is profitable for doctrine, for reproof, for correction, for instruction in RIGHTEOUSNESS"* (3:16).

Thus God speaks from Genesis to Revelation: GOD is the WORD; Jesus is the WORD.

What did the LORD say to Jeremiah, just the most major prophet ever.

> *For thou shalt go to all that I shall send thee, and whatsoever I command thee thou shalt speak. Be not afraid of their faces: for I am with thee to deliver thee, saith the Lord. Then the Lord put forth His hand, and touched my mouth. And the Lord said unto me, Behold, I have put MY WORDS in thy mouth. I have this day set thee over the nations and over the kingdoms."* (Jer. 1:7–10)

Thus, the Lord did with Ezekiel and Isaiah putting His WORDS in their mouths. Our church fathers have agreed from Jerome's Latin Vulgate to the present King James Version that these WORDS are GOD'S inspired WORDS: "Be not of a doubtful mind but believe."

Job says, *"I have esteemed the WORDS of his mouth more than my necessary food"* (Job 23:12).

In Psalm 12:6, the sweet psalmist of Israel undulates with truth saying, *"The WORDS of the LORD are pure WORDS: as silver tried in a furnace of Earth, purified seven times."* Wow!

Job is also considered one of the divines; he says, *"Oh that my WORDS were now written! Oh that they were printed in a book! That they were graven with an iron pen and lead in the ROCK FOREVER!"* (Job 19:23–24).

And guess what they are FOREVER. Jesus says heaven and Earth will pass but MY WORDS, the Holy Scriptures, shall endure forever. Job further states, *"How forcible are right words"* (6:25). The WORDS of the Lord endure forever for they are written in heaven, and God shall use these same WORDS at the LAST JUDGMENT to JUDGE MANKIND. These WORDS are the bar, wouldn't you like to know what they all say and be as Jesus and the Jews who are required to study, rewrite over and over and memorize. This is why Jesus had such a handle of the LAW. He knew and studied all the scriptures that were written up till then. This is why Paul was such a divine. He had impeccable training in the LAW under Gamalio, the most learned teacher of his day. Paul had a fabulous mind for the WORD, the apostles did not. They were unlearned fishermen but were eyewitnesses to Jesus's miracles.

The Book of Job is thought of as the oldest book of the Bible, and by some, the most popular. Job was so righteous that Ezekiel quotes the Lord as saying,

> *Though these three men, Noah, Daniel, and Job, were in it, they should deliver but their own souls by their righteousness, saith the Lord God. If I cause noisome beasts to pass through the land, and they spoil it, so that it be desolate, that no man may*

pass through because of the beasts: Though these three men were in it, as I live, saith the Lord God, they shall deliver neither sons nor daughters; they only shall be delivered, but the land shall be desolate. Or if I bring a sword upon that land, and say, Sword, go through the land; so that I cut off man and beast from it: Though these three men were in it, as I live, saith the Lord God, they shall deliver neither sons nor daughters, but they only shall be delivered themselves. Or if I send a pestilence into that land, and pour out my fury upon it in blood, to cut off from it man and beast: Though Noah, Daniel, and Job were in it, as I live, saith the Lord God, they shall deliver neither son nor daughter; they shall but deliver their own souls by their righteousness. (Ezek. 14:14–20)

"*Though these three men Noah, Daniel and Job were in it (Israel the land of Israel) they should but deliver their own souls by their righteousness saith the LORD GOD.*" Job is also one of many great scripture writers. The bar is soon to come, Jesus bar, it should behoove us to know how the script for our Judgment shall read by knowing what the Holy Writ contains. Then there will be no last-minute surprises. Jesus says, "I tell you before it happens" and the WORD also says, "Study to show thyself approved unto God a workman that needeth not be ashamed." Let's get on top of the program, folks. How were the Scribes and the Pharisees, how learned, how studied, how sharp was their scripture knowledge—very! And we, too, are required to study.

In Matthew 5:20, Jesus exclaimed, "*For I say unto you, that except your righteousness shall exceed the righteousness of the scribes and the pharisees, ye shall in no case enter into the Kingdom of Heaven.*" Think about it. Consider it; CONSIDER.

Every living soul will be accountable to the WORDS of Jesus everlasting Gospel. We conveniently have four beautiful Gospels:

St. Matthew
St. Mark
St. Luke
St. John

And John said (1:1), *"In the beginning was the WORD and the WORD was with God and the WORD was God."* So now just replace the word; WORD for Jesus, it is all one and the same, and those wonderful Gospels are salvation. Every page every verse shouts, "Read me."

John 12:47–50 Jesus says,

> *And if any man hear MY WORDS and believe not, I judge him not for I came not to judge the world, but to save the world. He that rejecteth me and recieveth not MY WORD, hath one that judgeth him: the WORD that I have spoken. The same shall judge him on that day! For I have not spoken of Myself; but the Father which sent Me, He gave Me a commandment what I should say, and what I should speak. And I know that His commandment is life everlasting: whatever I speak therefore, even as the Father said unto ME, so I speak."* Jesus plainly tells us that His WORDS will judge him in that Judgement Day. The Bible is the spoken WORDS of Jesus. He is no longer here in person, but these are His Words copied down for us. Jesus is the incarnate Word of God. It is not a choice but a command of God Almighty. *"And the times of this ignorance God winked at; but now commandeth all men everywhere to repent: Because He hath appointed a day in which he will judge the world in righteousness.* (Acts 17:30–31)

Even now He standeth at the door with the saints under the throne, crying day and night. "How long, Lord, until you avenge our blood?" Iran does not run the world, nor does Putin, nor Xi, nor Trump, nor the Queen, nor Boris Johnson but the Father in heaven ruleth over all. He ruleth over all the Kingdoms of the Earth. But the hour is late, we know; we must read the Master's good news so we will know the next move of His hand, we will then be ready.

> *"And now little children abide in Him that when He shall appear we may have confidence and not be ashamed before Him at His coming"* (1 John 2:28).

Stay upon thy God, friend; every other prop will fail, all other ground is sinking sand. Build your hopes upon the solid rock. Are you wiser than King David, who said,

> I will love thee O Lord, my strength. The Lord is my rock and my fortress,
>   and my Deliverer. My God, my strength, in whom I will trust; my buckler,
>   my shield and the horn of my salvation, and my high tower. (Ps. 18:1)

Who would know better than King David, the sweet psalmist of Israel, the apple of God's eye, the mighty warrior, the great father, the gentleman, and temple designer, the people's choice, the defender of the faith of the fathers, the king with an everlasting covenant from God, and Jesus's ancestry bloodlines. Who would know better than he; unto thee Lord shall all flesh come.

Let's see how Judgment Day looks from John's vision on the aisle of Patmos.

> *And I saw a great White Throne, and Him that sat on it, from whose face the Earth and heaven fled away. And there was found no place for them.*

And I saw the dead, small and great, stand before GOD ALMIGHTY. And the Books were opened. Another BOOK was opened, which is the Book of Life: and the dead were judged out of those things which were WRITTEN IN THE BOOKS according to his works. And death and hell were cast into the LAKE OF FIRE. And whosoever was NOT FOUND WRITTEN in the Book of Life was cast into the LAKE OF FIRE. (Rev. 20:11–12, 14–15)

Flee His wrath. Flee destruction.
Little children abide in Him.
Abide in His Word.
READ THE BOOK.

The WORD of God has never ever been diminished in importance. Right out of the gate, the Lord commanded Moses, "Write these WORDS down, write them in a book. So that they would have the standard, the record, the requirements, forever graven in stone, a guide, never to be forgotten. Because I am your God and I want you for my peculiar treasure, my inheritance forever, my people."

For the Lord's portion is HIS people; Jacob is the lot of His inheritance" And Moses said unto them, Set your hearts unto all the WORDS which I testify among you this day, which ye shall command your children to observe to do, all the WORDS of the LAW. For it is not a vain thing for you; because it is your LIFE; and through this thing ye shall prolong your days. (Deut. 32:9, 46–47)

And if thou shalt...do all His commandments which I command this day, the Lord thy God will set thee on high above all nations of the Earth: And all these blessings shall come on thee and overtake thee. The Lord shall establish thee an HOLY PEOPLE unto HIMSELF. (Deut. 28:1–2, 9)

The WORDS were to them LIFE if they would abide in them. All the blessings of heaven were theirs, peace, plenty, and victory over their enemies ALWAYS if they kept the Almighty's commands and WORDS. Their enemies would be faint of heart; the good treasures of heaven would rain down and fill their storehouses; to obey His WORD was the good life. The WORDS were a contract between God and His People, a blessing if they kept them and a curse if they did not.

> *"This BOOK OF THE LAW shall not depart out of thy mouth, but thou shalt meditate therein day and night, that thou mayest observe to do according to all that is written therein: for then thou shalt make thy way prosperous and then shalt thou have good success"* (Joshua 1:8).
>
> Also, Joshua, *"Wrote there upon the stones a copy of the LAW of Moses…in the presence of all Israel. And afterward he read all the WORDS of the Law, the blessings and curses… There was not a WORD of all that Moses commanded which Joshua read not before all the congregation of Israel"* (Josh. 8:32, 35).

God does not change; the WORD of God remains forever. The WORD is LIFE, He has magnified HIS WORD above His GREAT NAME. To trust and obey is LIFE, to obey His commands and believe is LIFE. Again He tells us and warns us that

> *[i]f thou wilt not observe to do all the WORDS of this LAW that are written in this BOOK, that thou mayest fear this glorious and fearful NAME, The Lord Thy God; Then the Lord will make thy plagues wonderful, and the plagues of thy seed, even great plagues, and of long continuance, and sore sicknesses, and of long continuance. Moreover he will bring upon thee all the diseases of Egypt, which*

thou wast afraid of; and they shall cleave unto thee. Also every sickness, and every plague, which is not written in the book of this law, them will the Lord bring upon thee, until thou be destroyed. (Deut. 28:58–61)

Jesus Christ is the same yesterday today and forever. His WORD is truth; His WORD is life. We must read it and obey it. It is the same today; His WORD is written in stone. When we turn from God and have no desire for Him, he also turns His back on us and in walks Satan with all the deals and packages of horror—sickness, disease, hunger, war, famine, perplexity of nations, confusion, and every evil spirit.

"For whatsoever things were written afore-time were written for our learning, that we through patience and comfort of the SCRIPTURES might have HOPE" (Rom. 15:4).

And how do we learn? Yes, yes, by studying. We go over and over and over the material maybe ten, twenty, one hundred, or one thousand times depending upon just how important that material is to us. We don't want to miss any angle, we want to know it well, we like to memorize it that we may remember it later on, when the book is not before us. We look, search, and make sure there is nothing we have missed.

John 8:31 instructs us, *"Then said Jesus to those Jews which believed on him, If ye CONTINUE IN MY WORD, then are ye my disciples indeed; And ye shall know the truth, and the truth shall make you free."* To continue is to dwell in, live in, to study that WORD and know it as an anchor for our soul. For it is the WORD that quickens; and makes us alive in Christ. Christ the Living WORD. But where can this WORD be found? Or heard?; Behind four walls on Sunday maybe, if you are lucky. Yes, this precious Word is scarce. It is written, that if we walk in the LIGHT as He is in the Light, we have fellowship one with another.

Years ago, the Catholics had a falling out with the idea of only laity reading Holy Writ, maybe because it was in Latin, which only scholars seem to understand. It was believed that the priests only were knowledgeable enough to rightly interpret Scripture. But this is contrary to God's teaching. Now that we have all the various Bibles in our own tongue, we need not have someone else spoon feed us. We are quite capable in this matter ourselves. As in the days of Augustine, people were paid well to mentor or teach, but the Lord says the Holy Spirit is our teacher and interpreter, and we need not that any person teach us; that is the SPIRIT'S job.

God from the beginning taught the Hebrew children the supreme importance of His WORD. It is your LIFE. It was so important that they never forgot God's WORDS. Moses went over and over this with the children. God carved His commandments with his finger in stone, two tablets of stone. And Moses said, "Take heed that you be not deceived and turn aside after other gods and ye perish quickly in the Lord's wrath." Moses said also,

Therefore shall ye lay up these my WORDS in your heart and in your soul, and bind them for a SIGN upon your hand, that they may be as front-lets between your eyes. And ye shall TEACH THEM your children, speaking of them when thou sittest in thine house, and when thou walkest by the way, when thou liest down, and when thou risest up. And thou shalt write them upon the door posts of thine house, and upon thy gates. (Deut. 11:18–20)

You see, today this would seem fanatical, but the Lord required it. His stamp or signet ring was to be all over them. They were His possession. He bought them out of bondage, and this was the Lord's ownership deal. And when the Lord looked down from heaven, His eyes would behold His obedient children that had vouched to obey and cleave to Him and Him alone. The SIGNS were a reminder to the children of the presence of God, that they were to live and breathe in His presence. Also their idol serving neighbors would have a witness that they served the Almighty Great God of heaven and Earth, the ONE TRUE God. These signs were far from fanatical they were routine. They were a special people unto God above all the nations of the Earth, and He wanted the enemies to know that. His WORD was an integral part of their lives, a blessing if they kept these WORDS or a curse if they did not. It is the same today for the Lord says, *"Heaven and Earth shall pass away, but my WORDS shall not pass away." "And of His own will begat He us with the WORD of Truth"* (James 1:18).

Begat means "to be born." We are born of the WORD. We are made alive in Christ by the WORD. Jesus said, *"marvel not that ye must be born again."* This is what He means: we are born to new life in Christ; we come alive because the WORDS are life, and they impart life, a new life in Christ. Whereas before I was blind, but now, I see. The old is past; the new is here. Jesus is that NEW LIFE. We are born of HIS SPIRIT. The children were reminded and reminded by the Man of God; Moses to cleave unto the Lord your God, for he is your LIFE.

> *"And that from a child thou hast known the Holy Scriptures, which are able to make thee wise unto salvation through FAITH which is in Christ Jesus"* (2 Tim. 3:15).

Grow up into the Lord for "Man shall not live by bread alone but by every WORD OF GOD." Jesus says, "Don't just feed the outer man. Feed the inner man with spirit food that he may become that strong spiritual man that hungers after righteousness." The Lord says be ye perfect as your Father in heaven is perfect. We can be perfect when we are covered by Jesus blood, His atoning package of Calvary. He turns none away. Throw yourself into His arms, that is where you belong. Jesus paid it all FOR YOU. The people thronged to listen to Jesus's WORDS; they pressed upon each other. Those same WORDS were carefully written down by those that loved Him most; His beloved disciples and the Great Apostle Paul. There is so much more if it had all been written down there would be hundreds and thousands more volumes; the disciples said the world itself would not be able to contain all the volumes.

Jesus's WORDS were so popular with the people of His day that they would gather in fields for days at a time to listen. Jesus tells us in Matthew that the people had been with Him for three days without eating. That is intense; three days solid without a thought for food. The Master was administering heavenly food, for He taught as one having authority and power, and the people ran after Him, even from city to city. His fame increased, for with His WORDS He healed and delivered the bound from demons. His WORDS were life and power, the disciples were amazed when Jesus spoke PEACE BE STILL to the raging storm at sea. They said even the elements, the wind and sea, obey His WORDS. What kind of man is this? Jesus gave marching orders to tens of thousands of demons with HIS WORDS. Why? Because His WORD is omnipotent and all power is His and the POWER is in His WORDS. Jesus had such fame and popularity with the majority that they wanted to make him their King.

> Let this mind be in you which was also in
> Chirst Jesus. (Phil. 2:5)
>> And again
>> But we have the mind of Christ. (1 Cor. 2:16)

Let's return to what Solomon said in Ecclesiastes 12:11: "A wise man's WORDS can put THE MIND OF one man into many a life."

Yes, this is the truth, we put on Christ Jesus when we take up His WORD. It is all one spirit and one truth; the spirit is ONE. We put on the MIND of Christ when we absorb ourselves in the WORD. We become one with GOD. He is not somewhere in outer space. He is in our hearts and minds through His WORD. I like what the prophet Hosea says,

> Then shall we know, if we follow on to know
> the Lord: But Israel slideth back as a backsliding
> heifer. (4:16)

Therefore have I hewed them by the prophets; I have slain them by the WORDS of MY MOUTH: And thy judgments are as the light that goeth forth. (6:5)

Now let's revisit the powerful WORDS of Paul to the Hebrews, a master in the WORD.

For the WORD of God is quick and powerful, and sharper than any two edged sword piercing even to the dividing asunder of soul and spirit, and of the joint and marrow, and is a discerner of the thoughts and intents of the heart. (4:12)

And John in Revelation saw.

And in the midst of the seven candlesticks one like unto the Son of man, clothed with a garment down to the foot, and girt about the paps with a golden girdle. His head and His hairs were white like wool, as white as snow; and His eyes were as a FLAME OF FIRE; And His feet like unto fine brass, as if they burned in a furnace; and HIS VOICE as the sound of many waters. And He had in His right hand seven stars: and out of His mouth went a sharp two edged sword: and His countenance was as the SUN shineth in His STRENGTH. And when I saw Him, I fell at his feet as dead. And He laid his right hand upon me, saying unto me, Fear not; I am the first and the last: I am HE that LIVETH, and was dead; and, behold, I am alive for evermore, Amen; and have the keys of hell and of death. WRITE the things which thou hast seen, and the things which are, and the things which shall be hereafter. (Rev. 1:13–19)

So the WORD of God is a sharp two-edged sword compliments of the old man on the isle of Patmos; the beloved John, disciple, and writer. John saw Jesus and His tongue was a two-edged sword. As HOSEA quotes the Lord saying He used the prophets to hew them and *"I have slain them by the WORDS of My Mouth,"* and as Paul says, the WORDS of GOD are a sharp sword going right into the soul and spirit of man. The WORD OF GOD is powerful, quick, sharper than a two-edged sword, causing you to totally UNFAILINGLY DISCERN the TRUTH. Jesus said, *"Ye do err not knowing the scriptures, nor the power of GOD"* (Matt. 22:29).

When we do not walk in the truths of the HOLY WORD of God we are susceptible to egregious errs. Jesus's WORDS are the truth.

So where can these WORDS of LIFE be found? Are they found in the land of the living? Are they behind four walls? Does your friend or neighbor know, your boss or colleagues? Who can point you to the truth. The world, my friend, is a desert wasteland. It's aims and ambitions are centered around self, not God. The world is riding a bullet train to no man's land. Knowing not either to where they are going or coming from. The blind leading the blind, looking for answers in all the wrong places, looking for answers in too many faces. The prophets foretold of this desert wasteland in Amos 8:11–13:

> *Behold, the days come, saith the Lord God, that I will send a FAMINE in the land, not a FAMINE of bread, nor a thirst for water, but of hearing the WORDS of the Lord: And they shall wander from sea to sea, and from the north even to the east, they shall run to and fro to seek the WORD of the Lord, and shall not find it. In that day shall the fair virgins and young men FAINT for thirst.*

We are in this very day, people; right now, it is that this goes on. Tourism and RVers running everywhere, searching for what they don't know. Because only God can satisfy the quench of a thirsty soul. Nothing satisfies the soul of man but God. And when he finally meets GOD, he is entirely swept off his feet. For now, he has met the lover of his soul. His lover, after so long a search, after decades in a waste howling wilderness GOD has appeared on the scene. Like Jesus told the Samaritan woman at the well if you knew who I was that asked drink of you, you would have asked ME, and I would give you LIVING WATER and you would NEVER thirst again. Jesus the Bread of Life, the Living Water, only He can satisfy the soul adrift at sea in a world of vanity. Isaiah in his fifth Gospel 55:1–3 gives us the best analogy!

> *Ho, every one that thirsteth, come ye to the waters, and he that hath no money; come ye, buy, and eat; yea, come, buy wine and milk without money and without price. Wherefore do ye SPEND MONEY for that which is not bread? and your LABOUR for that which satisfieth not? hearken diligently unto me, and eat ye that which is good, and let your soul delight itself in FATNESS. Incline your ear, and come UNTO ME: HEAR, and your soul shall live; and I will make an EVERLASTING covenant with you, even the sure mercies of David.*

The sure mercies of eternal life, now and forever.

You will hear a voice saying this is the way walk ye in it. Seek Him while He may be found, call upon Him while He is near. Draw nigh to God and He will draw nigh to you the scriptures say publish His WORD far and wide. Let the knowledge of God cover the Earth as the waters cover the sea. Bathe your soul in the fullness of HIS WORD and be satisfied. The Lord through his servants the prophets ever calls to us. But the WORD has perished the truth has fallen in the streets. Our leaders run to and fro for wisdom. They shout peace when there is none, for they have cast aside the very PRINCE of PEACE. Our iniquities have separated between us and our God, even our watchmen have become dumb dogs, failing to bark, failing to WARN of perilous times ahead.

> *"Yea, they are greedy dogs which can never have enough, and they are shepherds that cannot*

understand: they all look to their own way, every one for his gain, from his quarter" (Isa. 56:11).

First, covetousness is as idolatry, worshipping gain, can't have enough even though you already have too much. And the too much you have you spend without wisdom, restoring such animals as lions to the wilderness. Lions that have the taste of human blood in their bloodline. The saints that were torn apart and eaten by them are presently under Jesus's throne crying out for justice and revenge and you, my friend, celebrate their KILLER. Get some knowledge, wake up, and fly right, God expects wisdom of those with millions and billions. You restore lions while children in Africa are eaten by them on a daily basis. Children that have no food, no home, no shoes, no smiles, even the whole community has no water, no well. Drill a well for them. O, foolish man, and celebrate yourself with God. He will give you heavenly rewards for your love of obedience and wise charity. Wake up. Read the WORD: "Thy WORD is a light unto MY PATH." Read Psalm 119 please.

Furthermore and *second, "They are shepherds that cannot understand."* I will look at the church first. God help us here; we ordain priests and bishops that are women that are homosexuals; people have you no clue, I thought we read the same Bible? Women belong in the home, cleaning, baking, keeping the home, the children, the husband, but you say, "I have no children." Why? How can you? For two women cannot make children. Your conscience is gone; you are out of the way. And nowhere, nowhere do I see the early clergy, apostles, and disciples ordaining any women—none, none. Follow the older paths as Jeremiah commands.

Third, let's look at government and politics. Those lobbyists that corner and persuade you give gifts, give favors; in my Bible, this is bribery, the giving of favors or bribes that persuade men. But perhaps you have the NEW AGE BIBLE or the NEW WORLD ORDER BIBLE and you are also followers of Bill and Hillary and Obama that have written their own rules and thrown out the constitution and the ten commandments of God Almighty, or so it seems to me. I will tell you, Jesus Christ, I know. Paul, I know, but who are you? Common sense, people, like our beloved sons Jefferson and Paine who wrote *Common Sense.* Whose rule book ignorants? God's RULE BOOK, wake up! Our government is so corrupt and far off the correct path that every fowl bird, every sinful lying devil is exalted and hailed as politically correct. Dead wrong, friend. The communist and their party, and TV networks, and any stain of their impunity needs to be cast out of our mist—yesterday, today, and forever. Communism and atheism and the devil are bed partners and all such as are deceived thereby and the Chinese and all their cohorts hold Christians in their jails and intern Muslims. While they allow baby trafficking, child prostitution, and every evil bird of prey. These all such should not be allowed in our country brainwashing our young and tender next regeneration. Where is the rule book? Where can it be found. Where is the Book of books?

"I will speak of the glorious honour of Thy Majesty, and of Thy wondrous works" (Ps. 145:5).

Doth not wisdom cry? And understanding put forth her voice? Unto you, O man I cry, and My voice is to the sons of man My mouth shall speak TRUTH, and wickedness is an abomination to my lips Receive instruction and knowledge Rather than choice Gold. (Prov. 8:1, 4, 7, 10)

O, Earth, Earth, Earth, hear the WORD of the LORD, Ye sons of men, Ye sons made in the image of God, in the image of God you are created.

Hear me, hear me

Mr. Putin,

Mr. Xi,

Mr. Trudeau.

Your Majesty the Queen,

Our own Trump,

Mr. Netanyahu,

Mdm. Merkel, etc., etc., etc.

OBEY GOD, NOT MAN, and ye shall live.

The Lord possessed me (WISDOM) in the beginning of His way, before His works of old. I was set up from everlasting, from the beginning, or ever the earth was. When there were no depths, I was brought forth; when there were no fountains abounding with water. When He gave to the sea His decree, that the waters should not pass His commandment: when He appointed the foundations of the earth: Then I was by Him, as one brought up with Him: and I was daily His delight, rejoicing always before Him [I WISDOM]. (Prov. 8:22–24, 29, 30)

O Earth Earth Earth hear the WORD of the LORD. (Jer. 22:19)

"He that reproveth a scorner getteth to himself shame: and he that rebuketh a wicked man getteth

himself a blot. Reprove not a scorner, lest he hate thee: rebuke a WISE MAN, and he will love thee. Give instruction to a WISE MAN, and he will be yet wiser: teach a just man, and he will increase in learning." (Prov. 9:7–10)

OBEY GOD, OBEY GOD! His eyes are upon you.

Hear, O, leaders, ye kings and queens and princes, ye prime ministers, presidents all those in authority, and ye peoples. Listen to GOD, His way is perfect. His WORDS have been tried, proved, His ways cast up. Go toward God, friend, and escape hell beneath. Do not think to strive against God and succeed, your portion will be with the wicked who are as the troubled sea. They have no rest. I speak to the high ones, the top dogs, those in authority, and those that reign. I speak to you first because the world looks up to you as leaders. All eyes are upon you, to whom much is given to him shall much be required by the LORD of GLORY.

OBEY GOD rather than man.

Jesus's words are *"For what is a man profited if he shall gain the whole world and lose his own soul… For the SON OF MAN shall come in the glory of His Father with His Angels, and then He shall reward every man according to his works"* (Matt. 16:26–27).

"The first shall be last and the last first." Where have you been people, since when is good, evil and evil good? Since when is unrighteousness, righteous? Please common sense, folks, please, the Lord pleads.

The Lord pleads in Jeremiah 6:10,

> *To whom shall I speak, and give warning, that they may hear? behold, their ear is uncircumcised, and they cannot hearken: behold, the WORD of the Lord is unto them a REPROACH; they have no delight in it." "Thus saith the Lord, stand ye in the ways, and see and ask for the old paths, where is the good way and walk therein and ye shall find*

rest for your souls, but they said, we will not walk therein. (6:16)

Therefore, *"The Lord will reject them."* (6:30)

You think because you are a big shot here that you will have impunity with GOD? No, no, no, you like everyone else will crumble in His holy presence, your face will willingly be in the dirt. You will then be crying out for MERCY. Show mercy now, then He shall give you mercy. Obey the LORD'S commands, not your generals. Oh yes, you think to do their bidding I know, because if not they might overthrow you with a coup.

Fear not man but obey GOD, you leaders,
You BOSSES, or GOD will render likewise to you:
JUDGMENT WITHOUT MERCY equals HELL,
For you! Yes, you!

Listen up, friend, for GOD is talking to you. Yes, you, LEADERS, by His servant Beatrice. Do not say you were not told. I am myself telling you to get clued into GOD or you will end up in a merciless HELL. God has spoken. I am telling you leaders God's Words. Don't go to your grave being ignorant. This is the twentieth century, not 6,000 BC. Wake up to God's program or go to a devil's hell. And yes we, you, me and all else are equal, EQUAL BEFORE GOD, so listen up.

To reject GOD is to buy a front row seat in hell. Hell is eternal darkness, no light, always dark. Hell is all pain, all sorrow, all depression without any hope, all hope is lost, done away with, does not exist. Hell is torment forever and ever and ever. You cannot buy your soul out of hell; there are no exits, only one entrance guarded by the angels of GOD. Your soul is so important that Christ died to save your soul. The human man, flesh of Jesus was sentenced to death by Roman crucifixion. He suffered and died in your place. He took your punishment and put it upon Himself to set you free from the debt you owed and could not pay. Your salvation is a free gift from God; like I said, you cannot buy your way out of hell, but you can come to Jesus and ask, it is his free gift.

The things that were written aforementioned were written for our learning. What God says to one He says to all. Jeremiah is warning...

> *The SIN of Judah is written with a PEN OF IRON, and with the point of a diamond: it is graven upon the table of their heart... Thus saith the Lord; CURSED BE THE MAN that trusteth in man, and maketh flesh his arm, and whose heart DEPARTETH FROM THE LORD.* (Jer. 17:1, 5)

Mr. Putin, Mr. Xi, and all the rest, you cannot make nuclear weapons your defense of power, God must be your arm of power and defense. These weapons will count for nothing in the Day of God's wrath. If God be for me who can be against me. God is always the determining factor. The Lord holds the world in His hand. Return to your God Mr. Putin and Mr. Xi.

> *"Give glory to the Lord your God, BEFORE HE cause darkness, and before your feet stumble upon the dark mountains, and, while ye look for light, he turn it into the shadow of death, and make it gross darkness"* (Jer. 13:16).

There is only one way off this planet and that is through Jesus Christ. It's His planet and his show. And whosoever shall call upon the NAME OF THE LORD SHALL BE SAVED. Whosoever—whosoever! Thus saith the LORD.

The Lord hath exalted His WORD above His great NAME. We have only to know how great His NAME is to understand the glory of His WORD.

Paul's Epistles to the Philippians tells us how great...

> *And being found in fashion as a man, He humbled Himself, and became obedient unto death, even the death of the cross. Wherefore God also hath*

highly exalted HIM, and given HIM a NAME which is above every name: That at the NAME of JESUS every knee shall bow, of things in Heaven, and of things in Earth and all things under the Earth and every tongue will confess that Jesus Christ is the Lord to the glory of God the Father. (2:8–11)

So we see the hierarchy here and Jesus's Name reigns over all, all and everything. His NAME is Lord of lords and King of kings. There is nothing higher. He is the MOST HIGH, and He has set His WORD above his GREAT NAME. So now we arrive at the supreme legitimacy of HIS WORD. HIS WORD is LAW. Everything and body comes and goes through this fire; HIS WORD.

And Paul says in Romans 2:16, *"In that day when God shall judge the secrets of men by Jesus Christ according to my Gospel."* The Gospel is His Word; it is LAW and judgment is coming and as the crow flies that day does not seem far off.

All roads lead to Rome, right? Wake up! Hello! All roads lead to Jesus Christ through His WORD. Here is the WORD of the Lord as it came to Hosea. I like the book of Hosea it gets right down to nuts and bolts, and God really, really reveals His heart here. The Lord said to Hosea,

The land hath committed great whoredoms in departing from the LORD. Hear the WORD of the LORD…for the LORD hath a controversy with the inhabitants of the LAND because there is no truth, nor mercy, nor knowledge of GOD in the Land… My people are destroyed for lack of knowledge…they have forgotten the Law of Their God… there is none among them that calleth unto ME… That crieth unto ME with All their Heart… Sow to yourselves in righteousness, reap in mercy; break up your Fallow ground: for it is time to seek the LORD, til He come and rain righteousness upon you. Then

shall we know if we follow on to know the LORD.
(1:2, 4:1, 4:6, 10:12, 6:3)

IT IS TIME.

How do we call upon the LORD, we go to Psalms in the Bible and read David's WORDS of the LORD; they will tell us. How do we seek the LORD, by combing through all sixty-six books, especially the Gospels. Man shall not live by bread alone but by every WORD of GOD. How many times must Jesus tell us this? We take up the WORD into our hands and begin to digest His BREAD, His sustenance, His WORD. Believe me, King David had the lead here. Paul said, "Follow ME as I follow Christ." Let's follow David in His Psalms.

> So foolish was I and ignorant:
> I was as a beast before THEE.
> Nevertheless I am continually with THEE.
> Thou has holden me by my right hand.
> Thou shalt guide me with thy counsel. (73:23–24)

David's Psalm 119 is rather unique. All 176 verses of the Psalm talk of GOD's LAW, which is GOD'S WORD. If a person takes all the words that mean law in all 176 verses and substitute WORD or WORDS, it has the same meaning.

> *Quicken me after thy loving kindness so I shall keep the testimony of thy mouth. Forever O Lord, Thy word is settled in Heaven.* (119:88–89)
> *The Law of Thy Mouth is better unto me than thousands of gold and silver. Let my heart be sound in thy statutes; that I be not ashamed.* (72:80)
> *It is time for Thee, Lord to work. For they have made void thy LAW. I love thy commandments above gold… I also esteem all thy precepts concerning all things to be right.* (126–128)

My zeal hath consumed me, because mine enemies have forgotten THY WORDS. Thy WORD is very pure; therefore Thy servant loveth it... Thy righteousness is an everlasting righteousness and Thy LAW is the TRUTH. (139, 140, 142)

My heart standeth in awe of thy WORD. "I rejoice at Thy WORD as one that findeth great spoil." "Great peace have they which love THY LAW." (161, 162, 165)

I have gone astray like a lost sheep; seek Thy servant; For I do not forget THY COMMANDMENTS. (176)

The eyes of all wait upon Thee; and thou givest them their meat in due season. (Ps. 145:15)

All ye like sheep have gone astray; we have turned everyone to his own way and the LORD hath laid on HIM the INIQUITY OF US ALL. (Isa. 53:6)

Thy WORD is TRUE from the beginning: and everyone of Thy Righteous Judgments Endureth FOREVER. (Ps. 119:160)

Sanctify them through THY TRUTH: O Holy God Thy WORD is TRUTH. (John 17:17)

O Earth, Earth, Earth, HEAR THE WORD OF THE LORD. (Jer. 22:29)

I believe Thy WORD is TRUTH, O LORD.
My mind is enlightened.
I believe Thou art begetting ME,
Through THY TRUTH.
Thank you, Jesus,
Lord and Savior,
AMEN.

Ho everyone that thirsteth,…come buy wine and milk without money and without price.

—Isaiah 55:1

Knowest Thou Not

Art thou a master of Israel and knowest thou not these things?

—John 3:10

*For I say unto you, that except your righteousness, shall
exceed the righteousness of the scribes and Pharisees, ye
shall in no case enter into the kingdom of Heaven.*

—Mark 5:20

*Knowest thou not that whosoever shall not receive the Kingdom
of God as a little child, he shall not enter therein.*

—Mark 10:15

The Gospel is simple; it is plain, It is not convoluted; come out of the confusion of the world and put on the true holiness of the new man.

Knowest thou not. "The Good Samaritan" is someone helping an unfortunate in a tragic situation. Opening your door, your purse, your table, and going so far out of your way it hurts, and your pockets are empty.

Knowest thou not that the testimony of Cornelius like so pleased the Lord; his prayers and alms giving came before the face of Jesus and He sent an angel to his house. Be envious and use his example.

Knowest thou not that Jesus command *"to go and make disciples of all nations"* is to you. Did you say, "Here am I, Lord, send me"?

Knowest thou not that we are to tell the TRUTH; to our neighbor, if they hate you for speaking the truth, so be it.

Knowest thou not "that it is He (the Almighty) *that sitteth upon the circle of the Earth"* (Isa. 40:22)

And we are as nothing to Him.

Knowest thou not that the message is "repent for the kingdom of God is at hand." The confusion in our land would be dispelled if we repented. Repentance brings healing in Every quarter of the city.

"And He treadeth the wine press of the fierceness and WRATH of Almighty GOD" (Rev. 19:15).

"Art thou a master of Israel and knowest thou not these things." Think of all GOD'S PRECIOUS PROMISES to usward and still we want to argue and make excuses why we cannot abide in the presence of Jesus and have His will fulfilled through us. God help us, folks, for all the kings, prophets, and priests that have gone before us have desired to see and know the things we have witnessed through the disciples and apostles to this day. Make no excuse friend, Jesus Himself has given us the road map for our sojourning here below. Make no excuse, come before His GRACE bearing precious fruit that He may SAY, WELL DONE. Look into His precious face and behold the glory of your substitutionary sacrifice. He took your place. The man, the God, Jesus, tread Calvary's Road alone for you: *"I have trodden the winepress alone"* (Isa. 63:3).

What does that beautiful hymn say?

"Turn your eyes upon Jesus Look full in His wonderful face. And all the things of Earth Will grow strangely dim, in The light of His glory and grace." So let us lay our every sin aside and run this race with our confidence strong and sure in our solid ROCK, Jesus. We are more than conquerors, MORE, MORE than conquerors. For what does Ephesians advise us?

"Wherefore Jesus saith when He ascended up on high, He led captivity captive" (4:8).

THAT SOUNDS LIKE VICTORY TO ME!

> *And if so be that ye have heard Him and been taught by Him, (how through the WORD) as the truth is in Jesus (the WORD is truth), put off the old man…and put on the new man, which after Christ is created in righteousness and true Holiness.* (21–24)
>
> *And follow Peace with all men and Holiness, without which no man shall see the Lord.* (Heb. 12:14)

Again how do we get holiness? Yes, by putting on Jesus, staying in His Presence, by meditating in His yes, HOLY WORD, which is apt to make you holy if you stay with it and meditate long and often. Yes, Jesus can make the most vile sinner clean again, like a newborn baby. What does Newton say in "Amazing Grace." Ah yes, He saved a wretch like me. We are all wretches before Christ takes hold; we just wear different costumes. Beware if a man thinks he is some great one when he is nothing, he deceives himself.

> *For it is written, I will destroy the wisdom of the WISE, and will bring to nothing the understanding of the prudent. Where is the wise? where is the scribe? where is the disputer of this world? hath not God made foolish the WISDOM of this world? For after that in the wisdom of God the world by wisdom knew not God, it pleased God by the foolishness of preaching to save them that BELIEVE. For the Jews require a sign, and the Greeks seek after wisdom: But we preach Christ crucified, unto the Jews a stumblingblock, and unto the Greeks foolishness; But unto them which are called, both Jews and Greeks, Christ the POWER of God, and the WISDOM of God. Because the foolishness of God is wiser than men; and the weakness of God is stronger than men. For ye see your calling, brethren, how that not many wise men after the flesh, not many mighty, not many noble, are called: But God hath chosen the foolish things of the world to confound the wise; and God hath chosen the WEAK things of the world to confound the things which are mighty; And base things of the world, and things which are despised, hath God chosen, yea, and things which are not, to bring to nought things that are: THAT NO FLESH SHOULD GLORY IN HIS PRESENCE. But of Him are ye in Christ Jesus, who of God is made unto us wisdom, and righteousness, and sanctification, and redemption: That, according as it is written,*

HE THAT GLORIETH, LET HIM GLORY IN THE LORD. (1 Cor. 1:19–31)

No, there is none good no not one we are all as filthy rags. And even King Solomon in all His splendor was not, could not, even equal the beauty of the lily Jesus said. Now how is that for setting us straight. And the great ones and the rich think they have all sufficiency and know not that they are wretched, blind, naked, and worthless before God. They did not trust in God but trusted in their own merit. Many a deceived fool will say to Jesus on that day; well, I bet you are glad to see me Jesus. He will say, "How is it that you think you know me?" Do I know you? When was My Name ever on your lips? King Jesus will say, "Depart from Me. I do not know you." God wants us holy doing good and full of good works. If you know God, friend, then be ye Holy and put on Christ, who is your LIFE. Paul instructs us in Ephesians

> *Be ye therefore followers of God, as dear children; And walk in love, as Christ also hath loved us, and hath given himself for us an offering and a sacrifice to God for a sweet smelling savour… For ye were sometimes darkness, but now are ye LIGHT in the Lord: walk as children of LIGHT: (For the fruit of the Spirit is in all goodness and righteousness and truth;) Proving what is acceptable unto the Lord… See then that ye walk circumspectly, not as FOOLS, but as WISE, Redeeming the time, because the days are evil. Wherefore be ye not unwise, but understanding what the WILL of the Lord is… Submitting yourselves one to another in the fear of God. (5:1, 2, 8–10, 15–17, 21)*
>
> *Knowing that whatsoever good thing any man doeth, the SAME shall he receive of the Lord, whether he be bond or free. And, ye masters, do the same things unto them, forbearing threatening:*

*knowing that your Master also is in heaven; neither
is there respect of persons with GOD.* (6:8–9)

"Art thou a master of Israel and knowest thou not these things?"
Why then with all this knowledge do we keep hurting ourselves. Why
do we deprive ourselves of living on the mountain top, no instead we
wallow in the mire of the sewage ducts. Yes, like the one they sent our
Holy Prophet Jeremiah to, below the grates of the city street. Had it
not been for the righteous Ethiopian Eunuch Ebedmelech, he would
have died there and drowned in that mire.

> *Then took they Jeremiah, and cast him into
> the dungeon of Malchiah the son of Hammelech,
> that was in the court of the prison: and they let down
> Jeremiah with cords. And in the dungeon there was
> no water, but mire: so Jeremiah sunk in the mire.
> Now when Ebedmelech the Ethiopian, one of the
> eunuchs which was in the king's house, heard that
> they had put Jeremiah in the dungeon; the king then
> sitting in the gate of Benjamin; Ebedmelech went
> forth out of the king's house, and spake to the king
> saying, My lord the king, these men have done evil
> in all that they have done to Jeremiah the prophet,
> whom they have cast into the dungeon; and he is
> like to die for hunger in the place where he is: for
> there is no more bread in the city. Then the king
> commanded Ebedmelech the Ethiopian, saying,
> Take from hence thirty men with thee, and take up
> Jeremiah the prophet out of the dungeon, before he
> die.* (Jer. 38:6–10)

Love your neighbor as yourself; how many languages do I have
to write this in seeing ye are dull of hearing? What don't we get about
this North Korea, Malaysia, China, Africa, Russia, and most of Asia?
What don't we understand? And in every inhumane and dark place
of the globe where a brother is oppressed and denied civil liberties,

freedom of religion, and basic human needs? Why do we hurt ourselves so? We all came from one Mother and Dad, our first parents Adam and Eve. Like it or not they were the first two people on Earth, the beginning of all the HUMAN RACE. Now don't go into some scientific false malarkey, just believe Jesus's WORDS and you will understand we are all family; we are all cousins and brothers. And you can get the details from our Almighty Maker and Creator in heaven. Look up, folks, it's looking better all the time; Jesus said it. I believe it; that settles it, says Corrie Tenbaum. *"Heaven is nearer and the way groweth clearer, yes I'm in the Glory Land way"* says the old hymn. I am, I surely am, praise God!

> *God created man in His own IMAGE…male and female* [Adam and Eve]. *(Gen. 1:27)*
>
> *These are the families of the sons of Noah, after their generations, in their nations: by these were the Nations divided in the Earth after the flood. And the whole earth was of one language, and of one speech. And it came to pass, as they journeyed from the east, that they found a plain in the land of Shinar; and they dwelt there. And they said one to another, Go to, let us make brick, and burn them thoroughly. And they had brick for stone, and slime had they for mortar. And they said, Go to, let us build us a city and a tower, whose top may reach unto heaven; and let us make us a name, lest we be scattered abroad upon the face of the whole earth. And the Lord came down to see the city and the tower, which the children of men builded. And the Lord said, Behold, the people is one, and they have all one language; and this they begin to do: and now nothing will be restrained from them, which they have imagined to do. Go to, let us go down, and there confound their language, that they may not understand one another's speech. So the Lord scattered them abroad from thence upon the face of all the earth: and they*

left off to build the city. Therefore is the name of it called Babel; because the Lord did there confound the language of all the earth: and from thence did the Lord scatter them abroad upon the face of all the earth. (Gen. 11:1–9)

We will know all the details by and by so accept God's Word and realize the big picture is getting smaller. Our neighbor is anyone in the world. The two golden commandments are love God with all your heart mind and strength and love your neighbor as yourself. And this is the fulfillment of the LAW; all the law is fulfilled in this the Golden Rule. Jesus teaches us in St. Matthew's gospel.

Therefore all things whatsoever ye would that men should do to you, do ye even so to them: for this is the law and the prophets. (Matt. 7:12)
And the King shall answer and say unto them, Verily I say unto you, Inasmuch as ye have done it unto one of the least of these my brethren, ye have done it unto ME… Then shall He answer them, saying, Verily I say unto you, Inasmuch as ye did it not to one of the least of these, ye did it not to Me. (25:40, 45)

"Be ye PERFECT as your Father in Heaven is perfect." Jesus is our EXAMPLE, folks. He loved and loved and kept on loving. Now Jesus is in heaven. He ascended, His body ascended, but His Spirit is here in the hearts of those that choose Him as their Savior. And He left all the world for us to love. He said, "Do as I have done. Follow Me. I am the WAY. Open thine eyes please and smell the roses." Our Lord Jesus Christ wants all men to put on the robes of Sonship (by choice and the other choice is damnable). If we choose the Lord Jesus and His WAY, we become a SON OF GOD, a co-inheritor of all the Father has. He asks only one thing our love. When you do it to others you do it to Jesus. Wake up you heads of state you big bosses, Kings in the Earth. I'll tell you why because pretty soon you will

have to report in to your BOSS and that is JESUS, my friend. It is Jesus that you, YOU, YOU, will give account to. Hear me now; don't look back from the grave and tell me, "She was so, so, so very right" and "How did she know?" It's called the school of hard knocks. And, friend, I am so in love with Jesus, the words are causing fire to come out of my mouth, "Jesus, Jesus, Lord and Savior." No greater love no greater love than a man lay down His life for his friend. JESUS PAID IT ALL; all the debt I owed, HE PAID. He thrills me through and through. The way I feel makes me wonder how the disciples could keep their feet on the ground. He thrills me. Jesus does; nothing else only Jesus. Now hear again as Jesus tells us He is coming back to Earth one more time.

> *When the Son of man (Jesus) shall come in his glory, and all the holy angels with him, then shall he sit upon the throne of his glory: And before him shall be gathered ALL NATIONS: and he shall separate them one from another, as a shepherd divideth His sheep from the goats: And He shall set the sheep on His right hand, but the goats on the left. Then shall the King say unto them on His right hand, Come, ye Blessed of MY FATHER, INHERIT THE KINGDOM PREPARED FOR YOU FROM THE FOUNDATION OF THE WORLD: For I was an hungred, and ye gave me meat: I was thirsty, and ye gave me drink: I was a stranger, and ye took me in: Naked, and ye clothed me: I was sick, and ye visited me: I was in prison, and ye came unto me. Then shall the righteous answer him, saying, Lord, when saw we thee an hungred, and fed thee? or thirsty, and gave thee drink? When saw we thee a stranger, and took thee in? or naked, and clothed thee? Or when saw we thee sick, or in prison, and came unto thee? And the King shall answer and say unto them, Verily I say unto you, Inasmuch as ye have done it*

unto one of the least of these my brethren, YE HAVE DONE IT UNTO ME. (Matt. 25:31–40)

Does this sound like we should be throwing people into refugee camps and dislocating whole nations so we can build air defense stations and grab oil and other resources. Naked, you came into this world and naked you will leave it. So what are you bustin your arse about? NOTHING, NOTHING, hear me? NOTHING. If you had one ounce of common sense, you would pick up the Holy Book and begin to read about God, then give all your citizens that you hold prisoners in their own land, religious freedom. Back to the real world of Jesus folks.

Jesus is desperately wanting our love. He wants us to know Him and fall in love with Him. To KNOW and LOVE HIM IS TO HAVE IT ALL. As the lyrics go, "You know nothing until you know God and His love." Nothing, not a thing, all you have and know does not amount to a hill of beans. I don't care if your arse is sitting on a mountain of gold until you have arrived at Jesus, it's all zero. All of life for you is zero and in the Judgment Day (which looks to be soon); all you have done in this life will be burnt up. So kiss this world and everything in it goodbye; it will melt with a FERVENT HEAT. I see the lava flowing.

Jesus is the cornerstone that all this world stumbles around and until God knocks you off your high horse like Saul of Tarsus (Apostle Paul) and wakes you up; you ain't got nothin', babe. Nothing. All this world of vanity is going up in smoke when the Father pulls the plug in HIS CLOSING ACT. He's growing tired of this old, sinful world and the END is NEAR, so buckle up. Jesus says, "I am the best so you can forget the rest." Forget this world and get Jesus in your sights. The Jesus lens is due now for your life.

Let us not forget our brothers and sisters in those countries that have not a civil constitution; that is, one for the people by the people, just what kind of nonsense do you espouse in government? Yes, the government is to serve its citizens and help them and represent them. Instead, you have a party of one, a tyrant that serves a bunch of arrogant bullies that deprive the masses—the poor of a better life.

Are you for real? Are you maybe another Nero? Grow up, folks, this is not the STONE AGE, yet you act like it, using and abusing your poor. I mean really, really poor, to line your pockets. God will get you… God will avenge! This world is a mess, and you cannot fix it. Jesus does the fixing. He went to Calvary, and that is the ultimate FIX IT. For now, leave the work to Jesus and Father knows best. Jesus said you cannot change one hair of your head to white or gray. Why do you think you can do anything else? Jesus says, "Without me you can do nothing." Turn, turn now!

And you, Mr. Bolshevik General, you ol' farm boy, son of a gun. Your rap sheet reads a trail of blood, that was the old order and way; make them bow or take their head. It is a new order since Jesus coming, He shed the last blood that needed to be shed—no need, no need for such agony of soul, friend; find peace in Jesus. He is the Prince of Peace. It's hard to sleep at night, with nightmares as yours, hacking people to pieces, climbing the ladder of power on the blood of peasants who were better than you. My friend, God's Way is the right way. Embrace peace of mind with Jesus; there is no other path. The alternative is damnation in hell. "Come let us reason together," saith the Lord. You lust and war and have not because your way is the path of death and destruction. "There is no PEACE to the wicked," saith the Lord; he is as the troubled sea spitting up foam and gagging. Your way is sad, you thought; you were trained. Motherland, oh crap friend, your motherland will go up in smoke if you do not take hold of the nail-scarred hands of Jesus. When the God of heaven comes to Earth, dies on a cross and then resurrects Himself and preaches only love; this, this is what's worth looking into. He said, "My miracles themself testify that I am God." Wake up, pal, this is the twentieth century; we are not back in the stone age clubbing our neighbors over the head with a bat. But I see you are a stiff-necked, hard-nosed; die hard and would rather continue in your sins and grow sadder and more confused and troubled as the days wear on. We are all cousins; it's like killing your son or daughter. And God is not taking your willful ignorance lightly. Oh yes, you may sear the brain with vodka and soak what little conscience you have left, but beware, Job says beware…

> *Because there is wrath BEWARE Lest HE take thee away with His stroke: Then a great ransome cannot deliver thee. Thou hast fulfilled the judgment of the WICKED: JUDGMENT and JUSTICE take hold on thee.* (Job 37:18–19)
>
> *And so you meet the full doom (of your wicked ways) God's judgment grips you.* (Job 17 Moffatt)
>
> *The Lord loveth JUDGMENT.* (Ps. 37:28)
>
> *Know therefore that God Almighty exacteth of thee LESS, less, than thine iniquity deserveth.* (Job 11:6)
>
> *The wicked is reserved to the Day of Destruction, they shall be brought forth to the Day of Wrath.* (Job 21:30)
>
> *Is not thy wickedness great? And thine iniquities infinite? Thou hast…stripped the naked of their clothing. Thou hast not given water to the weary to drink, and thou hast witholden bread from the hungry.* (Job 22:5, 6)
>
> *Acquaint NOW thyself with HIM, and be at peace: Thereby good shall come unto thee. Receive, I pray thee, the law from His MOUTH, and lay up HIS WORDS in thine heart.* (22:21, 22)
>
> *As David says "Let death seize upon the wicked and let them go down quickly into Hell."* (Ps. 55:15)

It is time, it is time to REPENT; come out from among them, and be ye separate saith the Lord and your sins will be blotted out. There is only one good and right thing and that is God the Father, and you must come to Him through His son Jesus Christ of Nazareth, who paid the price to absolve your sins on the Cross of Calvary. And don't be some old fool that thinks to wait till his death bed to square things with the Almighty. Behold "today is the day of salvation." Right now, friend, you may be one breath away from eternity; you don't know. Make it right NOW.

> Seek ye the Lord while He may be found, call ye upon Him while He is near:
> Let the wicked forsake his way, and the unrighteous man his thoughts: and let him return unto the Lord, and He will have mercy upon him: and to our God, for He will abundantly pardon.
> For My thoughts are not your thoughts, neither are your ways MY WAYS, saith the LORD. For as the Heavens are higher than the Earth, so are MY WAYS higher than your ways, and MY THOUGHTS than your thoughts. (Isa. 56:6–9)

What does it say? My God, no, it says OUR GOD. He is your God too, so wise up get on the right team. Oh yeah, you thought you were doing right, in whose eyes? There is only ONE to consider, and that's Our Lord Jesus Christ. Who did you think baby Jesus was anyway, some little toy you take out at Christmas and Easter and then shelf Him for the rest of the year. No, no, no. Our help is in the NAME of the Lord; it is the Lord we serve first off, not ourselves and not our country. Besides, your country is corrupt—no religious freedom, no liberties. Wake up; this is now, that was then. Your soul is what is important, not the silly government. God reigns and if your government does not like the size of that, then do as Peter who says we ought to obey and serve God not man. God first, friend. Help yourself to some freedom. *"Whom the son sets FREE he is free indeed."* *"God is love."* He is pure love, fall into His arms now and behold His beauty.

This is the twentieth century, so get it right; we, each and every soul, are created in the image of God. You are to esteem others better than yourself. And as you do unto your brother so you do unto Me, "THUS SAITH THE LORD," and this is how God will judge you, hear me. Actually hear the beloved Prophet, and Priest Isaiah, of Royal Blood he was.

> *Ah sinful Nation, a people laden with iniquity, a seed of evildoers, children that are corrupters: they have forsaken the Lord, they have provoked the HOLY ONE of Israel unto anger, they are gone away backward... And when ye spread forth your hands, I will hide MINE EYES from you: yea, when ye make many prayers, I will not hear: your hands are full of BLOOD. Wash you, make you clean; put away the evil of your doings from before MINE EYES; CEASE TO DO EVIL; LEARN TO DO WELL; seek judgment, relieve the oppressed, judge the fatherless, plead for the widow. COME NOW, AND LET US REASON TOGETHER, saith the Lord: though your sins be as scarlet, they shall be as white as snow; though they be red like crimson, they shall be as wool. If ye be willing and obedient, ye shall eat the good of the land: But if ye refuse and rebel, ye shall be DEVOURED with the SWORD: for the mouth of the LORD HATH SPOKEN IT.* (Isa. 1:4, 15–20)

If you have taken away his religious freedom, you do not have a prayer pal. God will soon take away all your freedoms as you soon stand before the Almighty. This is not an audience with the pope, rather with the One to be feared, the King of kings, the ALMIGHTY. If you have beaten your brother with many stripes because of his faith, God will soon beat you with many stripes. Be not fooled. GOD IS THE AVENGER; HE IS THE ULTIMATE AVENGER. What God says He will most surely do!

> For the Day of Vengeance is in Mine Heart...for I will tread them in Mine Anger, and trample them in My fury; and their BLOOD

shall be upon My Garments, and I will stain all My Raiment. (Isa. 63:3–4)

For the Lord put on Righteousness as a breastplate…and He put on the garments of VENGEANCE for clothing, and was clad with ZEAL as a cloak. According to their deeds, accordingly He will repay, fury to His ADVERSARY, recompense to His enemies. So shall they fear the NAME of the Lord from the West, and His GLORY from the rising of the sun. (Isa. 59:17–19)

"He will not spare in the Day of Vengeance." (Prov. 6:34)

For we know Him that hath said, VENGEANCE belongeth unto ME, I will recompense saith the Lord. And again, The Lord shall judge His People. It is a fearful thing to fall into the HANDS OF THE LIVING GOD! So let us draw near with a true heart in full assurance of faith, having our hearts sprinkled from an EVIL conscience. (Heb. 10:30–31, 22)

What are you thinking? What kind of government is that? You may just as well set Satan up on a pedestal in your town square because he is running you and your country. You are just a pawn in Satan's hand, working his ill toward mankind. God forbid that you call evil, good and black, white; this is damnable before God. Wake up, folks. We shall soon be looking Jesus Christ Lord and Savior of the UNIVERSE, eye to eye. Then how arrogant and boastful will you be? You will crumble at HIS AWESOME MIGHTY POWER and PRESENCE, realizing you were on the wrong team.

Enter into the rock, and hide thee in the dust, for FEAR OF THE LORD, and for the glory of his majesty. The lofty looks of man shall be humbled, and the haughtiness of men shall be bowed down, and the LORD ALONE shall be EXALTED in that day. For the day of the Lord of hosts shall be upon every one that is PROUD and LOFTY, and upon every one that is LIFTED UP; and he shall be brought LOW. (Isa. 2:10–12)

Light is LIGHT, folks, not DARK. Jesus is LIGHT, all LIGHT. Come let us reason together, common sense, please. Turn the light upstairs on and behold Jesus and become the man you were meant to be an awesome man made in God's image. I repeat, *"in that ye have done, it unto the least of these ye have done it unto ME."* Thus saith the Lord.

"Art thou a master of Israel and knowest thou not these things?" When you get totally desperate sinner man, you will reach for your Bible because you know there God will have a conversation with you. Yes, that's right, a CONVERSATION and God will speak to you and you will faint for not knowing it was possible. Friend, God is a SPIRIT, and He is everywhere, and at any time you look or call or acknowledge Him with a head bowed or arms raised to heaven, even eyes closed, you just think Christ and He is there for you. He is always one step ahead of you, friend. He created all things; they only continue because He wishes it. The moment He does not want you to continue you are like so out of here. Like Job says, He will take thee away with His stroke. Then a very great ransom cannot give you a second more of life. And you will instantly be standing before Him, and your own conscience will bear witness as He gives you a thumbs-up or an outta here, begone into everlasting damnation. God is not mocked. He holds a second by second account of your life. Woe is me, friend, and woe is you as Paul says, "I press toward the mark," but not as though I had already attained; not even the Great Apostle is sure, how much less you and I. What did the Almighty say to Cain?

And the Lord said unto Cain, Why art thou wroth? and why is thy countenance fallen? If thou doest well, shalt thou not be accepted? and if thou DOEST NOT WELL, SIN LIETH AT THE

DOOR...in the field CAIN rose up and slew his brother Abel. And the Lord said unto Cain, Where is Abel thy brother? And he said, I know not: AM I MY BROTHER'S KEEPER? And the Lord said, What hast thou done? THE VOICE OF THY BROTHER'S BLOOD CRIETH UNTO ME FROM THE GROUND! And NOW THOU ART CURSED. (Gen. 4:6–11)

Friend, it is a serious thing to fall into the HANDS OF THE LIVING GOD. Yield unto Him today and find forgiveness of all thy sins. "Mark the end of the perfect man, his end is PEACE." Yield to God while He is still there. We are not promised any tomorrows; behold, today is the day of salvation. You cannot play Russian rou-lette with God; tarry not. You are outside the ark of safety. Only those souls within the ark were saved from the flood. Jesus is the ARK, come in and dine with Jesus.

Go to ye rich men weep and howl for the miseries that shall come upon you. Who hath warned you to flee the WRATH to come. There is that maketh himself rich, YET HATH NOTHING: There is that maketh himself poor, YET HATH GREAT RICHES. (Prov. 13:7)

He that oppresseth the poor reproacheth His MAKER: but he that honoureth the poor (honoureth His MAKER). (Prov. 14:31)

All the WAYS of a man are clean in his own eyes. (Prov. 12:15)

Ye do ERR not knowing the SCRIPTURE nor the power of God" "A good man obtaineth FAVOUR of the Lord. (Prov. 12:2)

The wrath of the King is as messengers of death: but a wise man will pacify it. (Prov. 16:14)

And he that sat upon the throne said, Behold, I make all things new. And he said unto me, WRITE:

FOR THESE WORDS ARE TRUE and faithful.
(Rev. 21:5)

*And I heard a great voice out of heaven say-
ing, Behold, the tabernacle of God is with men,
and he will dwell with them, and they shall be HIS
PEOPLE, and God himself shall be with them, and
be their God. And God shall wipe away all tears
from their eyes; and there shall be no more DEATH,
neither sorrow, nor crying, neither shall there be
any more pain: for the former things are PASSED
AWAY.* (Rev. 21:3, 4)

And he said unto me, IT IS DONE. I am
Alpha and Omega, the *beginning and the end. I will
give unto him that is athirst of the fountain of the
water of life freely. He that overcometh shall inherit all
things; and I will be his God, and he shall be My Son.
But the fearful, and unbelieving, and the abomina-
ble, and murderers, and whoremongers, and sorcerers,
and idolaters, and all liars, shall have their part in the
LAKE which burneth with FIRE and BRIMSTONE:
which is the second death.* (Rev. 21:6–8)

Choose you this day, friend. God has set before us life or death,
heaven or hell. We will all be there on JUDGMENT DAY. God will
resurrect us from the dead and set us down before Him. Every eye
shall see Him upon His throne; His throne was created for Judgment.

Why do you think you can get off scot-free with murder and
slaughter of the innocent. You should be prostrate before God crying
out, *"I am not worthy"* to even come before you. *"Have mercy on me O
Son of David."* Why you do so ERR dear one, open your eyes and behold
*your own misery and despair and emptiness and believe as St. Augustine,
"for thou hast made us for THYSELF and restless is our heart until it
comes to rest in THEE." The Confessions of St. Augustine,* pg. 5.[1]

*"And Peter boldly proclaims where could I go LORD, THOU hast
the WORDS of LIFE."* You knock yourself out and for what to leave
a fortune to your babes—wrong again. We are to labor for the Lord

not for children that have two good arms and legs and are gifted with many talents. God needs you working for Him, not oppressing the poor to gain more wealth. Wake up now, or you will wake up in the hot place. Jesus says, He who loses His life for My sake shall gain it. Only what's done for Jesus folks. If you are building treasure for an inheritance, you are wrong. Jesus says, "Lay up for yourselves treasure in heaven by giving, giving and giving."

Plainly, I can see dictators, tyrants, prime ministers, kings, queens, presidents, emperors, chiefs of the people, the unduly wealthy even chief surgeons and Wall Street hoity-toities, on and on the list goes. I see you all on a chain gang in hell unless you repent and flee the wrath to come. Did our sins not crucify HIS ONLY SON. Did we not attempt murder on Him for three and a half years? I recall Moses interceding for the whole nation of Israel and God was reluctant, but granted Moses His request but said the Almighty; I will remember and punish them some other more convenient time. You see, nothing escapes God. And Jesus Christ Our Lord said and commanded us, *"Seek ye first the kingdom of God and His righteousness."* He did not say work, play, govern, make money; no, He said, "Me first, seek Me first. My yoke is easy." He says and God is incapable of lying. Escape the WRATH to come, the last book, the apocalypse or Revelation as we call it, tells us about His WRATH that will be poured out.

How dare you communist nations infiltrate us and try to bring us down. Clearly you are in darkness, and you desire the LIGHT to be put out because your deeds are evil. If you were of the LIGHT you would come to the LIGHT. America is the world's hope of freedom, and you clearly hate that; misery likes company. We were founded on God. That is why you hate us. You covet our land and resources: you hate righteousness, you hate God, and you want to destroy or possess all things in your path. It is the fool, the fool that denies God, you deny all righteousness.

> *The fool hath said in his heart, there is no God. They are corrupt, they have done abominable works, there is none that doeth good. The Lord*

looked down from heaven upon the children of men to see if there were any that did understand and seek God. They are all gone aside, they are all together become filthy: There is none that doeth good, no, not one. Have all the workers of iniquity no knowledge? Who eat up my people as they eat bread, and CALL NOT UPON THE LORD (A Psalm of David 14:1–4)

It is not good to accept the person of the wicked to overthrow the righteous in judgment. (Prov. 18:5)

"He that justifieth the wicked and he that condemned the just, even they both are abomination to the Lord." (Prov. 17:15)

And what did the Master say? *"I do always those things that please My father."* Jesus is; He is our example. He said Himself that He is our example. We are to please the Lord God Maker of heaven and Earth, not our government, our country, our anything, Jesus God Creator, first and last is He. First, we make Him first. We put Him and Him alone on the Throne of our hearts, to let Him reign in our lives as King. King Jesus, *"Are you the king of the JEWS?"* I am, the great I am. He is a jealous God, no flesh shall stand in His sight; we all will bury our faces in the dirt before Him. He will be exalted in the Earth. He will be exalted in that day. He reigns, He rules, He is God Almighty. Come bow before Him. To you, folks, that are entranced with your beauty, your power, your wealth, He will not share His glory with another. He is the JEALOUS God and LORD over ALL CREATION.

"Art thou a Master of Israel and knowest not these things?" "Verily, verily, I say unto thee, we speak that we do know, and testify that we have seen… That whosoever believeth in Him should not perish, but have ETERNAL LIFE" (John 3:10–11, 15).

I believe the master declared it this way "All the WORD to all the WORLD," and anyone defying this command or obstructing it in any way is directly in DEFIANCE to the COMMAND OF GOD. Be converted to the cause or make yourself scarce, brother; this is GOD'S WORLD. The DAMNATION of hell rests on your head if you are obstructing the Gospel to anyone. Woe unto you, my friend. Did not Jesus call Judas friend? Hey, Mr. Bossman, governor in chief, dictator, tyrant, you know your way is wrong. While you still have a conscience, turn around, make your crooked paths straight and find praise from all. While you still have your sanity reach out to God, and He will heal your broken spirit. You know persecuting peace loving Christians is a sin; you know, that you know. Change. You are actually fighting against the Holy God of heaven, and He will knock you off your high horse like He did the Apostle Paul. You are fighting the wrong battle, *What wait I for, if God be for me, who can be against me.* God is love and those that know Him, LOVE. Woe is you to strive against the holiness of God, you vile, naked, depraved wretch. You think you are in a catch-22 now, but when God catches you, it will be your damnation. Fear God; He is your BOSS. Yes, yes you have an appointment to stand before Him, what will you say? If you are not standing with Jesus you are so very deluded, and of all men most miserable. How many souls have you led into hell by failing to be a godly leader that leads in the paths of righteousness. It is time for you to turn around before the wages of sin overwhelm you, and the confusion of terror overtake you, as it did King Nebuchadnezzar. From the chief to the beggar, we must all realize who RULES in the REALM of the MOST HIGH. The fear of God is the beginning of wisdom or is it the beginning of sanity? Come boldly to HIS THRONE OF GRACE and cast yourself down, while there is still time. Listen and see what happens to the proud and evil King of Babylon, Nebuchadnezzar.

The tree that thou sawest, which grew, and was strong, whose height reached unto the heaven, and the sight thereof to all the earth; Whose leaves were fair, and the fruit thereof much, and in it was meat for all; under which the beasts of the field dwelt, and upon whose branches the fowls of the heaven had their habitation: It is thou, O king, that art grown and become strong: for thy greatness is grown, and reacheth unto heaven, and thy dominion to the end of the earth. And whereas the King saw a Watcher and an Holy One coming down from Heaven, and saying, Hew the tree down, and destroy it; yet leave the stump of the roots thereof in the earth, even with a band of iron and brass, in the tender grass of the field; and let it be wet with the dew of heaven, and let his portion be with the beasts of the field, till seven times pass over him; This is the interpretation, O king, and this is the decree of the MOST HIGH, which is come upon my lord the king: That they shall drive thee from men, and thy dwelling shall be with the beasts of the field, and they shall make thee to eat grass AS OXEN, and they shall wet thee with the dew of heaven, and seven times shall pass over thee, till thou know that the MOST HIGH RULETH IN THE KINGDOM OF MEN, and giveth it to whomsoever he will. And whereas they commanded to leave the stump of the tree roots; thy kingdom shall be sure unto thee, after that thou shalt have known that the HEAVENS DO RULE. Wherefore, O king, let my counsel be acceptable unto thee, and BREAK OFF thy SINS BY RIGHTEOUSNESS, and thine iniquities by shewing mercy to the poor; if it may be a lengthening of thy tranquility. All this came upon the king Nebuchadnezzar. At the end of twelve months he walked in the palace of the king- dom of Babylon. The king spake, and said, Is not this great Babylon, that I have built for the house of the kingdom by the might of my power, and for the honour of my majesty? While the word was in the king's mouth, there FELL A VOICE FROM

HEAVEN, saying, O king Nebuchadnezzar, to thee it is spoken; The KINGDOM IS DEPARTED FROM THEE. And they shall drive thee from men, and thy dwelling shall be with the beasts of the field: they shall make thee to eat grass as oxen, and seven times shall pass over thee, until thou know that the MOST HIGH RULETH IN THE KINGDOM OF MEN, and giveth it to whomsoever he will. The same hour was the thing fulfilled upon Nebuchadnezzar: and he was driven from men, and did eat grass as oxen, and his body was wet with the dew of heaven, till his hairs were grown like eagles' feathers, and his nails like birds' claws. And at the end of the days I Nebuchadnezzar lifted up mine eyes unto heaven, and mine understanding returned unto me, AND I BLESSED THE MOST HIGH, and I PRAISED and HONOURED HIM that LIVETH FOR EVER, WHOSE DOMINION is an everlasting dominion, and HIS KINGDOM is from generation to generation: And all the inhabitants of the earth are reputed as NOTHING: and he doeth according to HIS WILL in the ARMY OF HEAVEN, and among the inhabitants of the EARTH: and NONE CAN STAY HIS HAND, or say unto HIM, WHAT DOEST THOU? At the same time my reason returned unto me; and for the glory of my kingdom, mine honour and brightness returned unto me; and my counsellors and my lords sought unto me; and I was established in my kingdom, and excellent majesty was added unto me. Now I Nebuchadnezzar praise and extol and honour the King of heaven, ALL WHOSE WORKS ARE TRUTH, and his WAYS JUDGMENT: and those that walk in PRIDE he is able to ABASE. (Dan. 4:20–37)

Do you get the message here? Why, oh, why do you try to beat Jesus at HIS OWN GAME? What a fatal situation, you are in to think any of us peons would even try to fight God. Absurd it is, friend, utterly. Yes, I am speaking to heads of state and country, to kings, queens, prime this, and governor in country that. You need to repent and set your kingdom in order. Then on the day that Great Judgment Day, you will not be ashamed. Why do you set yourself and your kingdom above Jesus? Jesus came to serve not to lord it over us; he that is first shall be last. He that is greatest must be minister of all Jesus says. Will Jesus say "well done" on Judgment day, or will He say, "I don't know you." We shall see Him face to face and behold His scars, His nail prints, will He be proud of your work and say well done? Let us not deceive ourselves, for the wisdom of this world is foolishness with God.

> *For it is written He taketh the WISE in their own craftiness, and again the Lord knoweth the thoughts of the wise, that they are vain.* (1 Cor. 3:18–19)
> *Man's goings are of the Lord; how then can a man understand his own way.* (Prov. 20:24)
> *The highway of the righteous is to depart from evil: he that keepeth his way preserveth his soul.* (Prov. 16:17)

REMEMBER

"The eyes of the Lord are in every place, beholding the evil and the good." We are never out of God's reach, we are ever before Him; do all things as though Jesus was standing right in front of you, because HE IS! Game on; Jesus is winning. HE DIED AT CALVARY! Make no mistake it is His game, His rules, HIS KINGDOM, stand in the way and He will mow you down. Jesus's last words on Earth were *"Go ye into all the world and preach the Gospel of the Kingdom, baptizing in the name of the FATHER, the SON, and the HOLY GHOST*

and he that believeth shall be saved, but he that believeth not shall be DAMNED" (Mark 16:15–16).

Will you with regret recall these WORDS as you stand before Jesus? Knowing that you stood in the way of salvation to hundreds of thousands and maybe millions of souls. Do we need to ask what your destiny is? Is it not the PLAIN TRUTH, idiot, that you were Satan's tool. Duh? Have you sent men and women, has your government and leaders of the past, sent men and women to Siberian prison camps: 60 degrees below zero, no shoes, no clothes, no heat, no food, no toilet, no water—JUST PURE PAIN. God will surely do the same to you. "With what measure you meet it shall be measured to you again." REPENT and be converted that your SINS may be washed away. It is never too late in God's game; remember, the thief on the right. "This day thou shalt be with Me in paradise Jesus said to him." Minutes before he died, amazing even on the cross Jesus is WORKING.

"Art thou a master of Israel, and knowest not these things?" Behold, Jesus parable of the help that was hired by the vineyard owner.

> *"And when the man had agreed with the labourers for a penny a day, he sent them into his vineyard"* (Matt. 20:2).

But the owner kept hiring throughout the day. So some worked all day while others worked six hours, some three hours and some one hour, but the owner paid them all the same as if they had put in a full day's work. This is Jesus, and he is giving us all the same wage, the same benefits, as if we struggled a lifetime in HIS VINEYARD. Crazy, isn't it? But this is God's great big, insane, possessive LOVE for us. A person can come through minutes before the clock strikes midnight and still be saved. What an awesome God we serve. Don't you just crazy love Him. Who is that? Patsy Cline that sings "Crazy." Crazy for loving you. That is God, a zillion times to infinity. Crazy to go to a dead man's CROSS, to go to a shameful grave marked as an outcast; Jeremiah nor Paul had nothing on Jesus. No, Jesus paid it all with His insane love for us. Let's just love Him back; let's just adore Him. No one is trying to condemn anyone. No Jesus did not descend to Earth from His Throne ON HIGH in GLORY to waste His time condemning.

Rather He brought the GOOD NEWS of His way of salvation, through His SON, JESUS Christ. He wants us to all repent and turn back to our MAKER, HIM, Jesus of Nazareth, the lowly carpenter, Joseph and Mary's Son. And if it were not for the grace of God Almighty, there go I. His grace, His saving grace is a fountain of LIFE.

No, no God forbid we are not condemning, RATHER pleading, begging that you too would set your heart to SEEKING GOD. Is not this the method that our great King David used to become great before God? He set his heart to seek the Lord, and the Lord was always found of him. Talk about giants, great men of the Earth this is one, God called him the apple of HIS EYE.

> *"David speaketh concerning Him, I foresaw the Lord always before my FACE, for He is on my right hand, that I should not be moved: Therefore did my heart rejoice, and my tongue was glad, moreover also my flesh shall REST IN HOPE"* (Acts 2:25–26).

(Think on Jesus constantly like King David.)

Yes, I am talking to you big ones, Wall Street hoity-toities, CEOs, bankers, aristocrats, kings in the Earth. Such as Israel called them heads of tribes, princes, lords, valiant, rich, powerful, wise men of the Earth, ready to lay down their lives for the cause. We are begging, pleading, see the LIGHT, look through the lens of Jesus. He is the greatest of the greatest of ALL MEN EVER to grace this Earth with his bodily presence. Are you getting the picture yet? Jesus, Jesus, Jesus!

Just give it a chance, friend. Jesus did not say, "Oh good, your beliefs are great. They are peaceful." No and no. He stated clearly, bluntly, profoundly, "I AM THE WAY." Don't tell me stupid and say all ways lead to the same thing. Jesus did not say I have a religion or a church for you to follow. No, He said, "FOLLOW ME, I AM THE WAY." Throughout the four Gospels, Jesus delivers parables concerning this WAY of His, the STRAIGHT and NARROW WAY, and few there be that find it He says. SO if God is tapping at your door, respond quickly, before the devil destroys the leading of the Holy Spirit.

Act quickly. REPENT is the WORD of the day and the hour. Come humbly before the King of kings. Draw nigh to HIM, and He will draw nigh to you. *"Come home, come home, ye who are weary come home,"* the song plays. Repent and find something you have never even dreamed about. *"Knowledge of the HOLY ONE!"* One might think knowing a worldly king would be hot. But even this is the lowest point on the totem pole compared to knowing King Jesus. Nothing compares. Repent and find out things you have never known or experienced.

> *The Lord hath made bare His Holy Arm in the eyes of all the Nations, and all the ends of the Earth shall see the SALVATION of our God. So shall He sprinkle many nations. The Kings shall shut their mouths at Him: for that which had not been told them shall they SEE. And that which they had not heard they shall CONSIDER.* (Isa. 52:10, 15)

For God and mankind's sake, REPENT now so I can stop writing and being enslaved to this notebook and pen. It's nice outside. I would like to smell the roses and plant a garden so I can have health to stay on this Earth a few more years, days, hours, whatever. This room is stuffy, and there is a nice breeze outside on this very hot day. Please REPENT so we can lay down our pens and fix dinner and walk the dog. It can be a lonely enterprise sitting all day with a pen or paintbrush; no one gets it till you've tried it.

And our beloved "Painter of Light"[2] is gone. How sad when selfish greed is the rule and we destroy our hometown heroes. Yes, he was fabulous. He was to painting what Elvis was to music. Like Elvis, he meant so much to so many. And some folks just had to have his next painting to add to their already robust collection. They loved his little speeches; they loved his paintings. They just loved the man. Now lots of folks have been deprived of their joy, sunshine and light. Sad a great loss of a wonderful soul, enough good things cannot be said about the man. "Painter of Light" pointing us to Jesus. Jesus is the LIGHT OF THE WORLD.

Great man, great loss, yes in his own words he was a modern-day Caravaggio.

So if we walk in the LIGHT as He is in the LIGHT, we will all REPENT. If we repent then we will humble ourselves and do all the above. Be a good Samaritan; give all, share the truth with friend, neighbor, and foe. Paul keeps using these words "in the END TIME, and Jesus said to discern the times." Watch and pray for it will be unexpected, at an hour that we know not. As in the days of Noah, Jesus said, "So shall it be, they laughed at Noah then suddenly rain lots of rain. Be ready be watching; it is a mind bender to me how some folks only open God's Book on the Sabbath; this idea has no urgency, no diligence.

The book is our roadmap, and every day is a journey. So HOW LOST ARE WE? The Book is our sword, our weapon of warfare. Keep it handy open on the table with a small size in your pocket, and you are more likely to war a good warfare. Like it or not, the devil wars against your soul; ignore this fact to your own detriment. The Book is our enlightenment; it is our wisdom. When we went to school, we read our textbooks to get the smarts. Likewise, GOD'S WORD makes the simple wise. God LAUGHS at the WISDOM OF THIS WORLD. We just don't get it, folks, it's deeper than all of us put together. "Oh, the depth of the RICHES and WISDOM of GOD." We have not even scratched the surface yet.

Oh, to linger always in His Presence.

Whom have I in Heaven but THEE? And there is none upon Earth that I desire besides Thee. (Ps. 73:25)

For they that are far from Thee shall perish.
Thou hast destroyed all them that go a whoring
from Thee. (Ps. 27)

Pretty strong WORDS. I would have thee cold or hot, so REPENT. Turn again to the living God, turn around, and keep your footsteps in the WAY EVERLASTING. Read, think Jesus, Jesus, and more Jesus. Don't let an opportunity slip to witness, get with the program, be working in the Master's vineyard. Freely ye have received; freely you should be witnessing, praying and gushing out those prayers and thoughts to the one that SAVES.

> *Little children, it is the last time.* (1 John 2:18)
> *The night is far spent, the day is at hand: let us therefore cast off the works of DARKNESS, and let us put on the armour of LIGHT.* (Rom. 13:12)
> *Thy word is a lamp unto my feet, and a light unto my path."* *"Come let us reason together."*

Friend, our righteousness must exceed that of the Scribes and Pharisees. Lord Jesus, grant it, amen.

"Art thou a Master of Israel and knowest thou not these things?"

Nothing But the Blood

1 What can wash a-way my sin? Noth-ing
but the blood of Je-sus;

What can make me whole a-gain? Noth-ing
but the blood of Je-sus.

2 For my par-don this I see—Noth-ing but
the blood of Je-sus;

For my cleans-ing, this my plea—Noth-ing
but the blood of Je-sus.

3 Noth-ing can for sin a-tone—Noth-ing
but the blood of Je-sus;

Naught of good that I have done—Nothing but the blood of Je-sus.

4 This is all my hope and peace—Nothing
but the blood of Je-sus;

This is all my righe-eous-ness—Nothing
but the blood of Je-sus.

(Refrain)

Oh! Precious is the flow That makes me
white as snow;

No oth-er fount I know, Noth-ing but the
blood of Je-sus. (Robert Lowry)

The Loss of All

But what things were gain to me, those I counted LOSS for Christ. Yea doubtless, and I count all things but LOSS for the excellency of the KNOWLEDGE OF CHRIST Jesus my Lord: for whom I have suffered the loss of all things and do count them but dung, that I may WIN CHRIST.

—Philippians 3:7–8

Mark his steps for when we run the race, we run all. Do we count as Paul counts? All things are dung in comparison to Christ. He put Christ on the pedestal of his heart and treasured Him and Him alone. He lost all; his place of honor in the temple, his high standing as a chief and zealous Pharisee, and says all those things were dung anyway. God made him blind for three days, and when he came to, he saw the world with Jesus's eyes. Are we of the same mind? We should be, for he says, "Follow me as I follow Christ, and not as though I had already attained either.

We cannot do enough. He says, lay down your distractions and idols; he says, so that Christ can be all in all to you. The flesh wars against the spirit, they blend like oil and water. Lay down your idols people and behold His wonderful face, and the things of Earth will grow strangely dim. Oh, how the gold has lost its glitter. Lay aside the robes of vanity and put on Jesus's cloak of humility and meekness.

For as many of you as have been baptized
into Christ have put on Christ.

For, brethren, you have been called into liberty; only use not liberty for an occasion to the flesh, but by love serve one another.

For all the LAW is fulfilled in one WORD, even in this; Thou shalt love thy neighbor as thyself. (Gal. 3:27, 5:13–14)

Christ has called us out of this world. "Be ye separate," saith the Lord. Walk the paths I walked. Jesus says, "I am your example. My NAME is JEALOUS for I am a JEALOUS God, have not those IDOLS before ME. Sell what you have and give to the poor and you shall have treasure in heaven." Cherish the fact that God has called you and given you the KNOWLEDGE of Himself; yes, the KNOWLEDGE of JESUS CHRIST. Cherish this fact, guard it with your life, lay your trophies down at His nail-scarred feet, and be as Mary and kiss those beloved feet. Hold on to the knowledge of Him as the hid treasure in the field that when the man found it he went and sold all that he had in order to purchase the field. Hold onto the knowledge of Him as the pearl—yes, the *Pearl of GREAT PRICE*, which the merchant was looking for.

> *"Who when he had found the one Pearl of Great Price went and sold all that he had, and bought it"* (Matt. 13:44–46).

And so it was with the Great Apostle Paul, when he had found the Hid Treasure and the Pearl of Great Price he traded in his filthy rags for the knowledge of Jesus Christ. He was now holding the costly Pearl; why would he even care about the dung of this world? For John says to love the world is to be the enemy of God, love not the world, he says, neither the things that are in the world. We cannot serve two masters, for either we will hate the one and love the other or vice versa. How hardly can we win Christ if we are clinging to the treasures and idols of this world. They are nothing. When we meet Jesus and Paul did, the gold of this world loses all its glitter. Thus, he says I have suffered the loss of all and do consider it all, but dung that; I may win my beloved Christ and Savior, my costly pearl, costly treasure, the Pearl of Great Price is Jesus Christ.

Our idols must go, our Lord is long suffering, *"And the times of this ignorance God winked at; but now commandeth all men everywhere to 'REPENT'"* (Acts 17:30).

Thou shalt have no other gods before ME, for I am a JEALOUS GOD. The idols are other gods; if you would know they are things we are privy to. In your heart, God must take preeminence; the heart must be swept and the idols thrown out.

> *Moses saw the calf and the dancing: Moses' anger waxed hot, and he cast the tables out of his hands, and brake them beneath the mount.* [Those tables Moses had received from God on Mt. Sinai, two tables of testimony, tables of stone written with the finger of God.]
>
> *And he took the calf which they had made and burnt it in the fire, and ground it to powder, and strawed it upon the water, and made the children of Israel drink of it.* (Ex. 32:19–20)

This is nothing compared to the dregs of the Lord's WRATH and FURY that the wicked and unbelieving shall soon be made to drink of. And furthermore, Moses commanded the priests to slay three thousand of them because of the molten calf they had worshipped and sacrificed to. We do the same friend; we are at ease in Zion. We take lightly the KNOWLEDGE of the HOLY ONE. And to our shame and ease, there are many who do not have the knowledge of God, they have one foot in hell's door and are petering on the other. What's that old expression, "Oh, holy cow, now you know the rest of the story." We are at ease as though the World will go on forever, and the Lord flatly states that it will melt at His return at His Holy presence, since the Earth did not receive Him and embrace Him at His first coming. No, Jesus Christ was hunted down like a LAMB for slaughter, by insane Herod's SS squad.

We are so relaxed and comfortable that the enemy has moved right in and set up radio and television stations to promote their propaganda, and we call it freedom of speech. God calls it laying down our arms and allowing the devil to rule and reign. We spend our days and hours worshipping our possessions as IDOLS. We worship our houses, our lands, properties, jewelry, cars, trucks, pools, gardens, and our accomplishments, as though we were Renaissance men, as Michelangelo, Da Vinci, Bach, Handel, or Mozart. Even these talented men held Jesus as LORD and GOD upon the table of their hearts, and that is doubtless why God so gifted them because they glorified GOD.

We are at ease in Zion and have sacrificed to the Golden Calf by giving all our time to obtain these objects of our fancy, which are now objects of our worship. Yes, we sacrifice to the golden calf of our harvested goods upon the Earth. Yes, we worship like the children of Israel, we worship the golden calf of our worldly possessions. And the LORD told Moses, *"Thou shalt worship no other god: for the LORD whose NAME is JEALOUS, is a JEALOUS GOD"* (Exod. 34:14).

And Job says, *"Naked I came out of my mother's womb, and naked I shall return thither: the LORD giveth and the LORD taketh away; blessed be the NAME of the Lord"* (Job 1:21).

Like the Great Apostle we MUST SAY. I have suffered the LOSS of all things and do count them as dung that, I may win Christ Jesus My LORD, my prize, my treasure, my reward, my CROWN. You will take none of this, has been stuff with you, *Job says.* And you will be oh so willing to give all your GOLD, just to have another year to do for Jesus. So let's wake up now, NOW, not then, the night surely cometh and is creeping upon us, when no man can work anymore.

Let us scrutinize JOB here for a little space. Job that rich man from the Land of UZ was a God-fearing, evil-despising, perfect man, as the Lord Himself testified to Satan. And Satan challenged God concerning JOB and said to God, but if you take away all he has,

> *He will curse thee to thy face... Now Satan came to present himself before the Lord, and the Lord said unto Satan, From whence comest thou?*

And Satan answered the Lord, and said, FROM GOING TO AND FRO IN THE EARTH, and from walking up and down in it. And the LORD said unto Satan, Hast thou considered MY servant JOB, that there is NONE like him in the Earth, a perfect and an upright man, one that feareth GOD, and eschewth, evil? And still he holdeth fast his integrity, although THOU movedst me against him, to destroy him without cause. (Job 2:1–3)

So God allowed Satan to have at him. And Satan through a course of events took all that Job had away. He, thus, suffered the LOSS OF ALL. Now Job was the RICHEST MAN in all of the east. He had tens of thousands of camels, sheep, oxen, many servants, and ten beautiful children, whom he deeply loved. But God allowed JOB'S love and loyalty to HIM to be tested by taking every last thing he possessed away, even his comforts and allowed him to be sacked with horrible pain. His wife says to him, "You are so finished, Job, just curse God and die, and it will all be over with." No, Job arose, rent his clothes, shaved his head, and threw himself in the dirt and worshipped GOD. He maintained his integrity and said,

My righteousness I hold fast and will not let it go as long as I live. (Job 27:6)
In all of this JOB sinned not, nor charged God Foolishly. (Job 1:22)

In fact, God-fearing Job said,

THOUGH HE SLAY ME, YET I WILL TRUST HIM. (Job 13:15, Job's most famous Words)

And reasoned with sound common sense that *"[m]an that is born of a woman is of few days and full of trouble as the sparks fly upward"* (Job 14:1).

Nevertheless, he said I will trust God; however, his lips were full of complaints, arguments, and justifications as we see here.

> *The Almighty hath destroyed me on every side... He hath stripped me of my glory, and taken the crown from my head.* (Job 19:9–10)
> *He hath put my brethren far from me and mine acquaintance are verily estranged from me.* [Hum, sounds familiar.] (Job 19:13)

Job continues his arguments:

> *Oh that my words were now written! Oh that they were printed in a book! That they were graven with an IRON PEN and LEAD in the ROCK FOREVER! For I know that my REDEEMER LIVETH, and that he shall stand at the latter days upon the Earth. And though after my skin worms destroy this body, yet in my flesh shall I see GOD (on His Judgement Day).* (Job 19:23–26)

Job only asks for a small platform so he can have his say; then he says you can *"mock on,"* after all he is the main character in this thesis. Now Job answered his friends' arguments this way.

> *Hear diligently my speech and let this be your consolation* [as it is mine he says]. (Job 21:2)
> The wicked is reserved to the day of the destruction of Almighty God, they shall be brought forth to the DAY of WRATH. (Job 21:30)
> *He knoweth the way that I take: when He hath tried me, I SHALL COME FORTH AS GOLD. My foot hath held HIS steps, HIS way have I kept and not declined. Neither have I come back from the commandment of His lips: I have esteemed the WORDS of HIS MOUTH MORE THAN MY*

NECESSARY FOOD." [same thing Jesus said].
(Job 23:10–12)

Hm, where have I heard that before. Mathew 4:4 perhaps? So Job not only withstood the LOSS OF ALL THINGS, the Lord also allowed Satan to put a continual reproach upon him. Job was smitten with boils from head to toe and sat in ashes scraping himself with a pot shard, and his three friends being *"miserable comforters"* accused him of sinning. False, false. Boo, they said these punishments and losses were due to sin in his life, totally opposite; that's old law thinking, because Job was the righteous sinless one, the apple of God's eye, and that is why God allowed Job this testing.

Job proved to God and Satan that his love was not just skin deep. His wife remember said, *"Dost thou still retain thine integrity, curse God and die."* Was she psychic? Did she have a little of the devil in her, for she knew if he cursed God, game over, with Satan declared as the winner. Thus, Job would have defeated his life's purpose and lost out with God in the final portion of the race. Disappointing GOD, his trainer who had allowed this wager against Job's soul. Can we even imagine what goes on in heaven and the conversations Satan has with Jesus about His servants here below.

Remember, Satan is the accuser of the brethren, the Father of Lies; goodbye Progressive left, hello, Jesus on the right. Satan upsets heaven night and day running a smear campaign against God's loving servants. But since our Lord's victory of the cross we are now cloaked in the SAVIOUR'S RIGHTEOUSNESS not our own. And it is no longer I that sin, for with our minds we serve Christ faithfully, but our flesh may keep on sinning rather unwillingly. Fear not, for we have an advocate with Jesus Christ the Righteous; thus, we can remain on the straight and narrow. Our old man, that old sinful nature wants to continually look back to the onions and leeks of Egypt, but we thank God for our continued victory in Jesus Christ.

Oh yes, the good ol' wife trial, so Job kindly reminds his wife.

Thou speakest as one of the foolish women
speak. What? Shall we receive good at the hand of

God, and shall we not receive evil? In all this did not Job sin with his lips. (Job 2:10)

I would seek unto God, and unto God would I commit my cause. [Memorize this please!] (Job 5:8)

Bravo, Job is staying the course and is keeping his garments unspotted from the sins of the world. Which has turned its back on JESUS CHRIST as its mainstay and is gone away backward stumbling in DARKNESS. Shh…don't mention the name JESUS in public (that is a mortal sin).

No pain, no gain, take for instance our beloved GENERAL and priest, JOSEPHUS, born to a precious lineage of theologians, scholars, lawyers, and aristocrats he perceived before he began the RACE to toughen his character against the weakness of the flesh. He thus made endurance training his prerequisite for running this race of life. Bunyan himself said this world is a desert wilderness, being interpreted to mean, not a great place to be if you do not possess God. Paul says, *"Lest by any means I should run, or had run in vain"* (Gal. 2:2). Josephus embraced the hardships of the desert testing grounds. For three years in his teens (sixteen to nineteen), he made the desert his home as a stoic, with minimal means of comfort for survival. I do absolutely mean minimal. Read for yourself in *The Works of Josephus* (p. 1).[1] It would be difficult to proclaim here all of Josephus's attributes. He was at once a general, a priest, a politician, a lawyer, and later, yes later he was the bishop of Jerusalem. Please read the book because he is so much more. This I want to say he was a great man of GOD, exhibiting qualities of wisdom, strength of character and understanding that only the rare and few have. Rich and rare he was, yes, rich and rare.

He quailed seditions and revolts all his life, trying to protect the Jewish people who thought that maybe, just maybe they were strong enough to take on the insanity of the Roman Empire with sticks and stones. Well done, Josephus. Can't wait to meet you, that is after I praise Jesus for ten thousand years.

I am telling you all that to tell you this; we must suffer the LOSS of all things, we must suffer the LOSS of our comforts. We must be girded with strength for our pilgrimage through this world of horrors. To the victor goes the crown, given by King Jesus, the way up is down, down on our knees. He that endures to the end the same shall be saved bringing his sheaves with him. Josephus, like Job, like the Apostle Paul was a strong man of endurance, for think of it. He commanded battalions of men for years. His character and pure wisdom like Paul brought him before kings, emperors, and tyrants and won him special favor with Rome and the Romans loved him. They admired his FAITH and TEACHINGS so much so that he had influence in planting and watering the precepts of Christianity with the Roman court. And many times was accused of treason by his fellow Jews for his strong bonds with Rome. The Scripture is true and says, *"When a man's ways PLEASE THE LORD, HE maketh even his enemies to be at PEACE with him"* (Prov. 6:7).

Like Paul who could list his hardships he suffered for Christ saying, you all have not yet resisted unto blood striving against sin and Paul states I bare in my body the scars of my pilgrimage, case stated. And Job with his boils, scars, and "miserable comforters" says, no I will not curse God.

> *"Till I die I will not remove mine integrity from me... My righteousness I hold fast"* (Job 27:5–6).

Job, like Paul, attests to his own worthy examples saying,

> *If I have made gold my HOPE, or have said to the fine gold, Thou art my confidence; If I rejoice because my wealth was great, and because mine hand had gotten much; If I beheld the sun when it shined, or the moon walking in brightness; And my heart has been secretly enticed, or my mouth hath kissed my hand: This also were an iniquity to be punished by the judge: for I should have denied the God that is above.* (Job 31; 24–28)

Then Job could justify all the evil beset him, and the LOSS of his comforts and wealth. No JOB was a just and perfect man as the text explains and like Father Abraham, God counted JOB'S faith as righteousness.

> *JOB delivered the poor that cried and the fatherless and him that had none to help him…"* *I caused the widow's heart to sing… I was a father to the poor, and the cause which I knew not I searched out. When the ear heard me, then it blessed me. They wanted and kept silence at my counsel. After my words they spake not again, and my speech dropped upon them. And they waited for me as for the RAIN…and I sat CHIEF, and dwelt as a KING in the ARMY, as one that comforteth the mourners.* (Job 29:11–25)

Pray tell me, is there any evil here? No, no, no, but I witness the best of the greatest of righteousness. No, Job is not going to take the three *"miserable comforters"* advice and confess sin because he did not sin. Instead Job is declaring I have worked righteousness and like our Father Abraham, it was righteousness by faith. So God's grace reigned in the LAND through the righteousness by faith in God by HIS servant JOB. I saved the best for the last, in verse 14 JOB says, "I PUT ON RIGHTEOUSNESS, AND IT CLOTHED ME: MY JUDGMENT WAS AS A ROBE AND A DIADEM."

Job has as he explains used his wealth and fortunes to take care of everything around him. He went the extra mile and used his wealth for the poor, the sick, the widows and *"THE CAUSE THAT I KNEW NOT I SEARCHED OUT"*—wow. No, his wealth was not an idol to him rather a tool for God's glory. He was God's hands and feet here, presiding like a monarch among men Moffatt says. And this monarch single-handedly took care of his Kingdom. He was the bank. He was the store. He was the social welfare system and the health care system. He was a distributor like the apostles were; everyone sold what they had and distributed to the poor churches. You see what we are fighting over today to do, or not to do, welfare, health care, food assistance, medicines, etc. JOB, all by himself, willingly took care for all the people around him. It has a flare of Solomon's reign to it. As Queen Sheba said, the half was not told me. The way you worship, the happiness of your servants, the bounty on your table, the beauty of it all and the DIVINE WISDOM with which you rule, takes my breath away, she says. Yep, sounds like JOB's KINGDOM—oh yes, the power of ONE MAN can make life so sweet.

> *"And I sought for a MAN among them, that should make up the hedge, and STAND IN THE GAP before ME for the LAND…but I found NONE"* (Ezek. 22:30).

Now GOD did not leave JOB in ruin. No, not even, our Gracious, Plentious GOD concluded His wager with Satan and blessed JOB's latter end more than before. And Satan was as usual defeated by our glorious KING as JOB patiently waded through his trials and held to his integrity by waiting upon the LORD. In the end, the LORD gave him twice as much as before and turned his captivity of evil when he prayed for his three friends (42:10). For a season Job suffered the loss of all things, even his health.

> *So the LORD blessed the latter end of JOB more than his beginning; for he had 14,000 sheep—now 6,000 camels—now 1,000 yokes of oxen—now 1,000 she asses—now He had again seven sons and three daughters. And in all the land were no women found so fair as the daughters of Job: and their father gave them an inheritance among their brothers. After this Job lived 140 years, and saw his sons, and his son's sons, even four genera-tions. "So Job died, being old and full of days."* (Job 42:12–17)

HOW GREAT IS OUR GOD!

HE HATH DONE ALL THINGS WELL!

This exemplary responsibility that JOB exercised over and toward the people around him in his LAND is an excellent model for solving world problems. The rich man, being lord to his LAND and kingdom spends his wealth to provide for all the needs around him, and the man still retained his wealth.

> *"Give and it shall be given unto you good measure pressed down, shaken together, and running over, shall men give into your bosom. For with the same measure that ye mete withal it shall be measured to you again"* (Luke 6:38).

The LORD promises this; it is a forever Promise, but greed is the way of the world lately, Remember

> *The LOVE of MONEY is the root of all evil.*
> (1 Timothy 6:10)
> *Will a man rob GOD? Ye have robbed ME. But ye say, Wherein have we robbed Thee? In tithes and offerings. Ye are cursed with a curse: for ye have robbed ME, even this whole NATION. Bring the tithes into the storehouse, that there may be meat in Mine House, and PROVE ME now herewith, saith the LORD of Hosts, if I will not open for you the windows of Heaven, and pour you out a blessing, that there shall not be room enough to receive it!*
> (Mal. 3:8–10)

You cannot out give God, folks, it all comes from Him in the first place. So can we solve world hunger and war, it is possible. With God all things are possible. Jesus speaks endlessly of giving in his Gospels, and of loving our fellow man as ourselves. So let's follow Josephus, Job, and Paul and solve our ever pressing world problems. Was Job a perfect man? The Almighty said he was perfect and wagered Satan over his integrity. "My perfect Job," God said, "will remain my perfect Job, in spite of Satan's torments." The Lord was betting on His man.

"No greater love than a man lay down his life for his brother." And this Job did a stellar job of leaving no rock unturned. And our beloved Paul also suffered the loss of all things that he might win Christ. He also won Christ for multiplied thousands of souls, and those thousands were multiplied over and over throughout the ages up till now. Paul laid the foundation for nearly the entire church of GOD, through his journeys into all the world in his time. He can rightly claim that he suffered the LOSS OF ALL THINGS and did count them but dung. They were nothing compared to the glory wrought through the Name of Christ Jesus for the Kingdom of Our Father. Does not the Proverb say, *"One soul saved is worth all this world's gold."* Are you worried about your gold? God is laughing.

God is so mighty; the little we sacrifice here we will laugh about on the other side. That we would even consider making an idol of such vain things as silver and gold or anything else of this world is so ridiculous to God. He sits in the heavens and laughs, yes. If he created the world in six days and God is all eternal and another NAME for God is the Creator, then what does he do? He creates! Do we think he has stopped creating because this is all we know; the Earth? And Jesus said in MY FATHER'S HOUSE are many mansions. There is no telling of it, folks; there is no end to God nor beginning. We cannot even begin to grasp the knowledge of Him. Paul says eye has not seen nor ear heard of those things God has prepared for us. And as Isaiah says, if the NATIONS are a mere drop in a bucket, compare, do the math, what else has God prepared for us, it goes on and on and never ends. He creates; he is the Creator. Isaiah attempts to put His Almighty Majesty into WORDS. Listen to what he says.

"God saw everything that He had made and behold it was very good" (Gen. 1:31).

Who hath directed the Spirit of the Lord, or being His counsellor hath taught Him?... Behold the Nations are as a drop of a bucket, and are counted as the small dust of the balance! Behold He taketh up the isles as a very little thing. (Isa. 40:14, 15)

He lifts lands like a straw, yes like a piece of straw. (Moffatt)

All nations before Him are as nothing; and they are counted to Him less than nothing and vanity. To whom then will you liken God? Or what likeness will you compare unto Him?... Hast thou not known? Hast thou not heard, that the everlasting God, the Lord, the Creator of the Ends of the Earth, fainteth not, neither is weary? There is no searching of his UNDERSTANDING. (Isa. 40:17–18, 28)

He is the CREATOR. He creates and He keeps on creating. He is still creating. God has no beginning nor end, and in six days, He created all this, so do the math again. Wake up! His universe never ends. Six days, six days, in six days, He made all we see, and He is forever. He keeps on creating because he is a creating God, why should he stop. He liked what he did in six days, seems like He will be doing a lot more of what He likes. And He that endures to the end shall inherit all things, and the longsuffering of the Lord is *SALVATION*.

So what is the loss of a few trinkets here for a moment or two, nothing, we shall inherit ALL THINGS.

Jesus is all we need be concerned about. Yes, He said it in ten thousand different ways. So did Peter, Paul, John, and all authors with an ounce of wisdom.

So if Jesus is not the biggest thing ever for you, then your game plan is all off. He has to be the switch you turn on in the morning and the one you turn off at night. The SCRIPTURE says, "Seek ye first the Kingdom of God." This condemned world we live in is all a mirage, it is not permanent, and this condemned mess is certainly not our home. Believe it or not, it will all be vaporized as Peter the

Apostle says. Remember, He is the creator and He wants to create new things for those that patiently endure unto the END OF DAYS. This Earth has received Jesus's blood in it. Is not that ALONE reason enough for the Father to destroy it? And then, think of all the thousands of prophets, saints, and martyrs whose blood has been spilt. Now think of all the disgraceful wars that have spilt rivers of young men's blood. War is a disgraceful act of humanity that rivals every virtue known to mankind and God. So again, what does Peter say in his Epistle,

> *In the last days there shall be scoffers saying Where is the promise of the Lord's coming? For all things seem the same as ever before Peter says in so many words and they are willingly ignorant of the fact that the old world that then was perished with a 40 day flood of water.* (2 Peter 3:3–6)

Peter is telling us remember that God has already, in the past, destroyed the whole Earth, and now, at the end of days, will again destroy it. It may seem strange when we look around at all our glorious infrastructure, but remember the Tower of Babel and Solomon's temple. Then remember how God had to destroy whole nations because they were devil worshipping entities which defiled GOD'S HOLINESS; they offered their infants as burning sacrifices to Baal. And recall that nothing that defiles shall enter God's Kingdom. That is why the universe will all be purged of uncleaness with FIRE. Let's continue,

> *But the Heavens and Earth which are now, by God's word are kept and RESERVED FOR FIRE AGAINST THE DAY OF JUDGMENT and Perdition of ungodly men. But beloved be not ignorant of the fact that one day is with the Lord as a thousand years and a thousand years as one day. The Lord is not slack concerning his promise, as some men count slackness; but is longsuffering*

to us-ward, not willing that any should perish, but that all should come to repentance. But the Day of the Lord will come as a thief in the night; in which the Heavens shall pass away with a great noise, and the elements shall melt with a fervent heat, and the EARTH also and the WORKS that are therein shall be BURNED UP. Seeing then that all these things shall be DISSOLVED, WHAT MANNER OF PERSONS ought ye to be in all HOLINESS and GODLINESS, Looking for and hastening the advent of the Day of GOD, wherein the heavens [universe] *being on FIRE shall be DISSOLVED, and the elements shall MELT WITH FERVENT HEAT?* (2 Pet. 3:7–12)

So this whole world with every single thing in it shall soon be vaporized. So why put so much weight by it, like it will last forever? IT IS TEMPORARY! This is not our real and lasting home. So stop building castles out of rock because the Lord that created rock will melt the ROCK. Yes, what about the lava beds, what are they? Molten rock, eh? So Jesus melts ROCK, so stop trying to fortify yourself here on this temporary planet, and quit making like it is everlasting. God and only God is EVERLASTING, so build your HOUSE on the DIVINE ROCK—JESUS CHRIST OF NAZARETH. I like saying Nazareth for the Jew's sake, that they might open their eyes and see their true Messiah. It is all going up in smoke folks. ALL of it! Every last bit. We are just traveling through and borrowing these TEMPORARY facilities. Wake up! Wake up! Our REDEMPTION DRAWETH NIGH.

And Jesus said,

Doth the master thank that servant because he did the things that were commanded him? I say not. So likewise you when you shall have done all those things which are commanded you, say, We are

*unprofitable servants: we have done that which was
our duty to do.* (Luke 17:9–10)

This is us. We are to say this after we have done all the Lord has
required of us to do. And Jesus said unto them,

> *As the Father has sent me* (into the world)
> *even so I send you* [into the world]. (John 20:24)
> *And Jesus came and spoke unto them, saying
> ALL POWER is given unto ME in Heaven and on
> Earth. Go therefore and teach all nations, baptizing
> them in the NAME of the FATHER and the SON,
> and of the HOLY GHOST.* (Matt. 28:18–19)
> *And Jesus said unto them, Go ye into all the
> world, and preach the gospel to every creature.
> He that believeth and is baptized shall be saved;
> but he that believeth shall not be damned.* (Mark
> 16:15–16)

Now I say this is our duty. Paul says follow me as I follow
Christ, and what did Paul do, he knocked himself out preaching and
teaching day and night. Jesus is our Great Example, and I ask you,
what did Jesus do? Yes, He preached His father's message of eternal
life unto Israel for three and a half years. This I tell you plainly is
our duty. We were not born to be a tourist, a movie star, or a carpenter; our main goal should be reaching the lost for Christ. This
is the Great Commission that our forefathers followed in coming
to the new world to spread the Gospel of Jesus to all who had not
heard it. We are Jesus disciples of this day and this hour, this will be
REQUIRED of us. Deny it not. Jesus said be FRUITFUL; seek ye
first His Kingdom, do first His will. His will is that we be fruitful.
We are to be stewards of the WORD OF GOD and let our lights
shine to the world. We are not to hide the Gospel and blend with the
world; we are to shout this Gospel from the very rooftops. O, fools
and slow of heart, to understand and obey all that the Master taught
us. Jesus said FOLLOW ME and I will make you fishers of men. I

think Jesus's most important parable is that of the sower; now the seed is the BLESSED WORD of the Kingdom of God, so hear what Jesus teaches,

> *Hear ye therefore the parable of the sower… He also that received seed among the thorns is he that heareth the WORD; and the cares of this world, and the deceitfulness of riches, choke the WORD, and he becometh unfruitful. But he that received seed into the good ground is he that heareth the WORD and UNDERSTANDETH it; which also beareth fruit, and bringeth forth some an hundredfold, some sixty, some thirty.* (Matt. 13:18, 22–23)

Jesus expects, expects, and expects us to be fruitful, profitable servants, and in doing so, we are doing that which is expected of us. Friend, if you are full of Jesus and His Spirit, your cup is going to bubble over automatically to all around you. It is no forced issue, for the LOVE OF GOD CONSTRAINETH US. When you are in love with Jesus, the Master, you just want to please Him and Jesus is most glorified in the salvation of souls. We want heaven to be packed out.

With many, the *"deceitful riches chokes the WORD and they become unfruitful."* It does seem that money is the god of this world and the gateway of luxury; thus, Jesus says we cannot have two masters: money and the Lord God. And Peter makes plain his feelings concerning riches by calling it *"filthy lucre."* He rather despises mammon, or money, and now I remember why. His precious Lord and Savior, Jesus Christ, was sold down the river for thirty awful pieces of silver. Yes, Peter hates the riches and the wealth and just like Jesus told the rich, young ruler, *"To sell all that he had and distribute unto the poor and he would have treasure in Heaven."* So likewise, Peter taught the early church to do the same to sell all that ye have and distribute to the poor, for the love of money is the root of all evil.

No, we are all just unprofitable servants doing our duty. Our DUTY is to keep his commandments and do those things that are pleasing to the Father.

> *"And this is His commandment, that we should believe in the NAME OF His Son Jesus Christ and love one another as He commanded us"* (1 John 3:23).

This is all our duty, and this fulfills all the law and the prophets. Then we need only look for HIS mercy after doing our duty, not some big reward because we think we have done something. No, it is our duty to LOVE God and our neighbor, and after doing all that we can, only HOPE for HIS MERCY. This is what we tie all our hopes to; His mercy. He owes us nothing, we and our sins crucified JESUS. He owes us nothing. We plead for His MERCY. Jude says, *"Keep yourselves in the love of God LOOKING FOR THE MERCY of our Lord Jesus Christ unto Eternal Life"* (Jude 1:21).

We are forgetting what manner of men we are, it is us who owe our Maker. We went out of bounds, not He. As the lyrics say, *"I owed a debt I could not pay He paid a debt He did not owe I needed Someone to wash my sins away."* It is we that owe Christ Jesus our Lord and nothing we or anyone else could do, could pay that debt. It took His blood and His alone to pay the price of reinstatement into God's Heavenly Kingdom. And that is why all the rest is DUNG, and that is why Peter's anger over riches because all the silver and gold of eternity could not EVEN buy or pay for our Blessed Saviour. Thirty pieces of silver, disgusting, a joke of the devil. It was, of course, a mockery. And all this is why we will be praising Christ Jesus, Our Saviour, throughout the ages of eternity with joyful and thankful hearts.

Singing like the angels the Hallelujah chorus.

> The kingdom of this world;
> is become the kingdom of our Lord,
> and of His Christ

and of His Christ
And He shall reign forever and ever
And he shall reign forever and ever
And he shall reign forever and ever
And he shall reign forever and ever
Forever and ever and all eternity. We will be sing-
ing and praising his majesty.
Christ Jesus
Our Lord God and Savior.

There Is Power in the Blood

1 Would you be free from the bur-den of sin? There's pow'r in the blood, pow'r in the blood;

Would you o'er e-vil a vic-to-ry win? There's won-der-ful pow'r in the blood.

2 Would you be free from your pas-sion and pride? There's pow'r in the blood, pow'r in the blood; Come for a cleans-ing to Cal-va-ry's tide; there's won-der-ful pow'r in the blood.

3 Would you be whit-er, much whiter than snow? There's pow'r in the blood, pow'r in the blood; Sin-stains are lost in its life-giv-ing flow; there's won-der-ful pow'r in the blood.

4 Would you do serv-ice for Je-sus your King? There's pow'r in the blood, pow'r in the blood; Would you live dai-ly His praises to sing? There's won-der-ful pow'r in the blood.

(chorus)

There is pow'r, pow'r, Wonder-working pow'r In the blood of the Lamb;

There is pow'r, pow'r. Won-der-work-ing Pow'r In the pre-cious blood

Of the Lamb. (L. E. Jones)

Repent

*And if the righteous scarcely be saved, where shall
the ungodly and the sinner appear?*

—1 Peter 4:18

*When once the longsuffering of GOD waited in the
days of Noah, while the ARK was a preparing, wherein
few, that is, eight souls were saved by water.*

—1 Peter 3:20

The like figure where unto even baptism doth also now save us.

—1 Peter 3:21

*But the END of ALL THINGS is at hand: be ye
therefore sober, and watch unto prayer.*

—1 Peter 4:7

These verses of Peter should strike fear into our hearts we should take heed to his warnings. For this is God's rock talking, Peter walked side by side with the Master, and three and a half years is a long time; it being every day for three and a half years. They became of one mind, one heart, one Spirit. Peter knew well, the teachings of Jesus and knew what was expected of a believer. He is saying that we must submit ourselves one to another in the fear of GOD in striving against evil and must fulfill as well as possible the doctrines of the Gospel Message. For perilous times are ahead, men being lovers of pleasure more than lovers of GOD. Deceiving and being easily deceived, growing soft and weak, not willing to stand for pure truth, afraid to be unpopular with vain persons.

Not much has changed since Peter's day. There were false teachers and prophets then and there are false teachers today. The blind leading the blind with false heresies and damnable doctrines of men, the feel-good false Gospel of everything goes. Perverting the truth to their own persuasion and running whichever way the wind will blow. Nothing seems to matter but our own ignorant gain. The Bible says that everything a man does is for his appetites and covetousness is idolatry (idol worship). No thought for the soul here, the lusts of the flesh are blinding, and the more we indulge the more our conscience is seared. Peter says, *"I beseech you as strangers and pilgrims, abstain from fleshly lusts, which* war *against the soul"* (2:11). And he continues, *"As obedient children, not fashioning yourselves according to the former lusts in your ignorance: But as He which hath called you is HOLY, so be ye Holy in all manner of conversation: Because it is written Be Ye Holy; for I AM HOLY saith the LORD"* (1:14–16). This is sound advice and John similarly warns,

> *Love not the world, neither the things that are in the world. If any man love the world, the love of the Father is not in him. For all that is in the world, the lust of the flesh, and the lust of the eyes, and the pride of life, is not of the Father, but is of the world. And the world passeth away, and the lust thereof: but he that doeth the will of GOD abideth forever. Little children, it is the LAST TIME: and as ye have heard that antichrist shall come, even now are there many antichrists, whereby we know that it is the LAST TIME.* (1 John 2:15–18)

We know it is the last time because there are many antichrists. The Cross of Christ has many enemies. And this old, bloodstained world is soon to be dissolved by the wrath and indignation of GOD ALMIGHTY. So what kind of men ought we to be, in all godliness and holiness seeing that the Earth and all its elements shall be dissolved, Peter says. It's dark, folks, it's dark out there. Without GOD, it is always midnight. Everyone just grabbing for that next rung of the ladder. But when the NAME of JESUS is lifted, LIGHT springs forth, because Jesus equals LIGHT. He is the LIGHT of the WORLD without Him we are as blind men fumbling in darkness for the light switch. Jesus is the Light of our lives, literally. He is Light for our path and Light for our journey. Some still don't get it, that without Jesus only darkness, gross darkness, zero light literally. God help you if your best friend's NAME is not JESUS, if not you are still lost. Jesus is the HOPE of all mankind; the only way out of here.

JESUS is the DOOR, the GATE to the fold. Jesus is our strong consolation, to us who have fled for refuge (from the darkness of this world) that we might lay hold upon that HOPE set before us: which HOPE we have as an anchor of our souls. JESUS CHRIST in person is that HOPE (Heb. 6:18–19). The door is now open to Christ, but as in Noah's Ark, the door was at the appointed hour pitched within and without and it began to rain. Christ's second appearance is at hand, but He is not willing that any should perish. His appointed times are at the command of His perfect will. There will come a cutoff time and He will say LAST CALL, LAST CALL. As the Father did in the times of Hosea, "God said unto Hosea, call her name Lo-Ruhamah: For I WILL NO MORE HAVE MERCY UPON THE HOUSE OF ISRAEL; BUT I WILL UTTERLY TAKE THEM AWAY. Then said God, call his name Lo-Ammi: FOR YE ARE NOT MY PEOPLE, AND I WILL NOT BE YOUR GOD" (1:6, 9).

The Spirit of GOD will not strive with men forever. His mercy has an exhaustion point, He will not plead forever. "Return now," He says, "before the door is closed. Work while it is light for night cometh when no man can work."

Take heed, Peter says, as unto a LIGHT that shineth in a DARK PLACE. That place is the world with all its glitz and glam and deceptions. Today he says heed His VOICE and harden not your hearts as in the wilderness. The Hebrew children continually chided with MOSES and Aaron and came to the door of the Tabernacle to stone them many times. Why did they do this? Because the heart is deceitfully wicked above all else who can know it the WORD warns. This, however, can be guarded against by a daily examining of the soul before GOD. Take heed, Peter says, lest any of you fall short of the grace of GOD and perish like those of Korah, who thought they were just as holy as MOSES. God showed them not to strive with His servant Moses. And they and all their loved ones and possessions got swallowed up as the Earth opened its mouth.

Their screaming and terror put the fear of GOD into the congregation and they fled for their lives fast, lest the LORD's anger come after them too. Be not as those of Korah, who tempted the LORD and proved His anger. God is not willing that any should perish. Today is the day of salvation; today is the day to hand the reigns over to your MAKER. What wait I for? It's only blessing and favor that you are missing. The Father of the wisest man ever to live said it this way; I would rather be a doorkeeper in the House of my God than to dwell in the tents of wickedness. King David a doorkeeper, yes if it is in GOD's house; GOD's ETERNAL HOME where no wicked shall ever step foot. David says,

> *The LORD heard my cry He brought me up out of an horrible pit, out of the miry clay, and set my feet upon a ROCK, and established my GOINGS He hath put a new song in my mouth even Praise unto our GOD. Blessed is the man that maketh the LORD his trust.* (Ps. 40:1–4)
>
> Solomon says, *"Man's goings are of the LORD; how can a man then understand his own way."* (Prov. 20:24)

You see, we cannot understand…

We cannot see and we are not in charge. Left to our digression we would be going in fifteen different directions and none of them right. But if we cleave unto our GOD, the psalmist says, *"That the steps of a good man are ordered by the LORD: and He delighteth in his way."* And "The Law of his GOD is in His heart and none of his steps shall slide" (Ps. 37:23, 31).

God is gracious, my friend, so let us turn again unto our GOD and lay hold of His great mercies. Let us plough that fallow ground of the heart by the constant cleansing of the WORD. The washing of the WORD whereby the mind is renewed and alive in Christ. David says, *"Let THY TRUTH continually preserve me"* (40:11). And in John's Gospel Jesus says, *"Now are ye clean through the WORD which I have spoken unto you"* (15:13), and *"Sanctify them through THY TRUTH: O GOD THY WORD is TRUTH"* (17:17).

There's revival folks, right there it starts with me and you *"is not MY WORD as a Hammer is not MY WORD as a Fire."* Pour it on, LORD. Leave me no room for my selfish ways. Time is short, I want to make the best of it for THY KINGDOM. Redeeming the time, taking it back from the enemy. Christ is our example; how well did He know the scripture? Yes, very well. He was not reading from a script or out of a book. It was in His heart and soul through much study. His cup ran over with the anointing oil of the WORD. Jesus said in Matthew 22:29, He said, *"Ye do ERR not knowing the Scriptures."* Peter says, "If we abide in Him and He in us we make it a sure deal that we will never fall and will be a wise and fruitful soul for Our LORD's Kingdom." Peter says we have a sure WORD of prophesy. David says, "God hath made with me an Everlasting Covenant, ordered in all things and sure: for this is all my Salvation, and all my desire" (2 Sam. 23:5).

God is not a man that He should lie, another WORDS God is incapable of sinning, so His WORD in all things is sure. *"Thy WORD is TRUTH."* There is nothing more true and sure and concrete than GOD'S WORDS. His everlasting promises are all yeah and amen. The things of GOD are invisible and are sure, the things of the world are visible and are so totally unsure that they will all pass away; unsure. Jesus is the sure deal. "COME FOLLOW ME," Jesus says. *"O fools and slow of heart to believe all that the Prophets have spoken"* (Luke 24:25).

Blessed is that man whom the LORD will find waiting and watching at His appearing. This man will be confident and not ashamed at Christ's sudden appearance. John the Apostle who has told us in one hundred different ways that *"GOD is LOVE"* says, *"He that saith he abideth in Him ought himself also to walk even as He walked. And whoso keepeth His WORD, in him verily is the love of GOD perfected: hereby know we that we are in Him"* (1 John 2:6, 5). And that is our goal total sanctification; the Love of GOD perfected in us; unspotted by the world. Thus we become *"partakers of the Divine Nature, having escaped the corruption that is in the world through LUST"* (2 Peter 1:4). How do we do this, *"line upon line, here a little there a little" "from faith to faith and from glory to glory,"* we are built up in the most Holy Faith. Fleeing worldly lusts which war against the soul. We are strangers and pilgrims here, using this world but not being obsessed with it. We need be obsessed with only one thing; JESUS and Him crucified. *"Disallowed indeed of men, but chosen of GOD and Precious."* He is our guiding LIGHT.

Jesus now, Jesus only, Jesus always.

> *Follow peace with all men and holiness without which no man shall see the LORD, Looking diligently lest any man fail of the grace of GOD.* (Heb. 12:14–15)
>
> *Take heed brethren lest there be in any of you an evil heart of unbelief in departing from the LIVING GOD. But exhort one another daily while it is called today; lest any of you be hardened through the deceitfulness of sin.* (Heb. 3:12–13)

If it were possible, the devil will try to deceive even the very elect with all deceivableness. We must lay fast hold on the LORD folks, cleaving to Him in desperation lest the enemy of our soul find some weak point with us, and allure us through the corruptible lusts, away from our Precious Savior, and His nail scarred hands. Cleave to Him; be one with Him. Let us not fail, let us not come short of the glory, let us not turn back and desire the leeks and cucumbers of Egypt. When the going gets tough, the tough get going. Not as Lot's wife who turned back, or as the pig goes back to his wallowing or the dog to his vomit. Let us follow on to know the LORD, steadfast, unmovable.

> *"How shall we escape if we turn away from Him that speaketh from Heaven. Whose voice then shook the Earth: but now He hath promised, saying yet once more I shake not the Earth only but also Heaven"* (Heb. 12:25–26).

Moses said it was frightful, terrifying—the fire, the smoke, the darkness, the shaking. The Hebrew children said, Moses you speak to GOD but let God not speak to us though because we might die. See how powerful just the Almighty's voice is; it crumbles mountains and melts rocks. Stand in terror, friend, because the world has never seen such power as His, GOD laughs at our power, which to Him is no power. How shall we escape? How shall we escape? Think about it; if He crumbles the mighty mountains. What shall the rest of the face of the Earth look like—all rubble, all rubble.

The Almighty intends to shake away and burn away all those things He finds displeasing, anything that defiles, anything that is not godly or holy. Take a deep breath, now what do you say will you keep denying His Holiness, will you even dare to deny everlasting happiness? Now no amount of good works, nor any amount of gold will not secure you before His Majesty, so bow now, friend; take off thy shoes and come humbly before Him. He is getting ready to shake this earth to pieces. But we, if we love Him, if we bow to Him now, if we serve him now, then those things which cannot be shaken will remain.

> *"Wherefore we receiving a KINGDOM which* cannot be moved, *let us have grace, whereby we may serve GOD ACCEPTABLY with Reverence and godly FEAR: FOR OUR GOD IS A CONSUMING FIRE"* (Heb. 12:28).

Yes, yes, yes, a consuming fire!

> *Now the GOD of Peace, that brought again from the dead our LORD JESUS, that Great Shepherd of the sheep, through the blood of the Everlasting Covenant, Make you perfect in every good work to do His will. Working in you that which is well pleasing in His sight, through Jesus Christ; to whom be glory forever and ever. Amen.* (Heb. 13:20–21)

(Oh, read this again and again and again, please!)

The matter before us, dear ones, is this: WHERE DO YOU STAND WITH THE ALMIGHTY? No, I am not asking you to get your house in order as if there is no tomorrow, but then again, I am because you know not what a day brings forth. There may be no tomorrow for all of us. With antichrists sitting on detonation switches that could bring this Earth down, there is no telling; here today, gone tomorrow. I'm just sayin', beware, don't put off till tomorrow what you can do today, you see then it's done. Now you are, you are clothed in Jesus's robes; yes, Jesus's robes. The robe He wore to Calvary, that robe of righteousness. Jesus sees through two lenses, one for the saved and robed and another for the unrobed and naked.

The robed are perfect because with Jesus's robe of righteousness that He secured at Calvary when He said, "it is FINISHED" that was the complete victory for all that believe in Him, He asks only that we BELIEVE. GOD cannot look on sin; that is why Jesus said it is FINISHED. My friend, work that was begun before the foundations of ever the Earth was FINISHED by that beautiful man/GOD that hung on that wretched, evil CROSS. Jesus completed a work so long in the making, so long, but in GOD's time, a short time. Who would have known, who would have known, that such a vile thing would be our VICTORY. I think only three in one, the Father, the Son, and the Holy Ghost. Thanks be to the Father for the victory we have through OUR LORD and SAVIOR JESUS CHRIST the KING and His Majesty; we are more than victors, more than conquerors through

Christ Jesus. He said it is FINISHED; JESUS PAID the price in full for our redemption through His spilt blood at Calvary. Let's look at the guilty world in Romans 3,

> *As it is written, there is none righteous, no, not one: There is none that understandeth, there is none that seeketh after GOD. They are all gone out of the way,…there is none that doeth good, no, not one* [we all have Adam's original sin and very original it is]. *Now the things the Law saith, it saith to them that are under the LAW:* [and the LAW could not; all those sacrifices could not justify anybody] *so that every mouth may be stopped; and all the world may become guilty before GOD."* [Even though all those Sacrifices of sheep and goats were being made, they did not take our sins away or justify us.] *"But now the Righteousness of GOD which is by faith in Jesus Christ is unto and upon all them that believe"* [this righteousness was manifested and performed by Jesus at Calvary]. Now we; *"Being justified freely by His grace through the REDEMPTION that is in Christ Jesus." "Whom GOD hath set forth to be a propitiation through FAITH in His BLOOD… for the Remission of sins…that He might be the JUSTIFIER of him which believeth in Jesus.* (Rom. 3:10–12, 19–26)

The Gospel in a nutshell, Jesus justified us, the LAMB of GOD slain before the foundations of the Earth. This was all planned for us six thousand or so years ago. *"Jesus PAID IT ALL, all to Him I owe."* We could not escape our sins; the animal sacrifices did not wash our sins away, but the perfect sacrifice did, Jesus the LAMB of GOD. Jesus the sacrificial Lamb paid the price for all sins, the sins of the WORLD. Jesus had those sins tagged on Him at Calvary; that is why Jesus said, *"Father why hast THOU forsaken ME."* The Father is SO HOLY He cannot even look on or at sin. So when the Father sees us now, we have on Jesus's robe of righteousness so He can now look at us; our sins are washed away by Jesus spilt blood. We are now righteous and the Father sees us as righteous, FORGIVEN. Forever, our sins are washed away as far as east is from west. The gift of GOD is ETERNAL LIFE through Jesus Christ our LORD. It's like someone sending you a gift a package in the mail, all you have to do is go to the post office and pick it up; it's yours free from Our Heavenly Father, the gift of Jesus Christ. He is ours and we are His. The knowledge of Jesus is salvation.

Just as Adam was the Son of GOD the first son so Jesus is the SON of GOD the second SON.

"And if by one man's offense (Adam*) death reigned by one,"* meaning, we had sin and had no access to Jesus or GOD, we were cut off from GOD; whereas Adam walked and talked with GOD and we would have too if Adam had not sinned and cut off our access to the Divine World. But we now having received pardon and put on Jesus Righteousness, we now *"REIGN in LIFE by ONE, JESUS CHRIST"* (Rom. 5:17). Yes, I said before we are VICTORS and have conquered sin and the devil by putting on Jesus Christ because we are temples of His actual, real to life—His Spirit, His Holy Spirit abides in our hearts, minds, and souls, through His WORD by His power. That's why He is called the LIVING WORD. He lives in our lives through His WORD.

Verse 18, *"Therefore as by the Offense of one* [Adam*] judgment came upon all men to condemnation; even so by the RIGHTEOUSNESS of one* [Jesus] *the free gift* [at your post office ready to pick up] *came upon all men unto justification of Life."* Verse 19, *"For as by one man's* [Adam's] *disobedience many were made sinners* [the whole world became sinners, cursed by sin and cut off] *so by the obedience of one* [JESUS] *shall many be made RIGHTEOUS.* [HOLY and pure and able to enter heaven]."

Verse 21, *That as sin hath reigned unto death* [cut us off from GOD], *even so might grace reign through RIGHTEOUSNESS* [grace brought us back into good standing with GOD and put us in His actual presence again] *unto eternal life by Jesus Christ OUR LORD."* Voila, GOD is great.

Now, forgive me if you think I repeat myself a lot. I am sorry, but not sorry and will continue to repeat the WORDS of LIFE until

I see genuine REVIVAL among us. For GOD is not willing that any should perish but that all men would come to His saving knowledge in Jesus Christ. There are just too many fainting by the way, too many at ease in Zion, too many complacent and ignorant. So yes, I will continue to repeat the WORDS of LIFE until we all see Jesus as the salvation of all of mankind. Repeat, repeat who? Pete no re*pete*?!

Through His Word and by His power, we are His. Now there are only two camps: Christ's and the anti-Christs'. Whosoever denieth the Father and the Son is anti-Christ. It is either "Yes, Jesus" or "No, Jesus." So get in the right camp. You sit on the median line, saying I'll make my move pretty soon. When I am secure and feeling good about things I'll check it out. No, friend, you make your move now; we move when Jesus calls—when the waters are troubled. He is calling now as John says, "Don't deny the SON." Now is the time Jesus is calling you now, "Come out from among them and be ye separate." Jesus now, Jesus all the time, take Jesus, be in His camp. Johnny, come latelys you will be sorry for not listening to the Captain sooner. What were Jesus exact WORDS; as I recall, ah, yes, He said, "Come, follow ME." And what was He doing? Yes, ministering to the LOST SHEEP. Do not let the glitz and glam deceive you; it can really get ahold of you and then you are like so gone, carried away, out of sight. Oh, I'm late for the therapist, for the plastic surgeon; GOD help us, folks. It's not easy unless you are the top-dog. Then you are all alone with the rest of the want-a-bees jealous of you and envy is cruel.

"I will be satisfied when I awake with THY
Likeness" (Ps. 17:15).

"Working my way back to you babe with a burning love inside," so the song goes. I pray the pages of your Bible are burning hot, those black and red letters just jumping off that rice paper and demolishing every evil in your heart, that you and I may serve GOD acceptably. And the crazy thought is that all comes from HIM and yet we think we can really do something for Him. That thought is inside and out. As David says,

> *But who am I, and what is my people, that we should be able to offer so willingly after this sort? For ALL THINGS COME OF THEE, and OF THINE OWN HAVE WE GIVEN THEE. For we are strangers before THEE, and sojourners, as were all our fathers: our days on Earth are as a shadow and there is none abiding. O LORD our God all this store that we have prepared to build THEE an house for THINE HOLY NAME cometh of THINE HAND, and IS ALL THINE OWN.* (1 Chron. 29:14–16)

"The Lord is good to all: and His tender mercies are over all His works" (Ps. 145:9).

Therefore, friend, we must prepare our hearts unto the LORD our GOD, that we might walk with a perfect heart before Him as our Father King David did. O, LORD, I want to be your slave. Whatever you can use me for Jesus, let me even be your doormat and I will be hilariously happy…forever. Your doormat, LORD, in your fabulous Kingdom that shall never end, in your heavenly city in your New Jerusalem. For Thou art the GREAT KING, and the Great God and Thou art the governor among the nations.

> *Blessed is the man whom THOU choosest and causeth to approach unto THEE. That he may dwell in Thy courts: We shall be satisfied with the goodness of THY HOUSE, even of thy Holy Temple.* (Ps. 65:4)

Blessed, blessed is THAT MAN!

Friend, there are more ways of telling you GOD's message than Carter's got pills. "Behold My tongue is the pen if a ready writer."

> *The LORD gave the WORD: great was the company of those that published it. Though ye have lien among the pots, yet shall ye be as the wings of a DOVE covered with silver, and her feathers with yellow gold.* (Ps. 68:11, 13)

What does Watchman Nee say "REVIVE us again Oh GOD"[1]?

Habakkuk the Prophet says, "Revive us in the midst of our days O LORD." Chapter 3 continues and concludes on this positive note.

> *Though the fig tree shall not blossom, though no fruit is on the vine, though the olive crop has failed, though the fields give us no food, though the folds have lost their flocks and in the stalls no cattle lie, yet in the Eternal we will find OUR JOY, we will rejoice in the GOD who SAVES US.* (Moffatt)

Job says it best of all: *"Though He slay me, yet will I trust in Him"* (13:15).

And again in Job 12:10, *"In whose Hand is the soul of every living thing, and the breath of ALL MANKIND."*

This sort of makes a person want to trust in Him and not the almighty dollar. And yes, whatever and whatever Habakkuk says, "We will still glory in the LORD, it does not matter, this way or that, because our time here is so fleeting anyway." Therefore to be put out a little for a short time is nothing compared to the eternity of bliss we will enjoy with Jesus our Savior. What does Hebrews tell us of GOD'S servant MOSES and his preferences.

> *"Choosing rather to suffer affliction with the people of GOD, than to enjoy the pleasures of sin for a season; Esteeming the reproach of Christ greater riches than the treasures in Egypt for he had respect unto the recompense of the Reward"* (11:25–26).

If this is not your favorite scripture, you are falling short. Revive us again O, LORD, and quickly, because MOSES was so HOT and this was his mantra. So I guess Moses said it best. Paul exhorts, *"Be not conformed to this world: but be ye transformed by the renewing of your mind, that ye may prove what is that good and acceptable, and perfect, will of GOD"* (Rom. 12:2).

The message is REPENT. It will always be REPENT. The LORD says our love is like a wilting flower or the dew of the morning; it vanishes quick. The allure of the world distracts us from Christ. It is amazing though to look at all the grandiose of this world—its buildings, its temples, gardens, estates, and all will soon be melted with a fervent heat Peter says. A surreal phenomenon, like a Salvador Dali painting, surreal. Evidently GOD has something millions of times better. He has promised that we will not be disappointed. For He said, "My Ways are higher than your ways and thoughts, as the heavens are higher than the Earth."

Jesus also said, *"The Father is greater than I."* Think about that. What does it mean? is the Father twenty feet tall? Jesus said, *"This is life Eternal that they might know THEE The ONLY TRUE GOD"* (John17:3), *"and Jesus Christ, whom Thou hast sent."* The old spiritual says, "He's got the whole world in His hands, He's got you and me sister, brother, babies in His hands… He's got the whole world in His hands." How is that for the big picture?

When the Almighty spoke from the top of the mountain to Moses and the Israelites, they were terrified at GOD's VOICE; it roared and thundered. Now if GOD is way up there in the heavens, how big would GOD have to be for His VOICE to be heard by the children of Israel down around the bottom of the mountain? How big? I say HUGE. Maybe God invented surround-sound or maybe He is in more than one place at a time. Whatever we know Him by His VOICE, and His Voice comes all the way from heaven on the day of Jesus's baptism in the JORDAN. The Voice roars from heaven, announcing, *"This is My Beloved SON in whom I am well pleased."* And at the transfiguration with Moses and Elijah the Father's Voice thunders clear from heaven. Psalm 29 says, *"The GOD of glory thundereth. The Voice of the LORD is full of majesty"* (verses 3–4). David should know He heard the LORD's VOICE often.

Moses speaks in Deuteronomy 4 of the LORD speaking to His people, *"And the LORD said unto me, Gather ME the people together, and I will* make them hear My WORDS *that they may Learn to* Fear ME… *And the LORD spake unto you out of the midst of the fire, ye heard the VOICE of the WORDS, but saw no similitude, only ye heard a VOICE"* (verses 10–12). And just as the Hebrew children feared for their lives when they heard GOD's VOICE, so will we be shaking and trembling before this all powerful GOD soon.

We need the fear of God in our hearts now that we will not be ashamed before Him or surprised on that Big Day. The fear of GOD is the beginning of wisdom; the fear of God is to depart from evil. Let us lay hold of the fear of God, let us possess it, own it, prize it. And above all, LORD GOD in Jesus Holy Name let me realize WHO, YOU ARE.

Yes, LORD, let me realize who You are and then who I am. I am a Son of God, if I want to be, if I make that choice and tell GOD, I want to be your son O, GOD. Then if a son, then are ye His Heir,

heir to all the Father has; in fact, ye are a joint heir and will reign with Jesus and sit in His Throne with Him. We need then not worry about the garbage down here, that's what it will look like compared to what He has in store for those that love Him. Wow, once I was blind, but now I see. Yes, LORD, I love you, I love you; don't go another minute if you have not uttered those WORDS in the last hour and Jesus said to Peter, "Do you love ME?"

How many souls were saved out of the first world, during the GREAT FLOOD—yes, eight souls, eight lonely souls pleased GOD and did not perish with that wicked generation. Jesus started a new world again with only, ONLY EIGHT SOULS. Think about it, consider it, ponder it; GOD got angry at the wicked and destroyed a world full of them in one stroke, by water. And by water, Noah and his family floated on top of the water and were saved by water, which is the like shadow of baptism, which saves us. And Jesus also says as it was in the days of Noah so shall it be in the days of the coming of the Son of Man. That should make us fear and tremble before such a HOLY GOD that cannot abide SIN. Yes, oh yes, the goodness and the severity of GOD is what we see. On the Egyptians and Pharaoh, we saw the severity of GOD, on GOD's children and MOSES we saw GOD's goodness. Romans 2 explains verse 20–22 and verse 1,

> *I say then, Hath God cast away His people?…*
> *Well because of unbelief they were broken off, and*
> *thou standest by Faith. Be not high minded, but*
> *Fear: For if God spared not the natural branches,*
> *take heed lest He also spare not thee. Behold there-*
> *fore the goodness and the severity of GOD: on them*
> *which fell, severity, but toward thee, goodness, if*
> *thou continue in His goodness: otherwise thou also*
> *shall be cut off.*

This was another later example of GOD's goodness versus His severity. The list is endless. God spared not Esau. He spared not the fallen angels, in the days of Daniel GOD spared not King Nebuchadnezzar but put him out to pasture as an ox to eat grass for seven years until he humbled himself, "Till thou know that the MOST HIGH ruleth in the kingdom of men" (Dan. 4:25).

The kingdom is the LORD's, and He ruleth among the Nations. God does as He pleases in the whole universe, and who is GOD's counselor that he should question Him. The World and all there is, is His. Be not high-minded then, but fear lest a promise being left you of entering in some would seem to fall short. We should not, as Paul says, "*Not to think of ourselves more highly than we ought to think*"; think humbleness. What did Job say, "He escaped by the skin of his teeth." Many are called few are chosen, not many mighty, not many great men are chosen. Jesus tells us in LUKE's GOSPEL 4:26, 27, "*But I tell you of a truth, there were many widows in Israel in the days of Elias* [during the three years and six months of famine]. *But to none was Elias sent but to the widow at Serepta, a city of Sidon* [again]. *And many lepers were in Israel in time of Eliseus the prophet and none of them was cleansed, saving Naaman the Syrian.*" You see not many are chosen. Thank you, LORD, that you called and chose me to be your own loving child. Thank you, LORD, you found me of all the millions of souls on the planet. You came and knocked at my door and said I will come in and dine with you dear, ME with you and you with ME. Thank you LORD for saving my soul.

If it were not for the grace of GOD; there go I. Why do the admonitions of Solomon tell us to get the "fear of GOD," because His fear will purify our steps. We will think before making any choices; does this please GOD? "The FEAR OF THE LORD is the beginning of WISDOM" (Prov. 9:10) and the knowledge of the HOLY is UNDERSTANDING." And if wisdom and understanding cloak your mortal being then you shall shake and tremble in the MOST HIGH's presence. It will lead you and keep you unto the Master's good pleasing, and great confidence it will lend you. The "fear of God" will keep you from evil and the evil way. It will cause you to flee, dread and hate all evil.

But certain naive people think of God as too loving and merciful to send the WICKED to hell. That is not what I read. God has made it clear that if we do not believe; we have sealed our own condemnation. All through the Bible, GOD shows His wrath against sin, disobedience, and unbelief, starting with Adam and Eve's dis-obedience and fall from grace. Then Isaiah, Jeremiah, and Ezekiel foretell of Israel's total and complete destruction because of their wicked sinning. Isaiah's "Thus saith the LORD" paints with hot hues GOD's intention.

> *"Woe to the rebellious children, saith the LORD...that add sin to sin... Behold the Name of the LORD cometh from far, burning with His anger; and the burden thereof is heavy: His Lips are full of INDIGNATION and His Tongue is as A DEVOURING FIRE"* (Isa. 30:27).

This is the same picture John the Beloved gives us in Revelation of God's great wrath. The Baptist warned them to repent and flee the wrath to come, quoting Isaiah. God has insane terrible wrath against evil. HE CANNOT ABIDE IT; His holiness will not allow it. So many times GOD told Moses to step aside and let Him destroy ALL the people. Moses fell on his face with a forty-day fast to intervene for their lives. God, on other occasions, however, destroyed tens of thousands at a time for murmuring complaining, lying, and disobeying. How is that for a tough Captain.

No, Jesus in the gospels makes it clear that there is a hell with unquenchable fire and torment where the LOST and unbelieving will be sent. In fact, the story of the rich man and Lazarus explains the rewards of good and evil perfectly. Jesus said,

> *There was a certain rich man, which was clothed in purple and fine linen, and fared sump-tuously everyday: And there was a certain beggar named Lazarus, which laid at his gate full of sores, and desiring to be fed with the crumbs which fell from the rich man's table: moreover the dogs came and licked his sores. And it came to pass that the beggar died, and was carried by the ANGELS INTO ABRAHAM'S BOSOM: the rich man also*

died and was buried; And in Hell he lift up his eyes in torments, and seeth Abraham afar off, and Lazarus in his bosom. And he cried and said, Father Abraham, have MERCY on me, and send Lazarus that he may dip the tip of his finger in water, and cool my tongue for I am tormented in this FLAME. (Luke 16:19–24)

In this what? In this FLAME. Sounds like hell to me. Jesus took the time to give this very vivid description of our scenario: HELL. The man had shown NO MERCY to Lazarus all his life, no he was reaping the evil he had sown. To him, that is merciful God will show him mercy. Even the dogs were kind to Lazarus, which further points out his evil heart. And if evil were not punished iniquity would abound. Our cities all over the world would look like Sodom and Gomorrah, there would be no incentive to do good. Remember the "wages of sin is death" and death is hell.

Paul says, I have not ceased to warn you day and night with tears. Jude says, *"The LORD cometh with ten thousands of His saints. To execute JUDGMENT upon ALL, And to convince ALL that are UNGODLY among them of ALL their UNGODLY deeds which they have ungodly committed, and of ALL their hard speeches which ungodly sinners have spoken against Him."* Does that sound like an easy, push-over, task master. Flee, flee for refuge against the day of the wrath of Almighty GOD. Jesus is the only refuge. Hell is never full. And His vengeance is like a cauldron of boiling water set upon coals of juniper, bubbling over, Ready to saturate the Earth with the wrath of His vengeance. Flee, flee, the Baptist says, flee the wrath to come. Flee into the arms of Jesus, friend. That's where you belong. And Jesus tells us, *"Fear not them which kill the body, but are not able to kill the soul: but rather fear HIM which is able to destroy both soul and body in HELL"* (Matt. 10:28). Now that is the sum total of what we have been chewing on, HELL and the *"FEAR OF GOD"* if we do not repent.

> *"Therefore HELL hath enlarged herself, and opened her mouth without measure: and their glory, and the multitude, and their pomp, and he that rejoiceth shall descend into it"* (Isa. 5:14).

But we that have fled from the devil unto Jesus Our LORD and Savior have a HOPE we can depend on. For GOD made a promise and swore by it that those that keep His WORDS and obey Him, wait for Him, and look for Him shall be able to make heaven their Home through repentance. Through repentance we flee sin and fall upon GOD's mercy into eternal life. This is promised us by GOD. Hebrews tells us, we have a strong consolation for GOD promised to Father Abraham with an oath that his heirs would receive the promise. Abraham is the Father of faith because he believed GOD. And so with us, by faith, we believe in GOD and His Promise of Everlasting Life for all those that turn from sin to serve the Living GOD. Paul explains, *"That by two immutable things (the promise and the oath) in which it is impossible for GOD to lie, we then have a strong consolation, who have fled for refuge to lay hold upon the hope set before us: Which hope we have as an anchor of the soul, both sure and steadfast"* (Heb. 6:18, 19).

I understand uncertainty; some mornings I lament before God and say, are you still there Jesus, are you with me today, that is an honest confession. I should say, thank you, Jesus, for being there every day, every hour for me. All I need do is turn my focus to you. We must rely on the promises, not what we see, but turn to our invisible GOD. All GOD's WORD is a promise, what did Jesus do all day every day for three and a half years. Yes, speak WORDS to the disciples and the crowds. We rely on the truth of His WORDS.

> *Thy WORD is TRUTH. Draw nigh to GOD and He will draw nigh to you. And He hath said I will never leave thee nor forsake thee.* (Heb. 13:6)

We wait for the redemption of our body (which is our full Sonship) For we are saved by HOPE: but HOPE that is seen is not HOPE... But if we HOPE for that which we see not, then do we with patience wait for it. (Rom. 8:23–25)

Our whole idea should center around making it to heaven, to be reunited with our LORD and MAKER. It is certain we will all go out of this world by death, even Jesus had to die. And the unknown is fearful at times. Our expectation is heaven but we must trust Jesus that he will carry us through to the other side. Jesus's constant WORDS were BELIEVE, HAVE FAITH; in other WORDS, TRUST ME, Jesus is saying. Believe in ME that I will do this for you. His first WORDS to His people were "REPENT for the Kingdom of God is at hand." Jesus does not mind if we REPENT All day. Jesus said to the Apostle, "How many times do we forgive our brother... yes, seventy times seventy," if need be. It is all right to ride the kneeling rail to heaven, it is good to examine ourselves daily to see if we are in the faith. JOB says,

> *How many are mine iniquities and sins? Make me to know my transgression and my sin... I am escaped with the skin of my teeth.* (Job 13:23, 19–20)
>
> *Bless the LORD, O my soul: and forget not all His benefits... Who forgiveth all thine iniquities; The LORD is merciful and gracious, slow to anger, and plenteous in mercy. He hath not dealt with us after our sins nor rewarded us according to our iniquities. As far as the East is from the West, so far hath He removed our transgressions from us.* (A Psalm of David, 103:2–3, 8, 10, 12)

It is Jesus's mercy that we hope in and the promises He has given us of eternal life with Him in Glory. We trust and know that He is not just a man that He will lie. His holiness only allows for truth.

He is who He says He is and so much more. He is all righteousness and pure justice and the mercy prevails over His Judgment Seat, but unless a man repent, he will not see the Kingdom of Heaven. Come boldly to His Throne and accept the free gift of His SON JESUS, Who is our Life and Glory.

> *"Keep yourselves in the love of GOD, looking for the mercy of OUR LORD JESUS CHRIST unto Eternal Life. And of some have compassion… And others save with Fear pulling them out of the Fire hating even the garment spotted by the flesh,"*
> Jude says.

Warn them the WORD says, warn them that they are in danger of hell fire unless they REPENT. There is no other way for a man to avoid destruction except by REPENTING. Don't just be that church going Christian that pays tithes and occupies a pew and thinks that is enough to cause the Gates of Heaven to swing wide. No we must have a WORK, being doers of the WORD not just churchgoers. *"Faith without WORKS is dead being alone."* Remember the devil believes and trembles; we must live out the gospel message and be doers with a work, a message, a song, something whatever your gift is whatever God inspires you to do.

Warn them for ME, Jesus says. Never be satisfied to do a little and just squeak by; we must be zealous for Jesus cause and do much. To whom much is given, of him shall much be required; the parable of the talents! (Read it.) *"The harvest is great and the Laborers are few."* I would rather be standing at the street corner handing out TRACKS, then be a praying one, locked away in solitude praying to the LORD for laborers for His harvest. Doers of the WORD please. Warn them, and if they repent, you have saved a lost soul from hell-fire and destruction. As I recall Jesus VERY LAST WORDS on Earth were, go out and preach, baptizing and discipling them, not find a cave and pray about it.

Common sense, people; please, more common sense.

The great Apostle says, *"Follow me as I follow Christ."* Good advice considering for certain, he is where we all want to be.

> *Yea doubtless I count all things but loss for the excellency of the knowledge of Christ Jesus MY LORD* (and the knowledge of Jesus is Salvation) *for whom I have suffered the loss of all things and do count them but dung, that I may win Christ.* (Phil. 3:8, 9)

> And remembering Peter's exhortations which were many. *"Give diligence to make your calling and election SURE: For IF YE DO THESE THINGS, YE SHALL NEVER FALL. For so an ENTRANCE shall be ministered unto you abundantly into the* Everlasting Kingdom of our LORD and SAVIOUR JESUS CHRIST" (2 Pet. 10:11)

> *Ye do well that ye take heed, as unto a LIGHT that shineth in a DARK PLACE.* (Verse 19)

THE WORLD IS A DARK PLACE

> *"And therefore will the LORD wait, that He may be gracious unto you, and therefore will He be exalted, that He may have MERCY upon you: for the LORD is a GOD of judgment blessed are all they that wait for Him."* In the glorious WORDS of ISAIAH 30:18,

May the LORD bless and keep us unto His Everlasting Kingdom in Jesus NAME, Amen.

Day Unto Day
By NICK KENNY

"WITH A FRIEND" was found on the body of an American boy killed in action on the other side. The Rev. Father Lucian Gallagher of the Church of St. Francis of Assisi had it printed, a copy falling into the hands of Ellen O'Grady, of 501 West 11th St., New York City, who sent it on to us. We thank her for it, so will you.

WITH A FRIEND

LOOK God, I have never spoken to You,
   But now I want to say "How do You do?"
   You see, God, they told me You didn't exist,
   And like a fool I believed all this.

Last night from a shell hole I saw Your sky
And figured then they had told me a lie.
   Had I taken time to see things You made
   I'd have known they weren't calling a spade a spade.

I wonder, God, if You'd shake my hand.
Somehow I feel You will understand.
   Funny I had to come to this hellish place
   Before I had time to see Your face.

Well, I guess there isn't much more to say
But I'm sure glad, God, that I met You today.
   I guess the zero hour will soon be here
   But I'm not afraid since I know You're near.

There's the signal—I've got to go . . .
I like You lots, I want You to know . . .
   Look now, this will be a horrible fight,
   Who knows? I may come to Your House tonight?

Though I wasn't friendly to You before,
I wonder, God, if You'd wait at Your door?
   Look, I'm crying—me!—shedding tears!
   I wish I had known You these many years.

Well, I have to go now, God, goodbye . . .
Strange, since I met You, I'm not afraid to die.
                    —Pfc. J. J. W.
                    *   *   *

PURISTS WOULD never call "With a Friend" poetry but to us it rates with the greatest poems ever written. As an expression of simple faith, in the language of a real American boy, it is priceless. May the brave lad on whose body it was found be in Heaven . . . safe in the Father's arms.

Joy Unspeakable

1 I have found His grace is all com-plete,
He sup-pli-eth ev-'ry need;
While I sit and learn at Je-sus' feet, I am
free, yes, free in-deed.

2 I have found the pleas-ure I once craved,
It is joy and peace with-in;
What a won-drous bless-ing! I am saved
From the aw-ful gulf of sin.

3 I have found that hope so bright and clear,
Liv-ing in the realm of grace Oh, the Sav-ior's
pres-ence is so near, I can see His smil-ing face.

4 I have found the joy no tongue can tell,
How its waves of glo-ry roll!
It is like a great o'er-flow-ing well, Springing
up with-in my soul.

(chorus)

It is joy un-speak-a-ble and full of glo-ry.
Full of glo-ry, full of glo-ry;
It is joy un-speak-a-ble and full of glo-ry.
Oh, the half has nev-er yet been told. (B. E.
Warren)

Jerusalem

*O Jerusalem, Jerusalem, thou that killest the prophets, and
stonest them which are sent unto thee, how often would I
have gathered thy children together, even as a hen gathereth
her chickens under her wings, and ye would not! Behold,
your house is left unto you desolate. For I say unto you,
Ye shall not see ME henceforth till ye shall say, Blessed is
HE THAT COMETH IN THE NAME of the LORD.*

—Matthew 23:37–39

I s there any lack of love here? I say nay, but it sounds more like a
lovers dirge, a lamentation of things gone south rather than like
a scourge. Jesus did assure them however that He would see them
again when He Returned to claim them as His own.

"*For thy Maker is thine husband; the LORD of Hosts is His Name;
and thy Redeemer the Holy One of Israel; the God of the whole Earth
Shall He be called. For a small moment have I forsaken thee; but with
great mercies will I gather thee*" (Isa. 54:5, 7). And David says, "*If I
forget thee O Jerusalem let my right hand forget her cunning. If I do not
remember thee and…if I do not prefer Jerusalem above my chief joys*"
(Ps. 137:5–6). And David represents the sentiments of all her people.
She is the center of Jewish life, the hub of all activity. Her temple is
her glory, and all citizens prided themselves with membership, for
the Jewish faith and religion was central to their culture, and she is
mother of all.

Psalm 87 declares that the "*Almighty Holy One founded her
upon the Holy Mountains.*" The Lord Himself has established her.

Dear city of GOD glorious things are spoken of thee everywhere in the Scriptures, and you are the talk of the media. If a pin drops in Jerusalem, fourteen journalists are stomping her grounds to see where. Henceforth we shall refer to her as Mother; saying this man or that one was born here, *"For every follower of Mine belongs to Her by birth."* Moffatt says, *"And the Eternal writes of every nation belonging to her by birth in His census and Prince or people, everyone has his home in Thee, O ZION"* (Ps. 87). And that is what all the hubbub is about. Now if the falling of her meant salvation to the Gentiles, what shall the springing forth of her be; but life evermore; for the LORD shall at His chosen time graft her back in. So fight over her, folks, and if you dare, claim her but she is what she is and stays where she stays and the Almighty Himself says, "SHE IS MINE."

Yes, at times, it all appears quarrelsome, so is history and politics, but all is love in war or peace. The LORD Himself says, *"I will make Jerusalem a cup of trembling unto all the people round about... and I will make Jerusalem a burdensome stone for ALL people."* I will *fight for her saith the LORD "I will open her eyes and Jerusalem shall Realize her strength lies in the LORD of Hosts"* (Zach. 12:2–3, 5, 8 Moffatt). And in the same breath, the LORD declares that He will destroy all those nations that come against her. This is a prophetic warning, and a firewall of the LORD'S defense for her. The LORD said it, that settles it. He says she is mine, trouble her not. Those that are encroaching in on her should back up, move back, and give Jerusalem the peace she needs. Move on, why press on her borders to the demise of your own souls. Go build another city; look out there is plenty of land everywhere or perhaps you be found working your own defeat against the very GOD you claim to love. Have faith, build another settlement out yonder. This is GOD'S Jerusalem, GOD's blood people, DON'T STRIVE AGAINST THE LORD, for that is what you are doing.

Jesus Christ the LORD GOD, Maker of heaven and Earth beneath is a Jew, of the tribe of Judah. It is an evil you do to fight against God. When Abraham and Lot's servants began to strive with each other Abraham says to LOT, "Let us distance ourselves from each other that we may have peace." The LAND is not big enough for all our cattle, if you go that way, I will go this way.

> *Now Abraham was very rich in cattle in silver, and in gold…and Lot also had flocks, herds and tents. And the LAND was not able to bear them, that they might dwell together: for their substance was great. And there was a strife between the herdsmen of each. And Abraham said unto LOT, let there be no strife, I pray thee, between me and thee, between my herdsmen and thy herdsmen; for WE BE BRETHREN. Is not the whole Land before thee? Separate thyself, I pray thee, from me: if thou wilt take the left hand, then I will go to the right, or if you go right I will go left. And Lot lifted up his eyes, and beheld all the plain of JORDAN, that it was well watered everywhere, before the LORD destroyed Sodom and Gomorrah, even as the GARDEN OF THE LORD… So Lot chose the plain and Abraham dwelled in the LAND of CANNAN… And the LORD said to Abraham… lift up thine eye and look at the place where thou art, look Northward, Southward, Eastward and Westward. FOR ALL THE LAND WHICH THOU SEEST TO THEE WILL I GIVE IT, AND TO THY SEED FOREVER. Arise walk through the LAND in the length of it and in the breadth of it; for I WILL GIVE IT UNTO THEE AND THY SEED.* (Genesis 13)

Now you see it is an unintelligent thing to hurt each other, waste resources, precious time, and to live in strife and misery by crowding each other. You are presently breathing down each others necks; move, create space; and see that peace will quickly ensue. Common sense, just plain old common sense. Abraham had it, so then have it to yourselves. You say Abraham is your Father; he would be ashamed of all this fighting. Use his good example and give yourselves space and rest and peace. He did not fight, and we and you are all cousins so WAKE UP!

And if you all stop your fighting, she shall remain and be there for GOD'S return to Earth just as He promised us. When He returns, the LORD Jesus Christ will set His feet on the Mount of Olives just like where He ascended from. And yes, Jesus has a New Jerusalem also, but until He wraps things up here, the old Jerusalem will remain and do for now. Jesus's plans are to reign here on Earth with His saints for one thousand years, while He puts Satan in the chains of hell. After the one thousand years expire, Satan will be loosed again for a season and then God will finalize all things on Earth. Until then keep calm and carry on. Don't push her into the sea; just give each other room.

Those whose eyes God has unveiled will understand; they will consider and abide by GOD'S Laws of LOVE. Let us rejoice with Jerusalem and all Israel as God continues to bring her people back. Let's support and encourage her with love and finances as we are able. For those that bless thee shall be blessed, and those that curse thee shall be cursed God told Abraham, and the promise is forever, as all of GOD'S covenants are. God is not slack concerning His promises, though it tarry, it shall be.

> *"Pray for the Peace of Jerusalem: They shall prosper that love thee. Peace be within thy walls, and prosperity within thy Palaces"* (Ps. 122:6–7).

Jesus was passionate about Jerusalem as all Jews are. His love brought tears to His eyes on Palm Sunday as He made His descent from the Mount of Olives.

> *"And when He was come near He beheld the city, and wept over it. Saying, If thou hadst known… the things which belong unto thy PEACE! But now are they hid from thine eyes"* (Luke 19:41–42).

Take heart, friend, for Jesus Himself wept, knowing all things. Jesus prophesied the destruction of the temple, and He told the women that were weeping for Him, "Weep not for ME but for yourselves and your children." The Holy City and Solomon's beautiful temple would be leveled to the ground. Jesus had grown up here. He taught and preached in this temple. It was His Father's house in two ways, and David His Father had commissioned the work, while Solomon David's son built it. This was one of the seven wonders of the world and was thirteen years in the making. And Jesus saw all this happening. He knew it would all be gone. Psalm 48 describes this for us,

> *Great is the LORD, and greatly to be praised in the city of our GOD, in the mountain of His Holiness. Beautiful for situation, the joy of the whole Earth, is mount ZION, on the sides of the North the city of the Great KING. GOD is known in her Palaces for a refuge. We have thought of Thy Loving kindness O GOD in the midst of Thy Temple. Let mount ZION rejoice. Walk about Zion, go round about her, tell the towers thereof. Mark ye well her bulwarks consider her palaces, that ye may tell it to the generation following. As we have heard, so have we seen in the city of the LORD of Hosts, in the city of our GOD: GOD will establish it forever. Selah.*

Through thick and thin, she will be forever lasting. God has not forsaken Jerusalem; she is the city of the Great King and of GOD'S people. And one thing have I desired and that is to see Solomon's Temple. In her making, not a hammer or saw was heard, for all parts were prepared aforehand. No real work was done in the Temple; all the parts were just put together there—no noisy hammers or saws; what awesome reverence this is. The stones for this massive monumental structure weighed in at thousands of tons. The undertaking and the labor were a huge project, Solomon was nearly overwhelmed, but the LORD'S guiding hand was with Solomon.

And King David said to Zadok the Priest, and Nathan the Prophet… take with you the servants of your lord, and cause Solomon my Son to ride upon mine own mule, and bring him down to Gihon: And let Zadok and Nathan anoint him there King over Israel: and blow ye the trumpet, and say, GOD SAVE King Solomon. (1 Kings 1:33–34)

And the house when it was in building was built of stone ready made before it was brought thither: so that there was neither hammer nor axe, nor any tool of iron heard in the house, while it was in building. (1 Kings 6:7)

Reverence overshadowed this work and GOD'S divine love guided all the minds and hands that were privileged to be a part of making a resting place for the Sacred Ark of the covenant. This was to be GOD'S holy house and every part of its work must be done with holy hands and hearts. For the LORD sees all things.

These are David's last words and instructions to his son Solomon and all the congregation of Israel.

Then David the king stood upon his feet and said Hear me my brethren and my people… I had it in mine heart to build a house of rest for the Ark… But GOD said unto me, Thou shalt not build an house for MY NAME, because thou hast been a man of war, and hast shed blood. How be it the LORD GOD of Israel chose me before all the house of my Father to be king over Israel forever:…for He Liked me to make me king over all ISRAEL. And of all my sons… He hath chosen Solomon my son to sit upon the throne of the Kingdom of the LORD over ISRAEL. And GOD said unto me, Solomon thy son, he shall build MY HOUSE and My courts; for I have chosen him to be My son, and I will be his Father. Then David gave to Solomon his son the pattern of… All that he had by the spirit, of the courts of the house of the LORD… All this said David, the LORD made me understand in writing by HIS HAND upon me, even all the works of this pattern. And David said to Solomon his son, Be strong and of good courage, and do it: fear not, nor be dismayed: for the LORD GOD, even my GOD,

*will be with thee; He will not fail thee, nor for-
sake thee, until thou hast finished all the work for
the service of the House of the LORD.* (1 Chron.
28:2–6, 9–12, 19–20)

*Furthermore David the king said… Solomon
my son, whom alone GOD hath chosen is yet young
and tender and the work is great: for the Palace is
not for man, but for the LORD GOD (and David
gave all his personal treasure of gold and silver to
the building fund)…and the people also offered willingly (and David prayed for Solomon and the people
on the next day)…and they anointed Solomon unto
the LORD to be the chief governor and made Zadok
his priest. Then Solomon sat on the Throne of the
LORD as king and prospered and all Israel obeyed
him. And the LORD magnified Solomon exceedingly in the sight of all Israel, and bestowed upon
him such Royal Majesty as had not been on any king
before him in Israel. Thus David reigned over all
Israel…for 40 years, 7 years in Hebron and 33 years
reigned he in Jerusalem.* (1 Chron. 29:1, 3, 22–27)

The temple was King David's dream and his son Solomon real-
ized it for him. This temple put Israel as a nation on the map. There
was no other building ever on Earth, built at this grand a scale, and
this grand of beauty that had ever been built; thus to this time, because
it was for a Great King and a Great GOD. Solomon foreknew that
the glory of the Almighty God of heaven and earth would be present
in this building. He had already experienced some of GOD'S glory.

#1 David, the Great King David was his father.

#2 God spoke to him in a dream:

*In Gibeon the LORD appeared to Solomon
in a dream by night: and GOD said, Ask what I
shall give thee"… And the LORD said, "I have
done according to thy words: lo I have given thee a*

wise and an understanding heart; so that there was none like thee before thee, neither after thee shall any arise like unto thee. (1 Kings 3:5, 12)

Solomon knew of the glorious magnificence of the LORD, and he wanted a temple fit for this King of kings and LORD of LORDS, so that God would come down and dwell with them, so that His presence would have a Resting place and be welcome.

> *And the priest brought in the ARK of the covenant of the LORD…into the most Holy Place… between the cherubim. And it came to pass when the priests came out of the holy place, a cloud filled the house of the LORD and the priests could not stand to minister because of the cloud: for the glory of the LORD had filled the House of the LORD. Then spake Solomon… I have surely built Thee an house to dwell in, a settled place for Thee to abide in forever.* (1 Kings 8:6, 10–13)

The ark of the covenant represented the presence of the LORD among His people. And up till now, it had always been in a tent. David struggled with this idea and thought, "Why should I have a house and My God has no house?" He wanted a house for His God. And Solomon said, "Now my God has a house among us." This is where the glorious LORD of Israel met with His people. The LORD was in the Ark. The Ark was in the holy place in the temple. And God dwelt among His people.

The fame of Solomon spread throughout the whole known world, and all the kings of the Earth came to witness Solomon, his wisdom, his temple, and all of his kingdom. So the ark was brought in by the priests and Solomon made a dedication prayer asking the LORD to hear Israel and all who prayed toward this Holy Temple forever; this lengthy prayer is recorded in 1 Kings 8. Then with all his buildings completed the LORD appeared to Solomon a second time.

> *The Eternal said I have heard your prayer and I have done for you all you desire; I hereby consecrate this temple you have built,* by fixing MY presence there for all time; *My eyes and MY heart shall constantly be there… If you will live under My eye, as your father David lived with upright heart…then I will make your Royal Throne sure over Israel for all time, as I promised your father David; that he would never be without a descendant on the Throne of Israel.* (1 Kings 9:3–5 Moffatt)

This is the Davidic Covenant God promised to David. And the covenant is for all time, God does not change His decrees; they are for all time, even until Jesus comes back to reclaim David's throne. God also promised His presence to be with them forever, and gave them promise of answered prayers if they kept His Holy Commandments. And all the LAW is fulfilled in this: "Thou shalt love the LORD your God with all your heart, mind, soul, and strength, and love your neighbor as yourself."

Solomon had many royal visitors, but none so telling as the queen of Sheba.

> *When the Queen of Sheba heard of the fame of Solomon concerning the Name of the LORD, she came to prove him with hard questions… And when she had seen all Solomon's wisdom, and the House that he had built…his ministers and servants…and his ascent by which he went up unto the House of the LORD (for worship); there was no more spirit in her. And she said to Solomon the king; It was a true report that I heard in mine own land of thy acts and thy wisdom. Howbeit I believed not the words, until I came and mine eyes had seen it: and behold*

the half was not told me… Blessed be the LORD thy God which delighted in thee to set thee on the Throne of Israel: because the LORD loved Israel forever*; therefore made He their king, to do justice and judgement.* (1 Kings 10:1–9)

So true, so true, you cannot make these things up. Here in black and white is a royal testimony to the hand of God at work. A picture is truly worth a thousand words. Without exaggeration, Solomon's buildings, his Temple, his robes, his manner all described for us as straight from the God of heaven. Now, she believed the God of Israel was the true God; only Almighty God could create such splendour. So magnificent was the sight of all, it took her breath away. This is the Jerusalem she came to see and she saw it all; she saw GOD at work, God Himself.

Solomon had turned Jerusalem into a wonderworld. And let us remember that Jesus refers to all this in His Gospel.

"The Queen of the south shall rise up in the judgment with the men of this generation and condemn them: for she came from the utmost parts of the Earth to hear (and see) *the wisdom of Solomon; and behold a greater than Solomon is here"* (Luke 11:31). So there now you have the rest of the story. The Temple, which Jesus loved, is the seventh wonder of the world and Solomon a wonder of God, but a GREATER than he is here, is HERE, and His NAME is Jesus Christ of Nazareth. Jesus said, "Is not He that built the building, greater than the building and every building is built by some man but He that built all things is GOD." God is the Creator of all things in heaven and Earth. God talked with King David and gave him the pattern for the temple, its courts, chambers, down to the very last detail. God is a wonder, Jesus is a wonder and He works His gracious wonders in the Earth.

Jerusalem is very old; we have no birth date for her. Jerusalem did not appear with Solomon or even with Moses, when the Hebrew children came into their inheritance promised to them by God through Abraham, Isaac, and Jacob. Jerusalem is a very, very ancient city. We first hear of her back in Genesis 14.

> *And Melchizedek King of Salem* (Jerusalem) *brought forth bread and wine: and he was the priest of the Most High God. And he blessed Abram, and said; Blessed be Abram of the Most High God, possessor of Heaven and Earth: And blessed be the Most High God which hath delivered thine enemies into thy hand. And he gave him tithes of all.* (Gen. 14:18–20)

Like Abraham and Genesis, the city has been there from the beginning of days. It has been rebuilt upon itself so many times we have lost track. I have heard a person can put a shovel to the ground nearly anywhere and find a treasure trove of antiquities. There is a lot of history here. When the Hebrew children came into possess the Land of Canaan with Joshua, Jerusalem was already a well-established city with walls and gardens, groves, and houses. Jesus Christ walked her streets preaching the Everlasting Gospel, healing the sick, raising the dead, and was found early in the morning and on the Sabbath in the temple preaching and teaching. She abides with us still and God is not finished with her yet. Pray for the Peace of Jerusalem. "And I will bless them that bless thee and curse them that curse thee, God said unto Abraham" (Gen. 12:3). These Words are Holy Writ and they imply a lot. So rock on, friends, and enemies, just don't try to rock GOD'S boat.

Jerusalem has many names, she can be referred to by any one of these, and is, throughout Scripture.

- Salem
- City of David
- City of God
- City of the Great King
- Zion
- City of Judah

- The Holy City
- The Holy Mount
- The Throne of the LORD
- The Perfection of Beauty

God does not start something and not finish it. It is finished when He says it's finished as on the Cross Jesus said, "It is finished," because He had completed His Earthly ministry. Surely He which hath begun a good work in you (Jerusalem) shall continue it until the day of our LORD. These are His chosen, His people; He started with them and will finish with them. God began with one man, Abraham and his household. This one man sojourned to Canaan and the LORD promised the LAND to his seed in an Everlasting Covenant. This is how God started with just this one man and built a nation. He then delivered them from the Egyptians and sanctified them in the wilderness and brought them into their promised LAND, the LAND of Canaan, with borders established by God.

Moses had warned them to cleave unto their God for *"He is thy LIFE,"* He said. But they were seduced with evil and began worshipping the idols of the heathen nations. Over the years, God sent His Holy Prophets to them to cry against their evils. Repent, amend your ways, and turn back to the living, breathing God. Israel spent many years in captivity and war because of their sin in forsaking GOD, but God did not utterly forsake them. God only punished them according to their ways and doings. In the days of Zechariah, God spoke to His prophet thus saying,

> *I am jealous for Jerusalem and for ZION with GREAT JEALOUSY… Therefore I am returned to Jerusalem with mercies. My House shall be built in it, saith the LORD of Hosts, and a line shall be stretched forth upon Jerusalem… My cities through prosperity shall yet be spread abroad; and the LORD shall yet comfort ZION, and shall yet choose JERUSALEM.* (1:14–18)

And the angel said unto me, measure Jerusalem (for breadth and length) *thereof... He said Jerusalem shall be inhabited as towns without walls for the multitude of men and cattle therein: For I, saith the LORD will be unto her a wall of fire round about, and will be the glory in the midst of her. Come forth and flee from the land of the North. Deliver thyself; O ZION that dwellest with the daughter of Babylon. For thus saith the LORD of Hosts; After the glory hath He sent me unto the nations which spoiled you: For he that toucheth you toucheth the APPLE OF HIS EYE. Sing and rejoice O daughter of ZION: For Lo I come, and I will dwell in the midst of thee, saith the LORD... And the LORD shall inherit Judah His Portion in the HOLY LAND, and shall choose JERUSALEM AGAIN.* (Zech. chap. 2)

"And I the LORD God Almighty shall do all this. Not one jot or one tittle of the WORD will fail." God will do it. JERUSALEM is His, is His now and forever. Wake up, people; has God done all these wonders in the Earth in vain? I think not. He is the Alpha and Omega, the beginning and the end of all things. He will work His works and who will stop Him. Keep your eyes peeled to Jerusalem for she is *God's time clock*. The Apostle says, has God forsaken Jerusalem? I think not; God forbid, he says. No she is God's portion; He is betrothed to her forever and ever and ever. We be but mortal men. He is GOD, a great God, and a great king. Who can know the mind of the LORD, or being His instructor, instruct Him. There is nothing too difficult for Him, He sits in the heavens and laughs at mere mortal man.

"Fear not Abraham I will bless thee and keep thee and make thee a great Nation and in thee shall all the nations of the Earth be blessed." She is to be the *example nation* to the whole Earth, for God made her thus, to reveal Himself through this tiny nation, and Jerusalem is her capital, the center of all life. He is telling Zechariah, "I will choose Jerusalem again," and she shall be glorious. Furthermore, I

the LORD Myself "shall be a firewall around her and I will again be the glory within her." My Jerusalem. Open your eyes, a FIREWALL, God Himself a firewall. God's Holy protection is here, and nothing will happen that God does not allow. We are clueless, friend; we have seen nothing yet, the program is only now beginning. Wake from your dead sleep and get on the right side of the firing line. Yes, I am speaking to you, Mr. Putin and Mr. Xi and all that want or even dare think to oppose her. God have mercy on your rebellious hearts. For the God of heaven reigns; He is the Great king of heaven and Earth; choose ye this day whom ye will serve. As Jesus Christ says in Luke chapter 11.

> *"Woe to you! You build tombs for the prophets whom your own fathers killed: thus you consent to what your fathers did, for they killed and you build." "And the blood of the prophets from Abel to Zechariah, who was slain between the altar and the House of God, yes I tell you it will all be charged upon this generation"* (47–51 Moffatt).

Nothing escapes God's watchful eye, so count the cost before you act. God is a firewall about His Holy City and about His Holy People.

There is no *"fear of God"* before their eyes. I will repay saith the LORD of Hosts. *"Vengeance is mine."* I will repay, though it tarry wait for it, it will surely come saith the LORD.

> *This is the WORD of the LORD unto Zerubbabel, Not by might, nor by power, but by MY SPIRIT saith the LORD of Hosts. Who art thou, O great mountain? Before Zerubbabel, thou shalt become a plain: and He shall bring forth the headstone thereof with shoutings, crying, Grace, grace unto it. Thy hands have laid the foundation of this house; and thy hands shall finish it...they shall see the plummet in the hand of Zerubbabel*

> *with those seven eyes: they are the eyes of the LORD,*
> *which run to and fro through the whole Earth…*
> *and thou shalt know that the LORD of Hosts hath*
> *sent me unto thee.* (Zech. 4:6–9)

The eyes of God see all and are upon all, how much more His Holy City. Still the enemy keeps blasting out threats of annihilation, but who art thou O great mountain… Thou shalt become a plain. How hard is it to fight against GOD; how hardly can you win? Don't be so blind; Jerusalem is the apple of God's eye another way of saying that is, she is the cat's meow. David sang of our love for her, and she is the instrument upon which GOD fills heaven with melodies. In the opposite breath, her enemies want to claim her, that's an oxymoron for sure.

All three of the major religions claim her. For here lies nearly all of Bible history, all or most of the holy sites of the kings, the prophets and our Fathers. Muslims, the Catholics, and the Jews all at odds over this little place on the map. God is her true owner, and God is not done with Jerusalem yet. There is exceedingly more to come and no Satan on Earth is big enough to stop God and His plans. Remember our arch foe was defeated at Calvary by the Precious Blood of our LORD and Savior; the LAMB slain before the foundations of the Earth. Oh yes, God has big plans for Jerusalem. Romans 11:12 says, "For if the falling out of them be the Salvation of the Gentiles (that's us) what shall the rejuvenation of them be but life from the dead." God's ultimate move. And Jesus is coming back to sit on His father David's throne. This shall be the throne from which Jesus Christ of Nazareth shall rule the world and all its nations, with a rod of IRON, this after He puts down all His enemies under His feet.

> *Thus saith the LORD: I am returned unto*
> *Zion, and will dwell in the midst of JERUSALEM.*
> *And Jerusalem shall be called a city of truth; and*
> *the mountain of the LORD of Hosts, the Holy*
> *Mountain.* (Zech. 8:3)

And I will bring them, and they shall dwell in the midst of JERUSALEM: and they shall be My People, and I will be their God... (Verse 8)

So again have I thought in these days to do well unto Jerusalem and to the house of Judah; fear ye not. (Verse 15)

"Fear ye not," the LORD says, "your time has come." God's intentions for Jerusalem are for peace and prosperity. God have mercy on those that will have an idea to fight against Him in His Holy LAND. The LORD says of His people, thou art My portion, my peculiar treasure, my great reward. Does the LORD change His mind, has He cast away His people? God forbid Romans tells us; they have the spirit of slumber. They still for the most part cannot see Jesus as Messiah. And Romans says, *"But as touching the election they are beloved for the Father's Sakes. And so all Israel shall be saved: as it is written, there shall come out of Zion the Deliverer, and shall turn away ungodliness from Jacob"* (Rom. 11:28, 26). And Isaiah reiterates the same prophesy.

In that day shall the BRANCH of the LORD be beautiful and glorious... And it shall come to pass, that he that is left in Zion, and he that remaineth in Jerusalem, shall be called HOLY, even everyone that is written among the living in Jerusalem. "When the LORD shall have washed away the filth of the daughters of Zion, and shall have purged the blood of Jerusalem from the midst thereof by the Spirit of judgement and the Spirit of burning. (Isa. 4:2–4)

Thou art My portion the LORD says though many are still concluded in slumber and blindness as to Jesus being the Messiah as Romans chapter 11 so aptly explains by the Great Apostle. In God's time, it has only been two days since Jesus was here. For the Word states that a thousand years are to the LORD as one day, and one day as a thousand years. The Jews sought for the answer but could not see this humble servant to be the Powerful Messiah they hoped for.

> *"And it was at Jerusalem the Feast of Dedication, and it was Winter, And Jesus walked in the temple in Solomon's porch. Then came the Jews round about Him, and said unto Him, How long dost Thou make us to doubt? If Thou be the Christ, tell us plainly"* (John 10:22–24).

For the most part, they still do not see, but worship and keep the Mosaic LAW. Now the LORD says He will make a quick work and cut it short for the sake of His elect and His GLORY. The LORD will return again for His people as He said and shall save them, He will return in His power.

> *Behold the Day of the LORD cometh... Then shall the LORD go forth, and fight against those nations that fight against Jerusalem, as when He fought in the Day of Battle. And His feet shall stand in that Day upon the Mount of Olives, which is before Jerusalem on the East... And the LORD shall be king over ALL the Earth: in that Day shall there be ONE LORD, AND HIS NAME ONE.* (Zech. 14:1, 3–4, 9)

God's glory upon Jerusalem is yet to be revealed. The Abrahamic blessing is, "I will bless those that bless you and curse those that curse you," watch out, O enemy of God. Maybe you should rethink your plans of annihilation. For God is not a God far off, but a God near at hand and Jesus shall appear and destroy His enemies with the breath of His mouth. As a birthday candle you blow out, they will be gone with this breath, cast into a devil's hell. The Grand Finale is getting close. Look up Jesus says, "For your redemption draweth nigh. It is close very close, keep your eye on the Eastern Sky."

I tell you and tell you BOLDLY, Jerusalem is not an old actor that is just going to fade away into the side wings.

CAMERA, ACTION, GO…

No, Jerusalem will wax greater and greater because there is no one like her. Her popularity is going to soar; she will become so wealthy that even those poor little exiles returning will be clothed in gold. Their tables will be set as a banquet set for kings. Her people will be strengthened and become bold and proud of their heritage. How say ye? First, through the LORD her God and second through tourism because she is the Land of Mystery to many.

She is the Holy City of Our LORD and Savior, and Our Lord shall return here to the Mount of Olives from whence He left from on the Day of His Ascension into heaven. Jerusalem is the City of His people. Yes, there are many popular sites around the globe, like the Vatican City, Queen Elizabeth's castles, Moscow and St. Petersburg. Washington, DC, Tokyo, and the Peking Gardens too. But nothing, none of these even touch the hem of Jerusalem's garment. For everyone knows that to visit her is addictive; it is a life changer. One is never the same after visiting the holy city, with all her holy sites and seeing the effects all her, kings and holy prophets and fathers have had on her. The Holy One was born here, walked in the streets here, sat on the wells. Prayed in her gardens, feasted with friends, raised her dead, Jesus is what makes her the Holy City. He was born, died and was resurrected here, the Holy One was here and is still here in presence. He is here!

Yes, this is the land and the city God chose to manifest Himself to the world from. John the Baptist at the River Jordan has knowledge of Jesus Christ first, and seeing Him approaching he says, *"Behold the LAMB of GOD which taketh away the sin of the World."* John knew that Jesus was to be manifest to Israel as their Redeemer, yes, Jesus made His debut right here. John baptized Jesus in the Holy River Jordan. Why holy? Because everything that Jesus touches becomes holy. Has He touched you yet? And John baptized Jesus and said, *"I saw and bare record that this is the SON OF GOD."* Yes, the King of kings debuted in Israel and her cities. *"And I say unto you, Swear not at all; Neither by heaven; for it is GOD's THRONE: Nor by the Earth;*

for it is His footstool: neither by JERUSALEM; for it is the City of the Great King" (Matt. 5:34–35).

Can you say this about any other city, state, or country? No, because God chose Israel, the Jews, and Jerusalem as His own. To be His birthplace, His home, His workshop. This is where Jesus displayed God's power, worked His miracles, taught in her temple and preached His WORDS from city to city, all over Israel and Jerusalem. This is a most blessed place and a visitor can only pray, that some of these blessings might cling to him. No other city can boast of the blessings gotten here, nowhere on the face of God's green Earth.

> *For the LORD hath chosen Zion; He hath desired it for His habitation. This is My rest forever; here will I dwell for I have desired it.* (Ps. 132:13–14)
>
> *The LORD shall bless thee out of Zion; and thou shalt see the good of Jerusalem all the days of thy life. Yea thou shalt see…peace upon Israel.* (128:5–6)
>
> *They that trust in the LORD shall be as Mount Zion which cannot be removed, but abideth Forever. As the mountains are round about JERUSALEM, so the LORD is round about His people…forever.* (125:1–2)
>
> *When the LORD turned again the captivity of Zion, we were like them that dream.* (126:1)
>
> *Blessed be the LORD out of Zion which dwelleth at Jerusalem, Praise ye the LORD… Ye that stand in the House of the Lord, in the courts of the House of the LORD. Praise the LORD for the LORD is good sing praises unto His Name.* (Ps. 135:1–2, 21)
>
> *He saved them for His Name's sake that He might make His mighty power to be known.* (106:8)
>
> *Declare the Name of the LORD in Zion and His Praise in JERUSALEM.* (99:21)

Except the LORD build the House, they labor in vain that build it: Except the LORD keep the City, the watchmen waketh but in vain. (127:1)

Jerusalem is the beauty of the whole Earth, so don't be jealous people, countries, and kingdoms. Be happy. She is as close as a plane ticket and her lasting effects are meant for all. Come wash in the pool of Shiloam and be healed. Be baptized in the River Jordan like Jesus. Pray in her temples; listen to her rabbis. Learn more about the foundations of your faith, walk the paths that Jesus trod. Partake in her festivals. Pray at the Western Wall; Jerusalem's most holy site and feel the presence of God. Most of the holy sites and cities of interest are also close by, such as Bethlehem, Nazareth, Tel Aviv, and much, much more.

God has not forsaken Jerusalem; she is on hold for the moment for she is still the apple of God's eye. And we have yet to see the restoration of God's Temple in His Holy City. The rebuilding of the temple has exciting implications, especially if she is a replica of Solomon's wonder. This would be a gift from on high for these Jewish descendants of Abraham, to have the former glory restored. A true place like the original temple. All things are possible with God, Jesus says. God is mindful of all these things, and God shall restore and rebuild, her latter glory shall be greater than her former glory. Do we dare limit the MOST HIGH.

My righteousness is near, My Salvation is gone forth, for the LORD shall comfort Zion: He will make her wilderness like Eden, and her desert like the garden of the LORD. Therefore the redeemed of the LORD shall return and come with singing unto Zion. (Isa. 51:3, 5, 11)

Awake, awake, put on thy strength, O Zion; put on thy beautiful garments, O Jerusalem the HOLY CITY… Shake thyself from the dust; arise and sit down, O Jerusalem: loose thyself… O captive daughter of ZION. Therefore My People shall know MY NAME: they shall know in that day that I AM

He that doth speak: behold IT IS I. How beautiful…are the feet of him that…publisheth Salvation; that saith to Zion, THY GOD REIGNETH!

They shall sing…when the LORD shall again bring Zion. Break forth into joy and sing, ye waste places of JERUSALEM: for the LORD hath comforted His People, He hath redeemed JERUSALEM. The LORD hath made bare His Holy Arm in the eyes of all nations; and all the ends of the Earth shall see the SALVATION OF GOD. (Isa. 52:1–10)

As the Baptist says,

O generation of vipers, who hath warned you to flee from the wrath to come. (Luke 3:7)
Bring forth fruits worthy of repentance… (Verse 8)
And so ALL ISRAEL shall be saved: as it is written, there shall come out of Zion the DELIVERER, and shall turn away ungodliness from Jacob: For this is MY COVENANT unto them, when I shall take away their sins…for they are the Beloved *of the Father."* (Rom. 11:26–28)
Touch not Mine Anointed and do My Prophets no harm. He that toucheth thee toucheth the apple of Mine Eye.

Jesus is now standing at the threshold of heaven's gate, ready to descend upon her Mount of Olives in a moment's notice.

So watch, wait, and be ready for her king, our king, to appear, and to set up His kingdom right in the heart of Jerusalem; GOD'S Royal City.

Goodbye enemies, hello, Savior.

KING of KINGS, LORD of LORD'S.

What I say unto you,

I say unto all:

WATCH!

"Yes, salvation is of the Jews!"

God created Salvation for the Gentiles (that's us), by using the Jewish Nation, through them GOD brought Salvation into being.

The LORD told Abraham in Genesis 12:

> *Get thee out of thy country...and from thy father's house, unto a LAND that I will show thee: and I will make of thee a great* Nation, *and I will bless thee, and make thy name great: and thou shalt be a blessing: And I will bless them that bless thee, and curse them that curse thee: and in thee* shall all the families of the Earth be blessed... *Abram departed...and went into the Land of Canaan. And the LORD appeared unto Abram and said, unto thy seed will I give this LAND: and there builded he an altar unto the LORD.* (Gen. 12:1–8)
>
> *The book of the generation of Jesus Christ of Nazareth, Saviour of all mankind, was the son of David who was the son of Abraham.* (Matt. 1:1)

"Salvation is of the Jews"; Jesus says in His Gospel
Do you have Jewish salvation yet?
Is the Messiah your salvation, your life's blood?
Come to Jerusalem the city of kings and priests.
The Royal City of King David and King Solomon.
The Royal Capital City of Israel.
The City of Our Great God.
The City of our Great King, JESUS THE MESSIAH.

> *And whosoever shall call upon the Name of the LORD* (Jesus Christ) *shall be saved.*

COME SEE JERUSALEM

enter into Her Gates with Praise!

O Jerusalem, Jerusalem, which killest the prophets, and stonest them that are sent unto thee; how often would I have gathered thy children together, as a HEN doth gather her brood under her wings, and ye would not! (Mat. 23:37)

When Johnny Comes Marching Home

1 When Johnny comes marching home again, Hurrah, hur-rah!

We'll give him a heart-y Wel-come then, Hur-rah, hur-rah!

The men will cheer, the boys will shout, The la-dies, They will all turn out,

And we'll all feel gay, When Johnny comes marching home

2 The old church bell will peal with joy, Hurrah, hur-rah!

To wel-come home our dar-ling boy, Hur-rah, hur-rah!

The vil-lage lads and las-sies say, with roses they will strew the Way,

And we'll all feel gay, when Johnny comes marching home.

3 Get rea-dy for the Ju-bi-lee, Hurrah, hur-rah!

We'll give the he-ro three times three; Hur-rah, hur-rah!

The lau-rel wreath is rea-dy now To place up-on his loy-al brow,

And we'll all feel gay, When Johnny comes marching home.

Nation shall not lift up sword against Nation, neither shall they learn WAR anymore.

Come ye, and let us walk in the Light of the LORD. (Isa. 2:4–5)

Bibliography

Charles Haddon Spurgeon, *Spurgeon's Sermons*, volume 7–8. Hendrickson Publishers, Peabody Massachusetts: August 2017.

Watchman Nee, *Revive Thy Work*, Christian Fellowship Publishers Inc., New York.

James Moffatt, A New Translation of The Bible, Harper & Brothers Publishers: 1935.

Flavius Josephus, *The Works of Josephus*, Hendrickson Publishers, Peabody, Massachusetts: 1987.

St. Augustine, *The Confessions*, Hendrickson Publishers Marketing, LLC, Peabody, Massachusetts: 2004.

John Cardinal McCloskey, Archbishop of New York, New York, *Baltimore Catechism Two*, Tanbooks, Saint Benedict Press, Tan Books: 2010. Online at www.tanbooks.com, www.saintbenedictpress.com.

The Holy Bible, King James Version, Hendrickson Publishers, Peabody, Massachusetts:
The New Amplified *Pilgrim's Progress*, adapted from John Bunyan's Original Text by James Pappas Jr., Destiny Image Publishing, Sheppenburg Pennsylvania: 1999. Online at www.destinyimage.com.

Dietrich Bonhoeffer, *The Cost of Discipleship*, Touchstone, 1230 Avenue of the Americas (translated from the German Nachfolge, first published in 1937): 1959, SCM Ltd.

G. Eric Kuskey with Bettina Gilois, *Billion Dollar Painter*, The Triumph and Tragedy of Thomas Kinkade, Painter of light, Weinstein Books, 250 West 57th Street, 15th floor, New York, NY 10107: 2014. Online at www.weinsteinbooks.com.

George F. Muller, *The Autobiography of George Muller*, Whitaker House, 1030 Hunt Valley Circle, New Kensington, PA, 15068.

The Complete Works of E. M. Bounds on Prayer, Baker Books, a division of Baker Publishing, PO Box 6287, Grand Rapids, MI, 49516: 1990.

EVANGEL SONGS, The Gospel Publishing House, Springfield, MO: 1931.

Tabernacle Hymns Number Three, Tabernacle Publishing Company, Corner Lake St. and Waller Ave., Chicago, Ill.: 1934.

The New Blue Book of Favorite Songs, Hall & McCreary Company, Chicago, Ill.: 1941.

(All text is King James Version unless otherwise indicated as Moffatt translation.)

Notes

Chapter 2: His Name
[1] John Cardinal McCloskey, Archbishop of New York, New York, Baltimore Catechism Two, Saint Benedict Press, Tan Books: 2010. Online at www. tanbooks.com, www.saintbenedictpress.com.

Chapter 3: His Word
[1] George F. Muller, The Autobiography of George Muller, Whitaker House, 1030 Hunt Valley Circle, New Kensington, PA, 15068.
[2] The Complete Works of E.M. Bounds on Prayer, Baker Books, PO Box 6287, Grand Rapids, MI, 49516: 1990.
[3] St. Augustine, The Confessions, Hendrickson Publishers Marketing, LLC, Peabody Massachusetts: 2004.

Chapter 5: The Voice
[1] The New Amplified Pilgrim's Progress, adapted from John Bunyan's Original Text by James Pappas Jr., Destiny Image Publishing, Sheppenburg Pennsylvania: 1999. Online at www.destinyimage.com.

Chapter 7: Hell
[1] The New Amplified Pilgrim's Progress, adapted from John Bunyan's Original Text by James Pappas Jr., Destiny Image Publishing, Sheppenburg Pennsylvania: 1999. Online at www.destinyimage.com.
[2] Charles Haddon Spurgeon, Spurgeon's Sermons, Volume 7–8, Hendrickson Publishers, Peabody Massachusetts: August 2017.
[3] Dietrich Bonhoeffer, The Cost of Discipleship, Touchstone, 1230 Avenue of the Americas (translated from the German Nachfolge, first published in 1937): 1959, SCM Ltd.

Chapter 9: Knowest Thou Not
[1] St. Augustine, The Confessions, Hendrickson Publishers Marketing, LLC, Peabody Massachusetts: 2004.

[2]   G. Eric Kuskey with Bettina Gilois, Billion Dollar Painter, The Triumph and Tragedy of Thomas Kinkade, Painter of light. Weinstein Books, 250 West 57th Street, 15th floor, New York, NY 10107: 2014. Online at www.weinsteinbooks.com.

Chapter 10: Loss of All
[1]   Flavius Josephus, The Works of Josephus, Hendrickson Publishers, Peabody Massachusetts: 1987.

Chapter 11: Repent
[1]   Watchman Nee, Revive Thy Work, Christian Fellowship Publishers Inc., New York.

BOOK NOW AVAILABLE AT THESE LOCATIONS

Amazon - Barnes & Noble - Apple iTunes - Google Play

GET INSPIRED

BOOK NOW AVAILABLE AT THESE LOCATIONS

Amazon - Barnes & Noble - Apple iTunes - Google Play

GET INSPIRED

AVAILABLE SOON AT THESE LOCATIONS

Amazon - Barnes & Noble - Apple iTunes - Google Play

GET INSPIRED

About the Author

Unapologetically, we say Beatrice is a Jesus fanatic and, after years of reading James's Epistle, she has decided to write about Jesus Christ the Nazarene. With true faith in all God's Words of the Bible she writes, hoping that the public will be blessed, encouraged, and enlightened through her work about the One and the only Savior of the Universe. Her teacher in this undertaking has been Jesus Christ our Lord, who has instructed us in the Scriptures that He is indeed our example. He said, "Come follow Me." With Jesus's Words and those of St. James, she has felt inspired to write.

James says, "Thou believest that there is one God; thou doest well: the devils also believe and tremble. But wilt thou know, O vain man, that faith without works is dead?"

I am convinced that Beatrice is speaking truths here with all humility of mind and love for mankind. Like what the old sixties slogan said, "PEACE," so she has also imparted to us through these words, "Peace," which only comes through the Prince of Peace, JESUS CHRIST. Enjoy!

If you are enjoying This book so far feel free to write us a Review at our amazon author page by scanning the QR code below.

You can reach us on Instagram and Facebook, look for "Jesus Books" also.

Your love goes a long ways. Thanks for buying and showing your interest in this kind of book and spreading the Good news further.

www.ingramcontent.com/pod-product-compliance
Lightning Source LLC
Chambersburg PA
CBHW051132120626
46547CB00012B/770